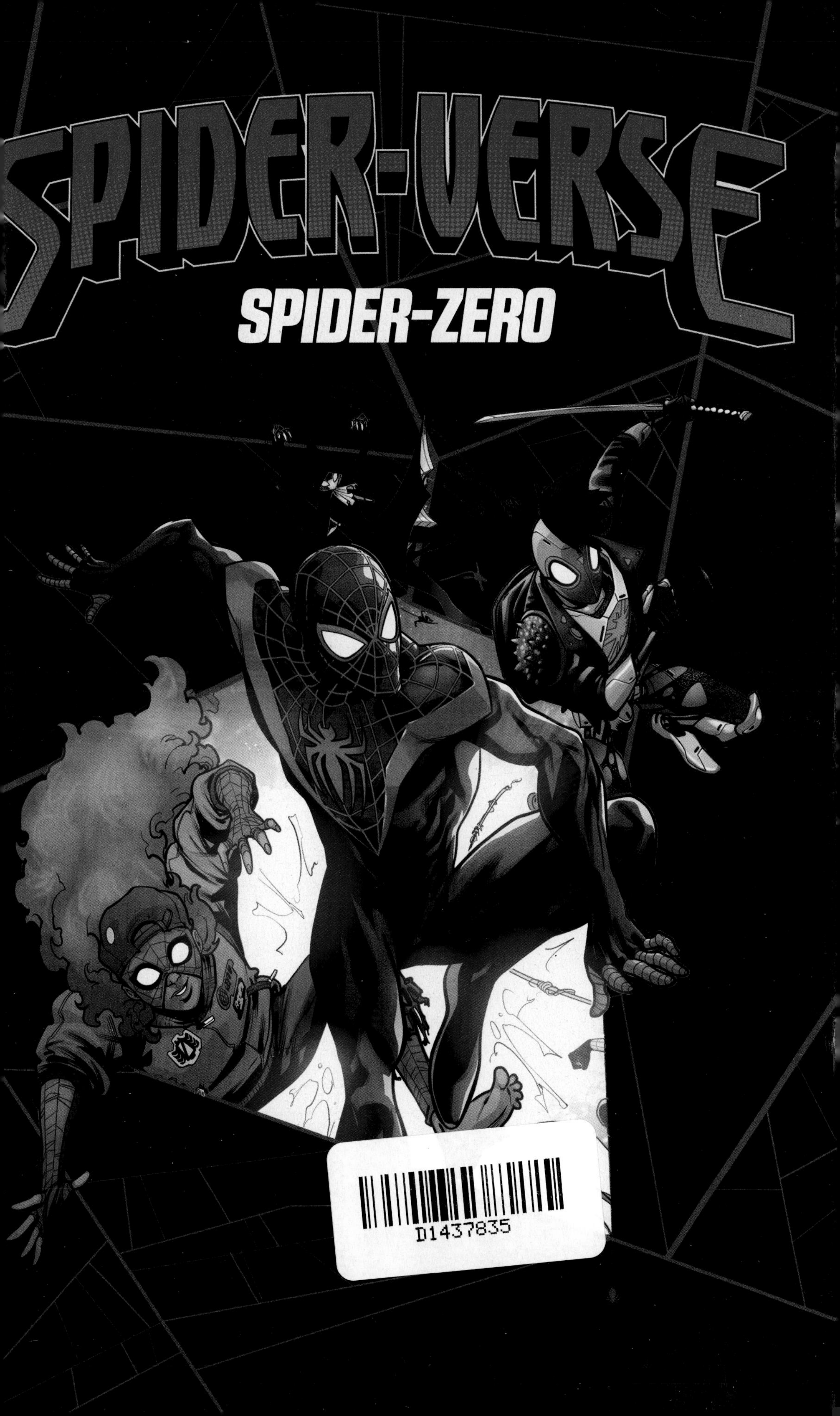
SPIDER-VERSE
SPIDER-ZERO

HIGH SCHOOL STUDENT MILES MORALES WAS BITTEN BY A GENETICALLY ALTERED SPIDER AND GAINED INCREDIBLE ARACHNID-LIKE ABILITIES. HE HID THESE ABILITIES AT FIRST, UNTIL A HERO INSPIRED HIM TO USE THEM TO TRY TO MAKE THE WORLD MORE JUST.

MILES WAS RECENTLY SUMMONED TO EARTH-001, THE LOCATION OF THE WEB OF LIFE AND DESTINY, A NEXUS POINT BETWEEN UNIVERSES THAT STABILIZES EACH REALITY AND MAKES IT POSSIBLE TO TRAVEL BETWEEN THEM. ONCE MILES REACHED THE WEB, SPIDER-ZERO, THE NOMAD SPIDER WITH NO WORLD TO CALL HOME, EXPLAINED THAT A CORRUPTION WAS SPREADING THROUGH THE WEB, AND THE ONLY ONE WHO CAN REPAIR IT, ANNIE MAY PARKER, WAS MISSING. WITH THE WEB IN NEED OF HEALING, MILES AND SPIDER-ZERO TEAMED UP TO FIND ANNIE AND SAVE THE UNIVERSE!

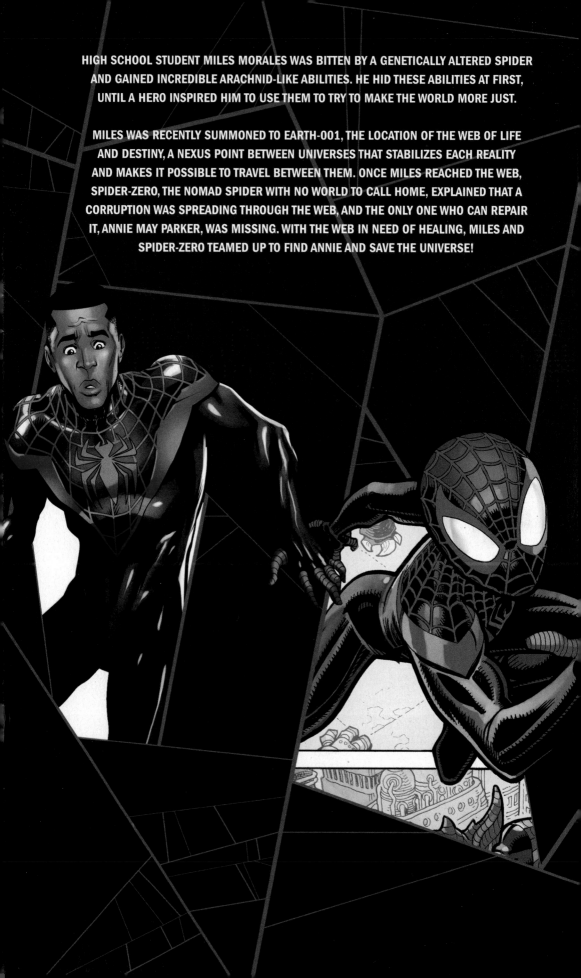

SPIDER-VERSE

SPIDER-ZERO

SPIDER-VERSE #1

WRITER: JED MacKAY

ARTISTS/COLOR ARTISTS: JUAN FRIGERI & CARLOS LOPEZ (PP. 1-4, 16-17), STACEY LEE (PP. 5-6), ARTHUR ADAMS & FEDERICO BLEE (PP. 7-8), JAMES HARREN & DAVE STEWART (PP. 9-10), DIKE RUAN & CARLOS LOPEZ (PP. 11-12), SHELDON VELLA (PP. 13-15)

SPIDERSONAS: COTTON VALENT, ANTONIO DEMICO & V-0-3

SPIDER-VERSE #2

WRITER: RYAN NORTH

PENCILER: PERE PÉREZ

INKER: JORDI TARRAGONA GARCIA

COLOR ARTIST: MARTE GRACIA

SPIDERSONAS: DICE SHIMI, JAMES GIFFORD & TORI APIRADEE

SPIDER-VERSE #3

WRITER: JED MacKAY

ARTIST: DIKE RUAN

COLOR ARTIST: IAN HERRING

SPIDERSONAS: DAYNA BRODER, AL¥SSA RAGNI & CARLY HENSON

SPIDER-VERSE #4

WRITER: TARAN KILLAM

ARTIST: JUAN GEDEON

COLOR ARTIST: BRIAN REBER

SPIDERSONAS: AUDRA AUCLAIR, C.R. SCANNELL & ABRAHAM LOPEZ

SPIDER-VERSE #5

WRITER: CHRISTOS GAGE

ARTIST: JUAN FERREYRA

SPIDERSONAS: STEVE POOLE, DAVID "KOPFSTOFF" MÜLLER & OH SHEEPS

SPIDER-VERSE #6

WRITER: JED MacKAY

ARTIST: ZÉ CARLOS

COLOR ARTIST: CHRIS SOTOMAYOR

SPIDERSONAS: KEVIN BOLK, CHRIS WILSON & CAIT ZELLERS

LETTERER: VC'S CORY PETIT

COVER ART: WENDELL DALIT (#1) & DAVE RAPOZA (#2-6)

ASSISTANT EDITORS: KATHLEEN WISNESKI, MARTIN BIRO & DANNY KHAZEM

EDITORS: NICK LOWE & DEVIN LEWIS

SPIDER-MAN CREATED BY **STAN LEE** & **STEVE DITKO**

COLLECTION EDITOR **JENNIFER GRÜNWALD** ASSISTANT EDITOR: **DANIEL KIRCHHOFFER** ASSISTANT MANAGING EDITOR: **MAIA LOY**
ASSOCIATE MANAGER, TALENT RELATIONS **LISA MONTALBANO** VP PRODUCTION & SPECIAL PROJECTS **JEFF YOUNGQUIST**
BOOK DESIGNERS **STACIE ZUCKER** & **ADAM DEL RE** WITH **JAY BOWEN**

SVP PRINT, SALES & MARKETING **DAVID GABRIEL** EDITOR IN CHIEF **C.B. CEBULSKI**

SPIDER-VERSE: SPIDER-ZERO. Contains material originally published in magazine form as SPIDER-VERSE (2019) #1-6. Second printing 2022. ISBN 978-1-302-92026-5. Published by MARVEL WORLDWIDE, INC., a subsidiary of MARVEL ENTERTAINMENT, LLC. OFFICE OF PUBLICATION: 1290 Avenue of the Americas, New York, NY 10104. **Printed in Canada.** KEVIN FEIGE, Chief Creative Officer; DAN BUCKLEY, President, Marvel Entertainment; JOE QUESADA, EVP & Creative Director; DAVID BOGART, Associate Publisher & SVP of Talent Affairs; TOM BREVOORT, VP, Executive Editor; NICK LOWE, Executive Editor, VP of Content, Digital Publishing; DAVID GABRIEL, VP of Print & Digital Publishing; SVEN LARSEN, VP of Licensed Publishing; MARK ANNUNZIATO, VP of Planning & Forecasting; JEFF YOUNGQUIST, VP of Production & Special Projects; ALEX MORALES, Director of Publishing Operations; DAN EDINGTON, Director of Editorial Operations; RICKEY PURDIN, Director of Talent Relations; JENNIFER GRÜNWALD, Director of Production & Special Projects; SUSAN CRESPI, Production Manager; STAN LEE, Chairman Emeritus. For information regarding advertising in Marvel Comics or on Marvel.com, please contact Vit DeBellis, Custom Solutions & Integrated Advertising Manager, at vdebellis@marvel.com. For Marvel subscription inquiries, please call 888-511-5480. **Manufactured between 4/15/2022 and 5/17/2022 by SOLISCO PRINTERS, SCOTT, QC, CANADA.**

10 9 8 7 6 5 4 3 2

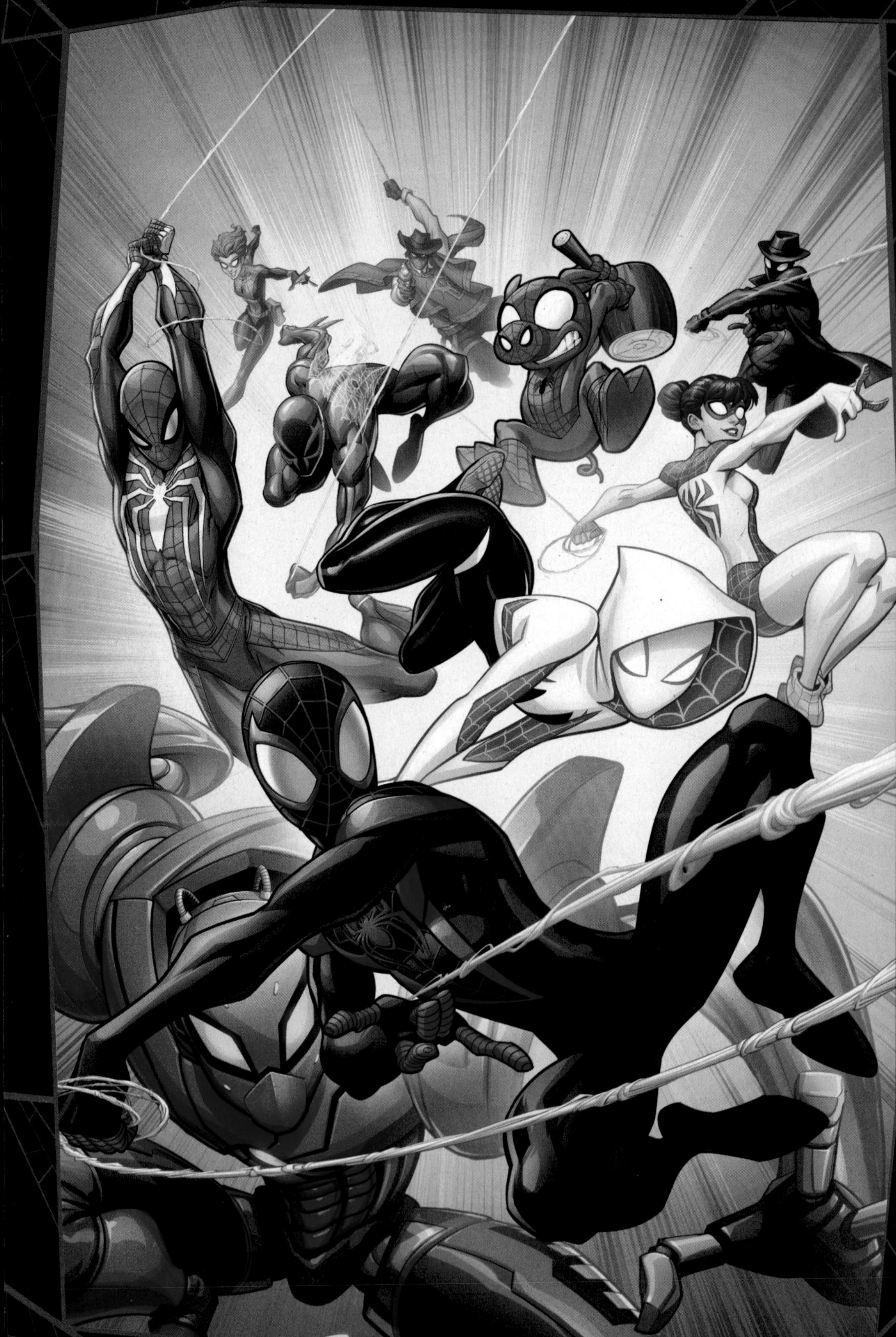

SPIDER-VERSE #1 VARIANT BY
PATRICK BROWN

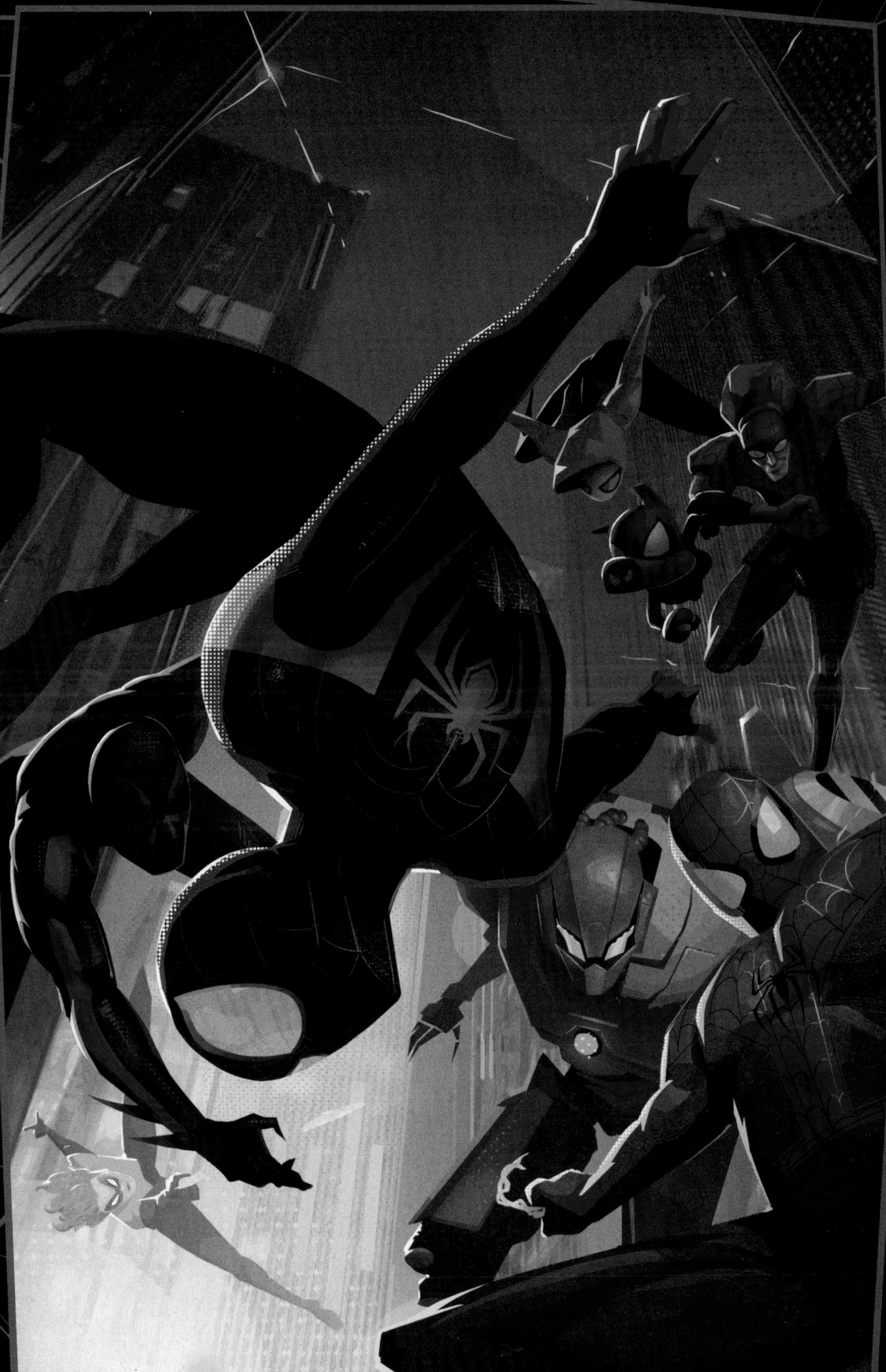

SPIDER-VERSE #1

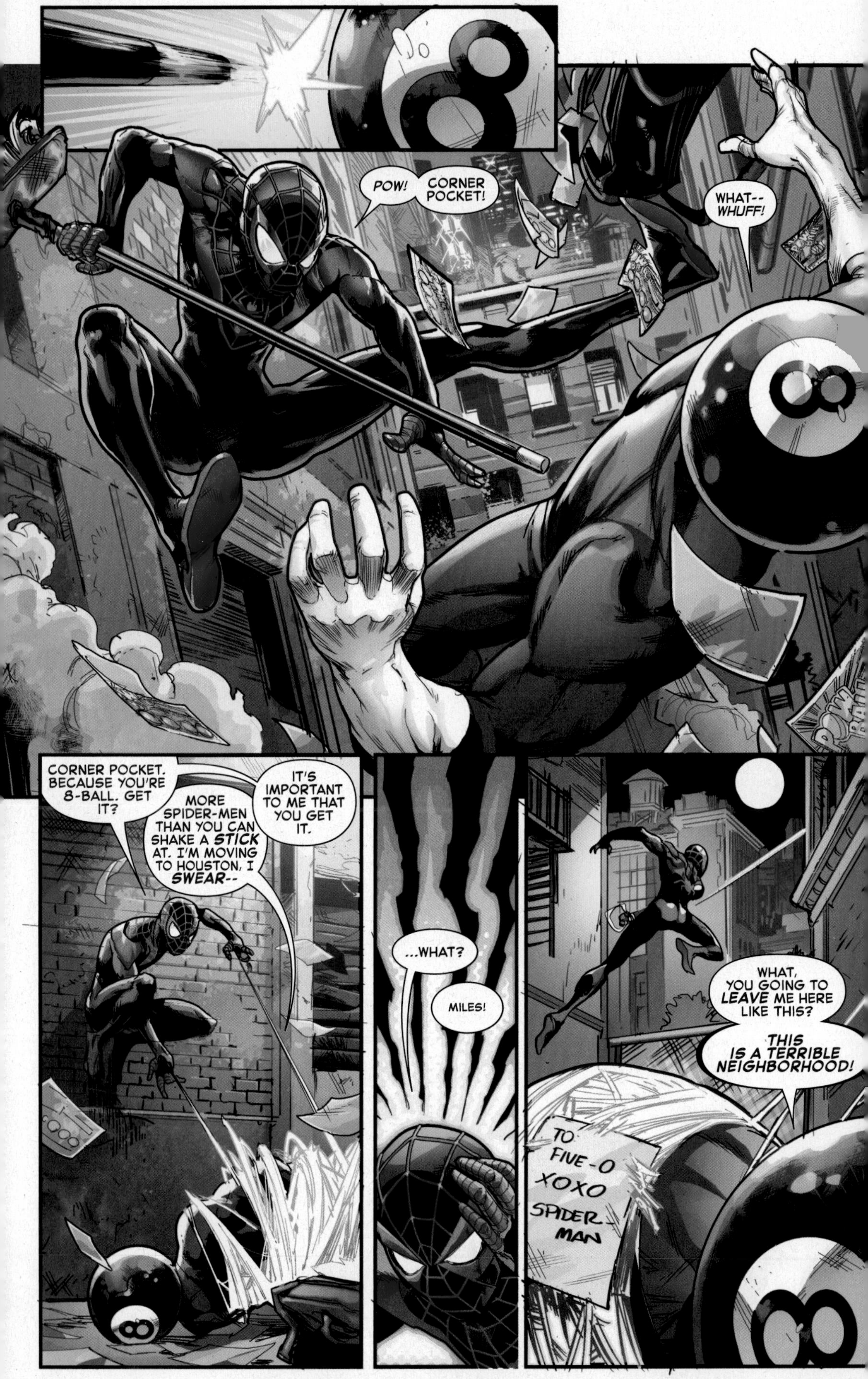
POW!
CORNER POCKET!
WHAT-- WHUFF!
CORNER POCKET. BECAUSE YOU'RE 8-BALL. GET IT?
IT'S IMPORTANT TO ME THAT YOU GET IT.
MORE SPIDER-MEN THAN YOU CAN SHAKE A STICK AT. I'M MOVING TO HOUSTON, I SWEAR--
...WHAT?
MILES!
WHAT, YOU GOING TO LEAVE ME HERE LIKE THIS?
THIS IS A TERRIBLE NEIGHBORHOOD!
TO FIVE-O XOXO SPIDER-MAN

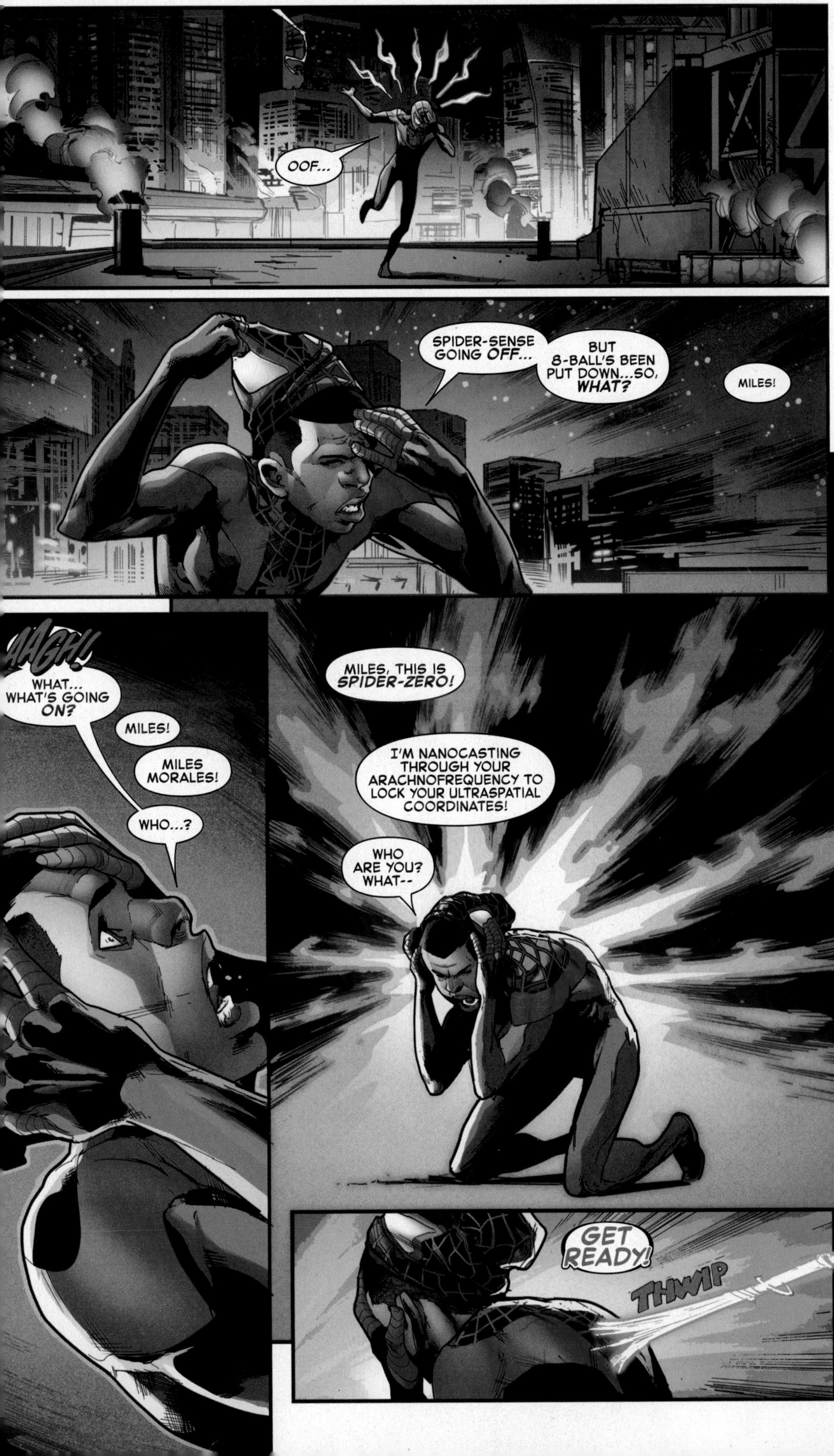
OOF...
SPIDER-SENSE GOING OFF...
BUT 8-BALL'S BEEN PUT DOWN...SO, WHAT?
MILES!
AAGH!
WHAT... WHAT'S GOING ON?
MILES!
MILES MORALES!
WHO...?
MILES, THIS IS SPIDER-ZERO!
I'M NANOCASTING THROUGH YOUR ARACHNOFREQUENCY TO LOCK YOUR ULTRASPATIAL COORDINATES!
WHO ARE YOU? WHAT--
GET READY!
THWIP

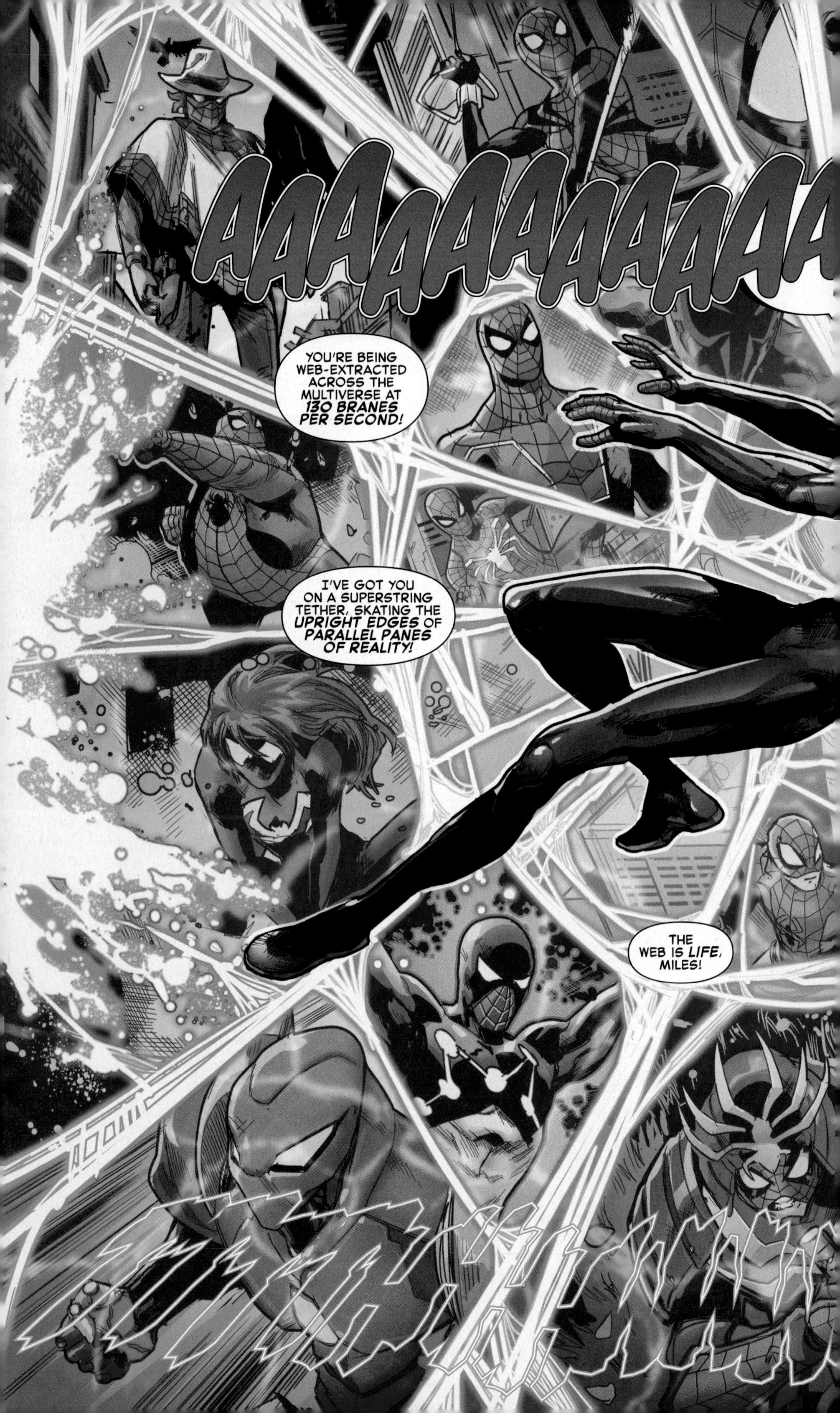
AAAAAAAAAAAA
YOU'RE BEING WEB-EXTRACTED ACROSS THE MULTIVERSE AT *130 BRANES PER SECOND!*
I'VE GOT YOU ON A SUPERSTRING TETHER, SKATING THE *UPRIGHT EDGES* OF *PARALLEL PANES OF REALITY!*
THE WEB IS *LIFE,* MILES!

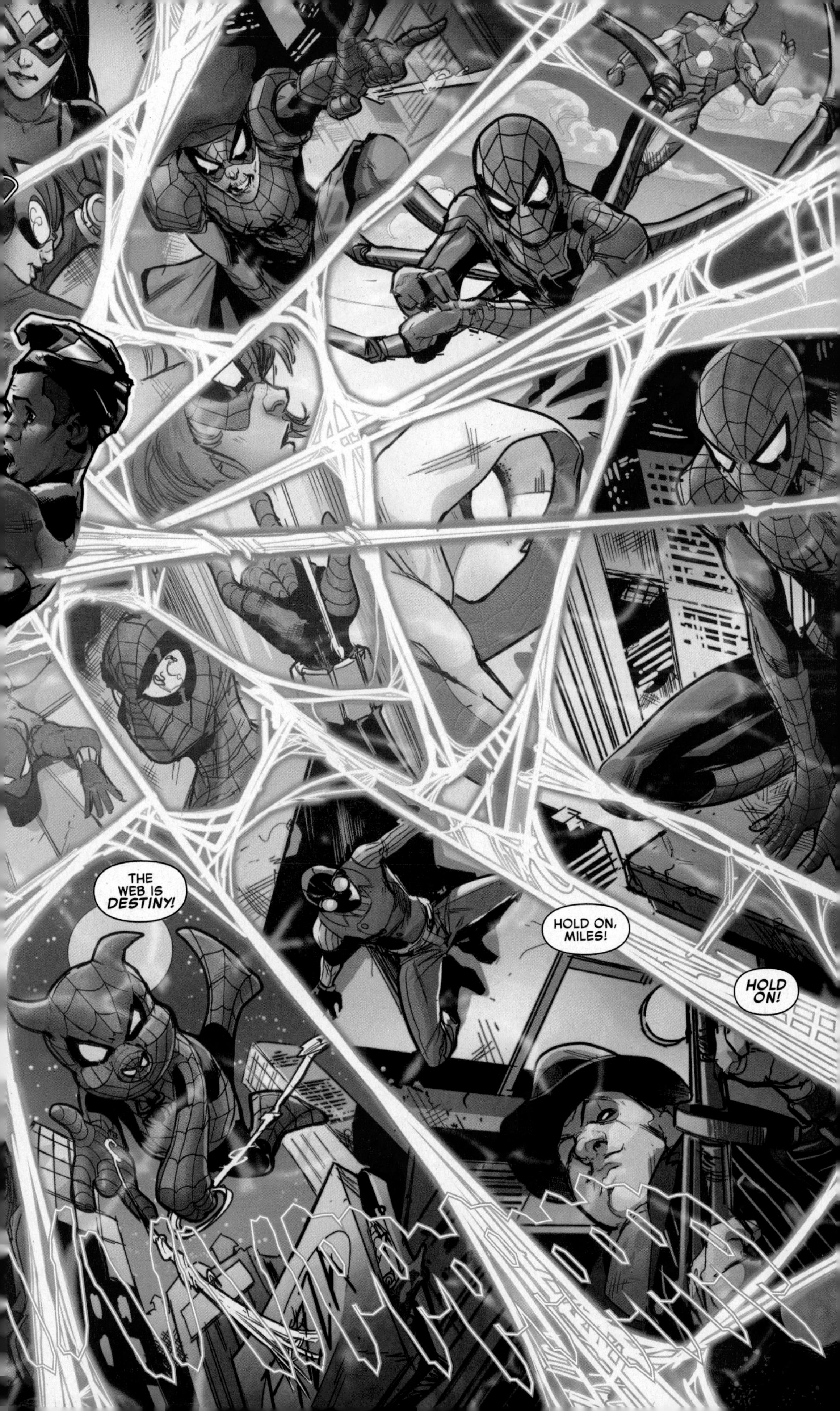
THE WEB IS DESTINY!
HOLD ON, MILES!
HOLD ON!

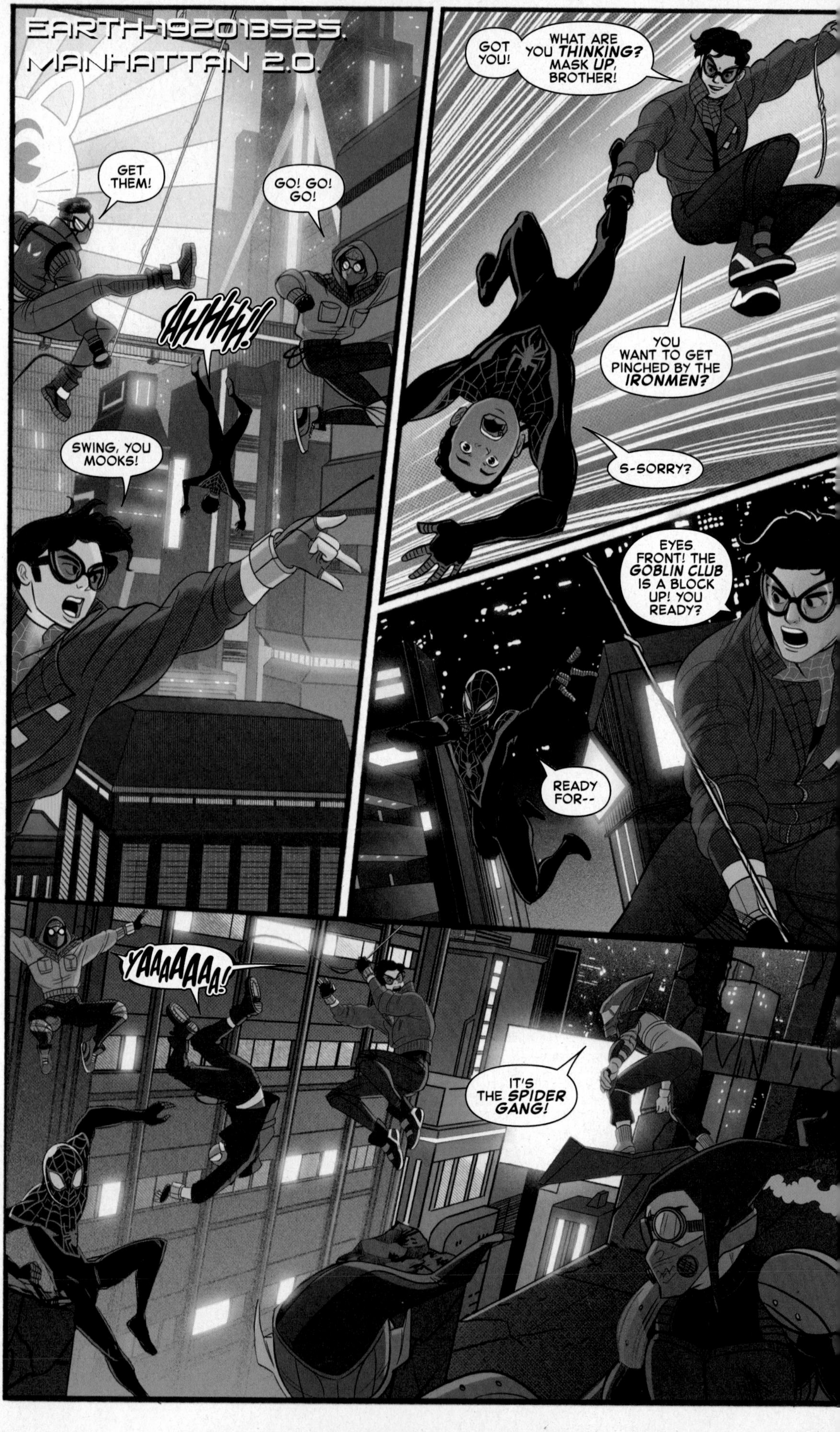
EARTH-1920135255.
MANHATTAN 2.0.
GET THEM!
GO! GO! GO!
AHHHH!
SWING, YOU MOOKS!
GOT YOU!
WHAT ARE YOU THINKING? MASK UP, BROTHER!
YOU WANT TO GET PINCHED BY THE IRONMEN?
S-SORRY?
EYES FRONT! THE GOBLIN CLUB IS A BLOCK UP! YOU READY?
READY FOR--
YAAAAAAA!
IT'S THE SPIDER GANG!

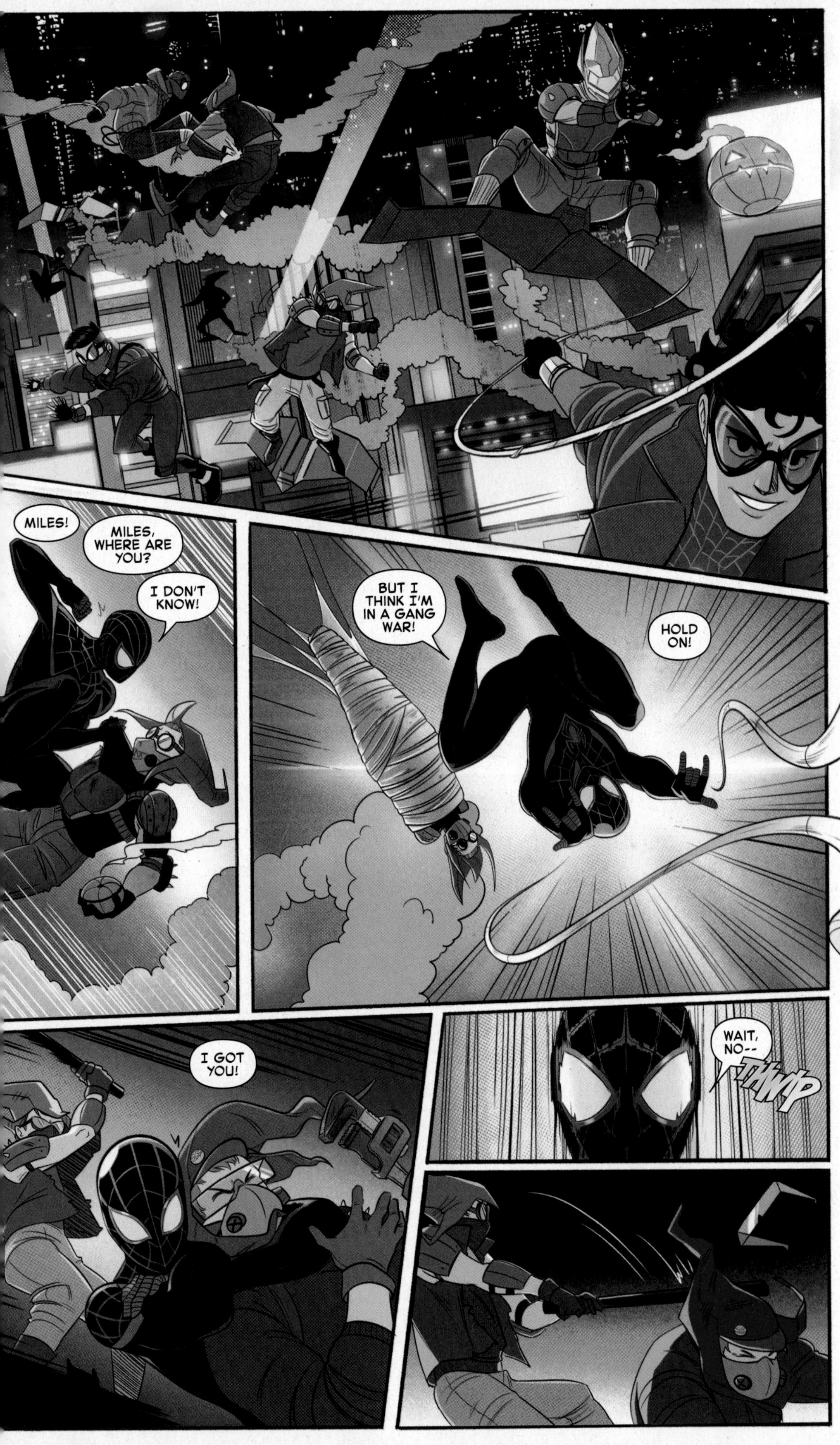
MILES!
MILES, WHERE ARE YOU?
I DON'T KNOW!
BUT I THINK I'M IN A GANG WAR!
HOLD ON!
I GOT YOU!
WAIT, NO--
THWIP

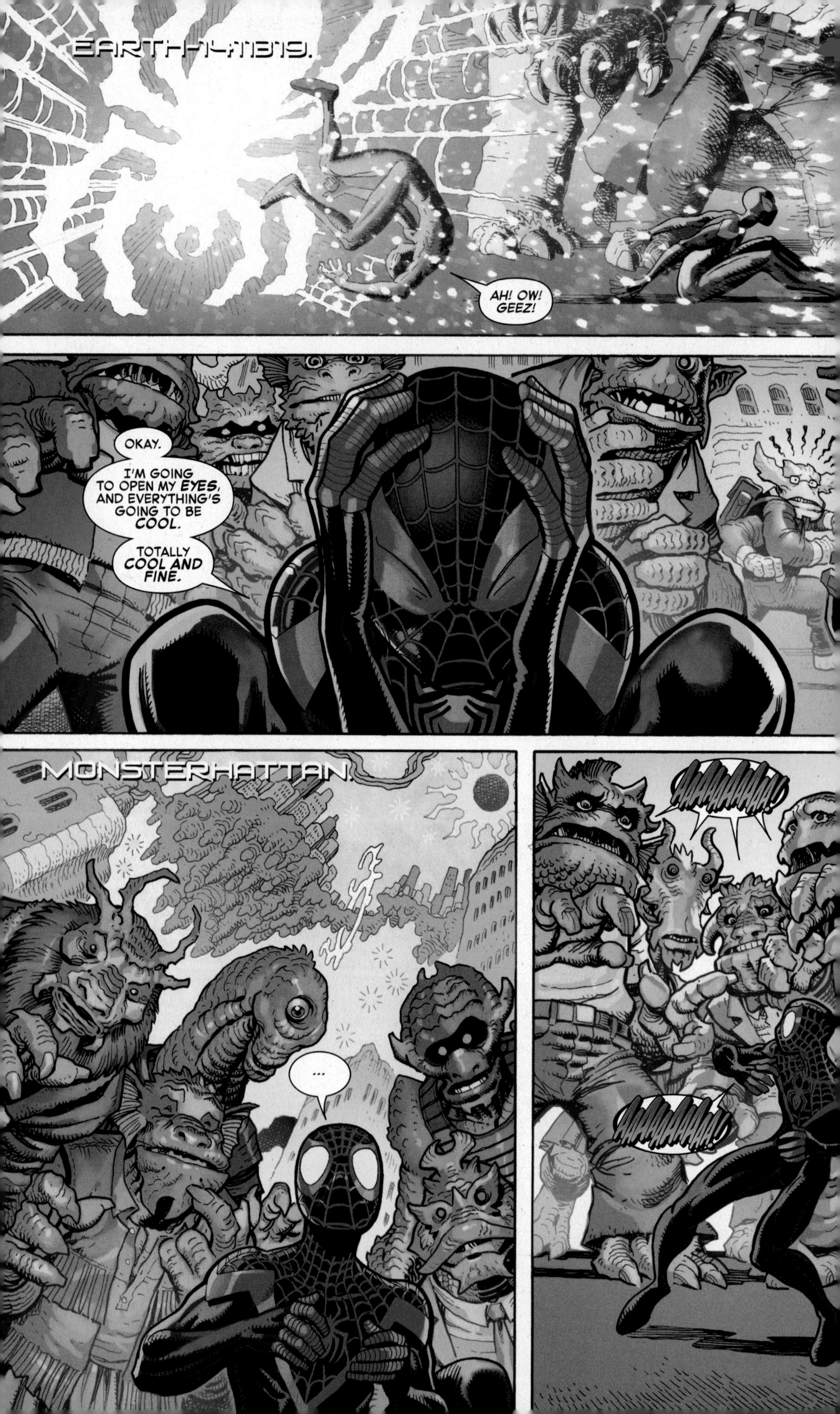
EARTH-1411319.
AH! OW! GEEZ!
OKAY.
I'M GOING TO OPEN MY *EYES*, AND EVERYTHING'S GOING TO BE *COOL*.
TOTALLY *COOL AND FINE*.
MONSTERHATTAN.
...
AAAAAAAAAAA!
AAAAAAAAAA!

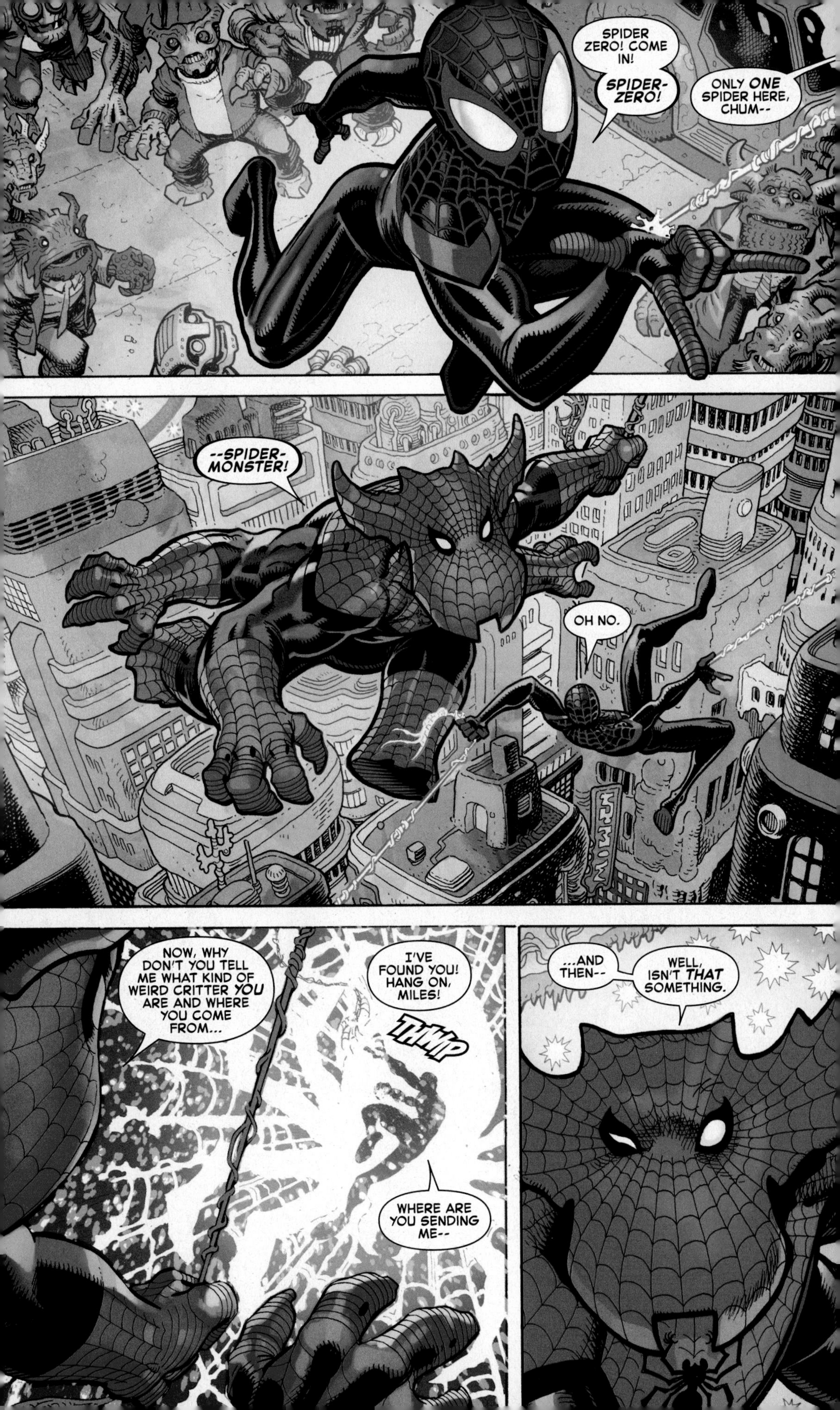

SPIDER ZERO! COME IN!
SPIDER-ZERO!
ONLY ONE SPIDER HERE, CHUM--
--SPIDER-MONSTER!
OH NO.
NOW, WHY DON'T YOU TELL ME WHAT KIND OF WEIRD CRITTER YOU ARE AND WHERE YOU COME FROM...
I'VE FOUND YOU! HANG ON, MILES!
THMP
WHERE ARE YOU SENDING ME--
...AND THEN--
WELL, ISN'T THAT SOMETHING.

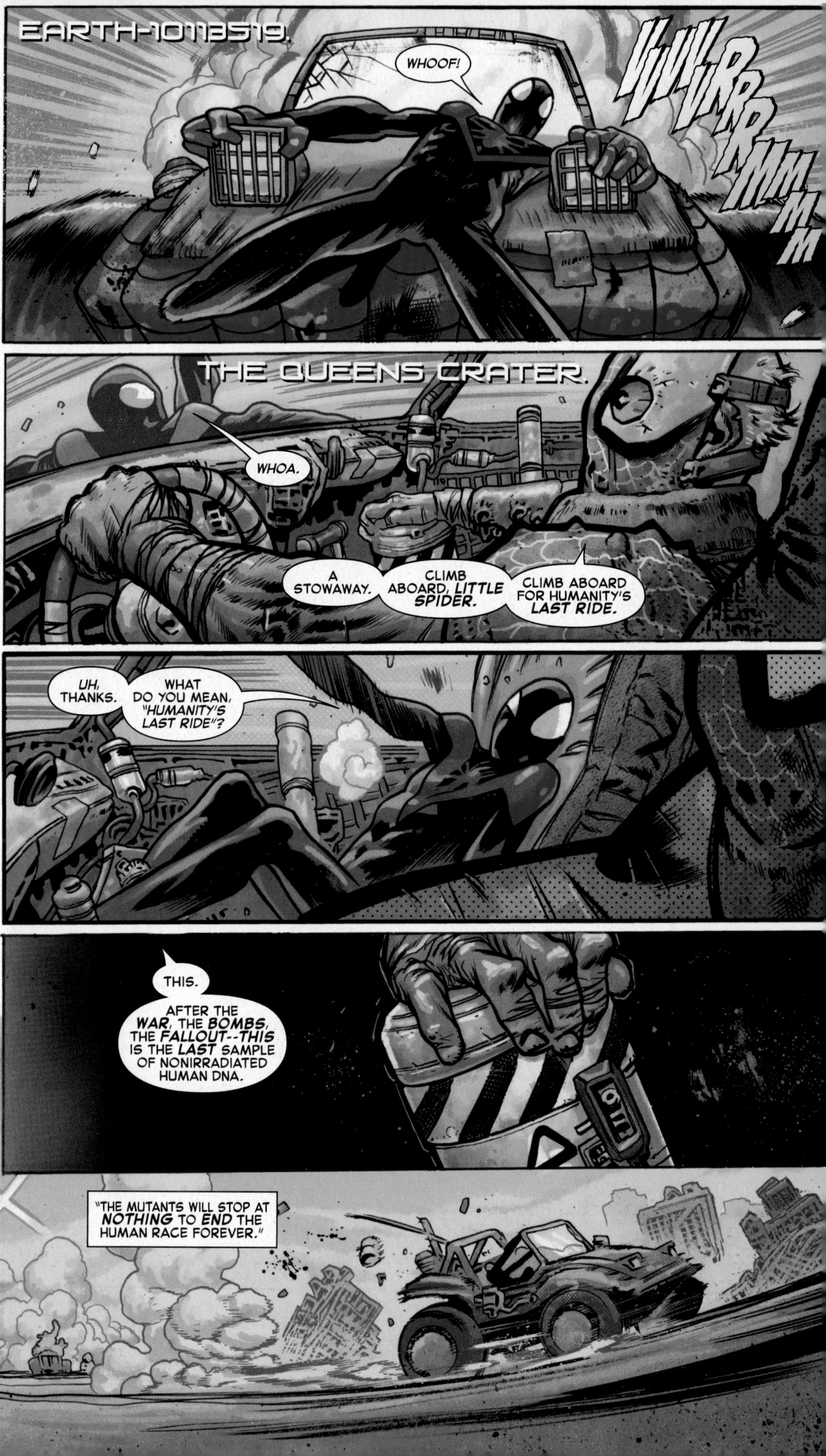
EARTH-10113519.
WHOOF!
VVVRRRMMMM
THE QUEENS CRATER.
WHOA.
A STOWAWAY.
CLIMB ABOARD, LITTLE SPIDER.
CLIMB ABOARD FOR HUMANITY'S LAST RIDE.
UH, THANKS.
WHAT DO YOU MEAN, "HUMANITY'S LAST RIDE"?
THIS.
AFTER THE WAR, THE BOMBS, THE FALLOUT--THIS IS THE LAST SAMPLE OF NONIRRADIATED HUMAN DNA.
"THE MUTANTS WILL STOP AT NOTHING TO END THE HUMAN RACE FOREVER."

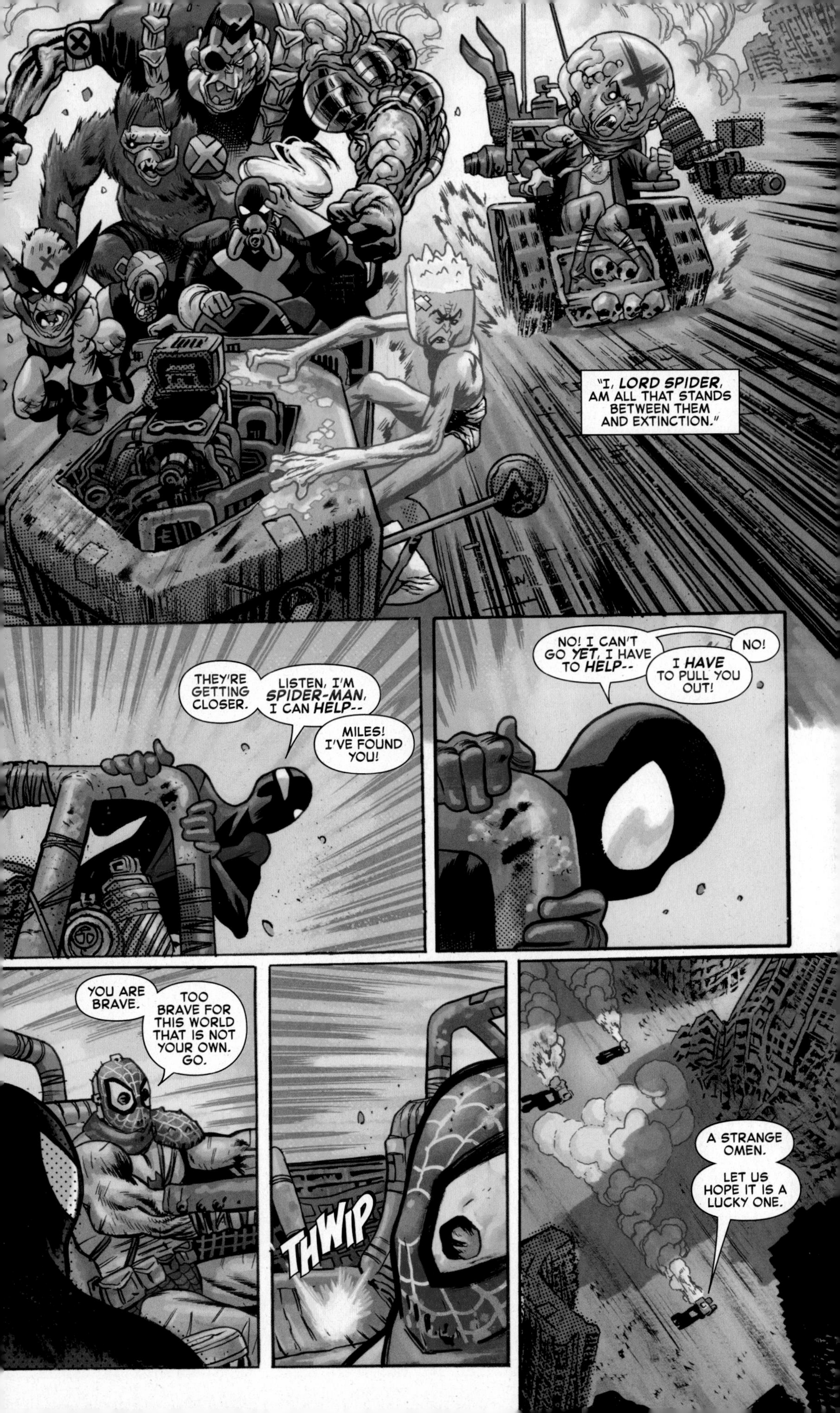
"I, LORD SPIDER, AM ALL THAT STANDS BETWEEN THEM AND EXTINCTION."
THEY'RE GETTING CLOSER.
LISTEN, I'M SPIDER-MAN, I CAN HELP--
MILES! I'VE FOUND YOU!
NO! I CAN'T GO YET, I HAVE TO HELP--
NO!
I HAVE TO PULL YOU OUT!
YOU ARE BRAVE.
TOO BRAVE FOR THIS WORLD THAT IS NOT YOUR OWN. GO.
THWIP
A STRANGE OMEN.
LET US HOPE IT IS A LUCKY ONE.

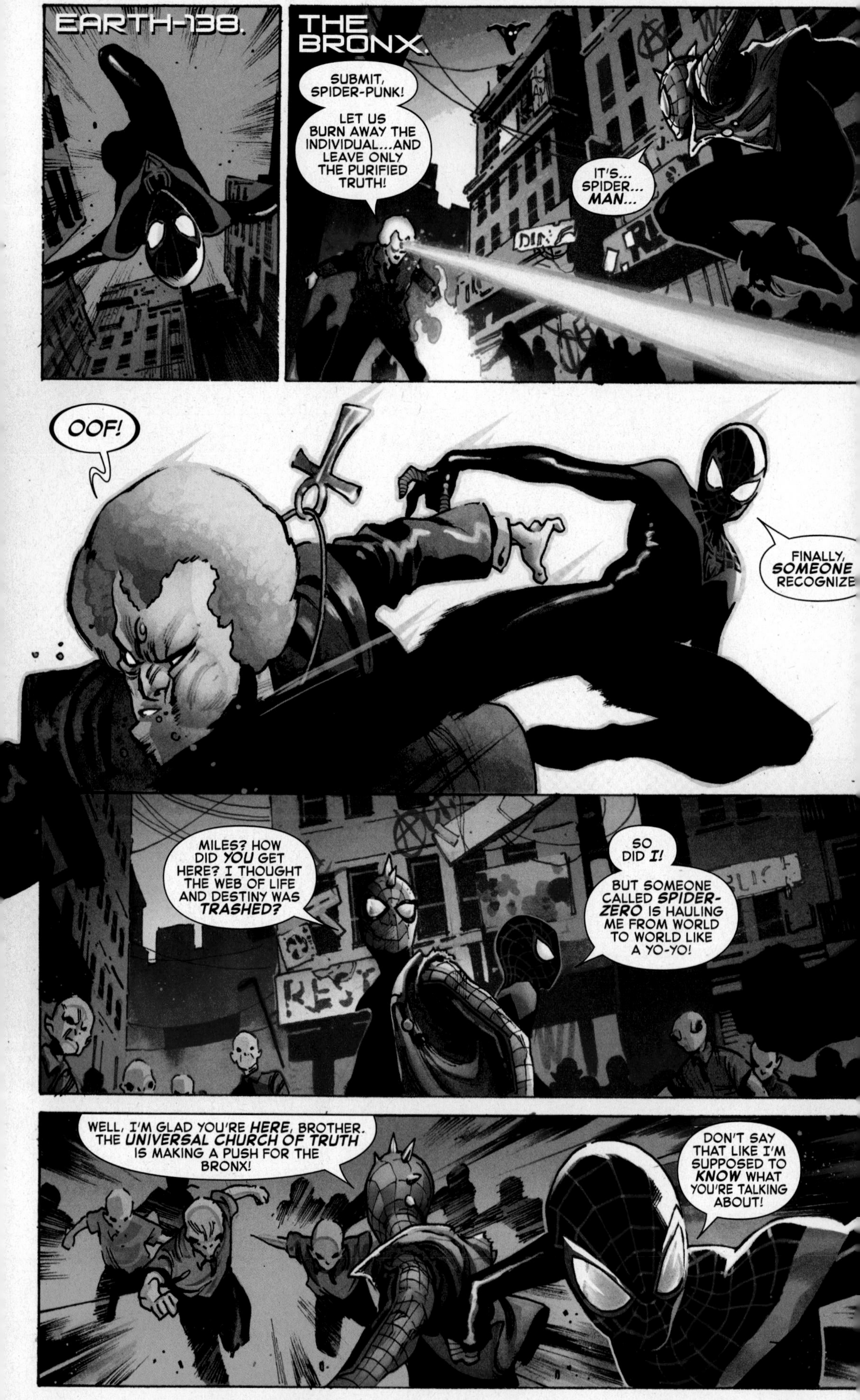
EARTH-138.
THE BRONX.
SUBMIT, SPIDER-PUNK!
LET US BURN AWAY THE INDIVIDUAL...AND LEAVE ONLY THE PURIFIED TRUTH!
IT'S... SPIDER... MAN...
OOF!
FINALLY, SOMEONE RECOGNIZE
MILES? HOW DID YOU GET HERE? I THOUGHT THE WEB OF LIFE AND DESTINY WAS TRASHED?
SO DID I!
BUT SOMEONE CALLED SPIDER-ZERO IS HAULING ME FROM WORLD TO WORLD LIKE A YO-YO!
WELL, I'M GLAD YOU'RE HERE, BROTHER. THE UNIVERSAL CHURCH OF TRUTH IS MAKING A PUSH FOR THE BRONX!
DON'T SAY THAT LIKE I'M SUPPOSED TO KNOW WHAT YOU'RE TALKING ABOUT!

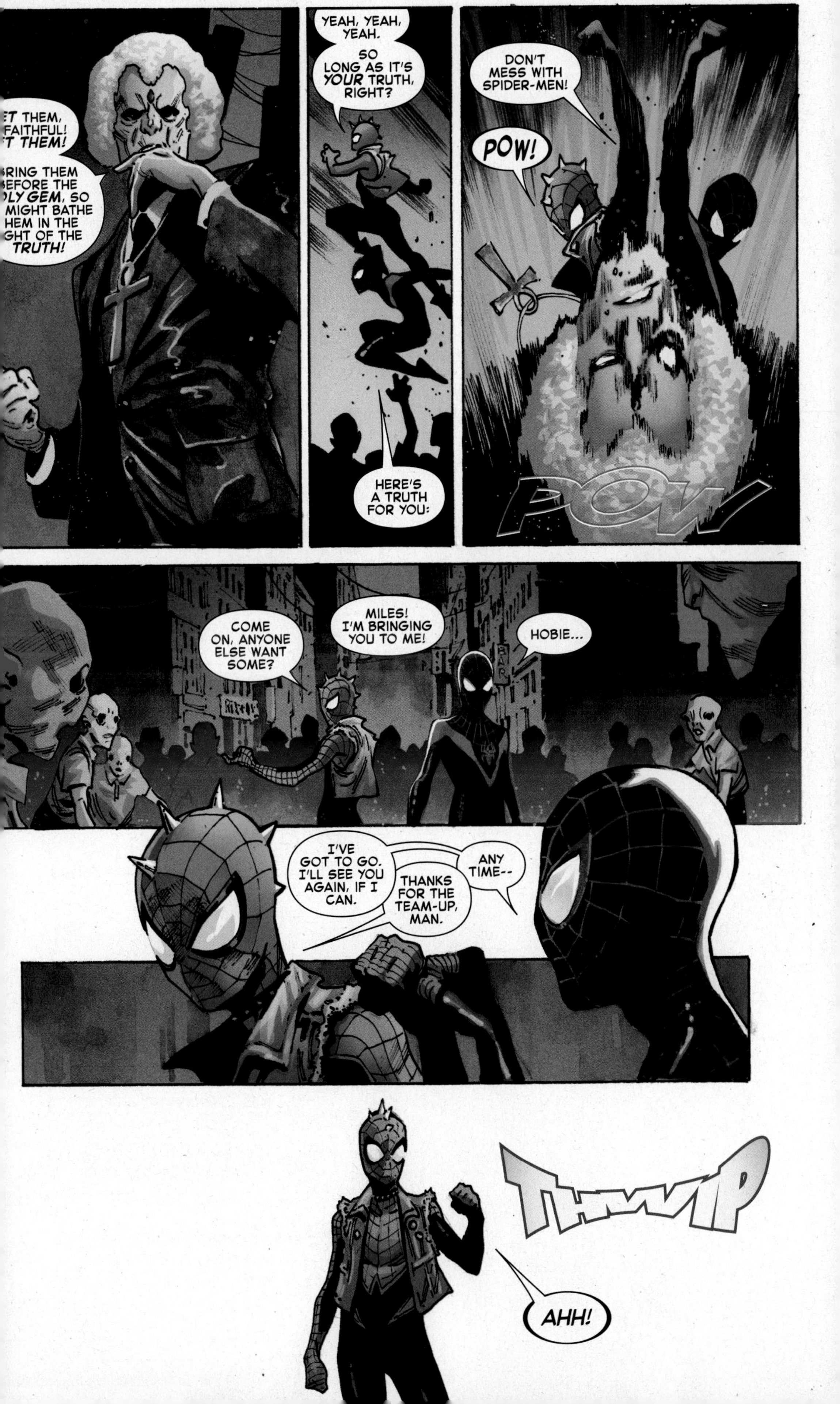
ET THEM, FAITHFUL! T THEM!
RING THEM BEFORE THE LY GEM, SO MIGHT BATHE HEM IN THE GHT OF THE TRUTH!
YEAH, YEAH, YEAH.
SO LONG AS IT'S YOUR TRUTH, RIGHT?
HERE'S A TRUTH FOR YOU:
DON'T MESS WITH SPIDER-MEN!
POW!
POW
COME ON, ANYONE ELSE WANT SOME?
MILES! I'M BRINGING YOU TO ME!
HOBIE...
BAR
I'VE GOT TO GO. I'LL SEE YOU AGAIN, IF I CAN.
THANKS FOR THE TEAM-UP, MAN.
ANY TIME--
THWIP
AHH!

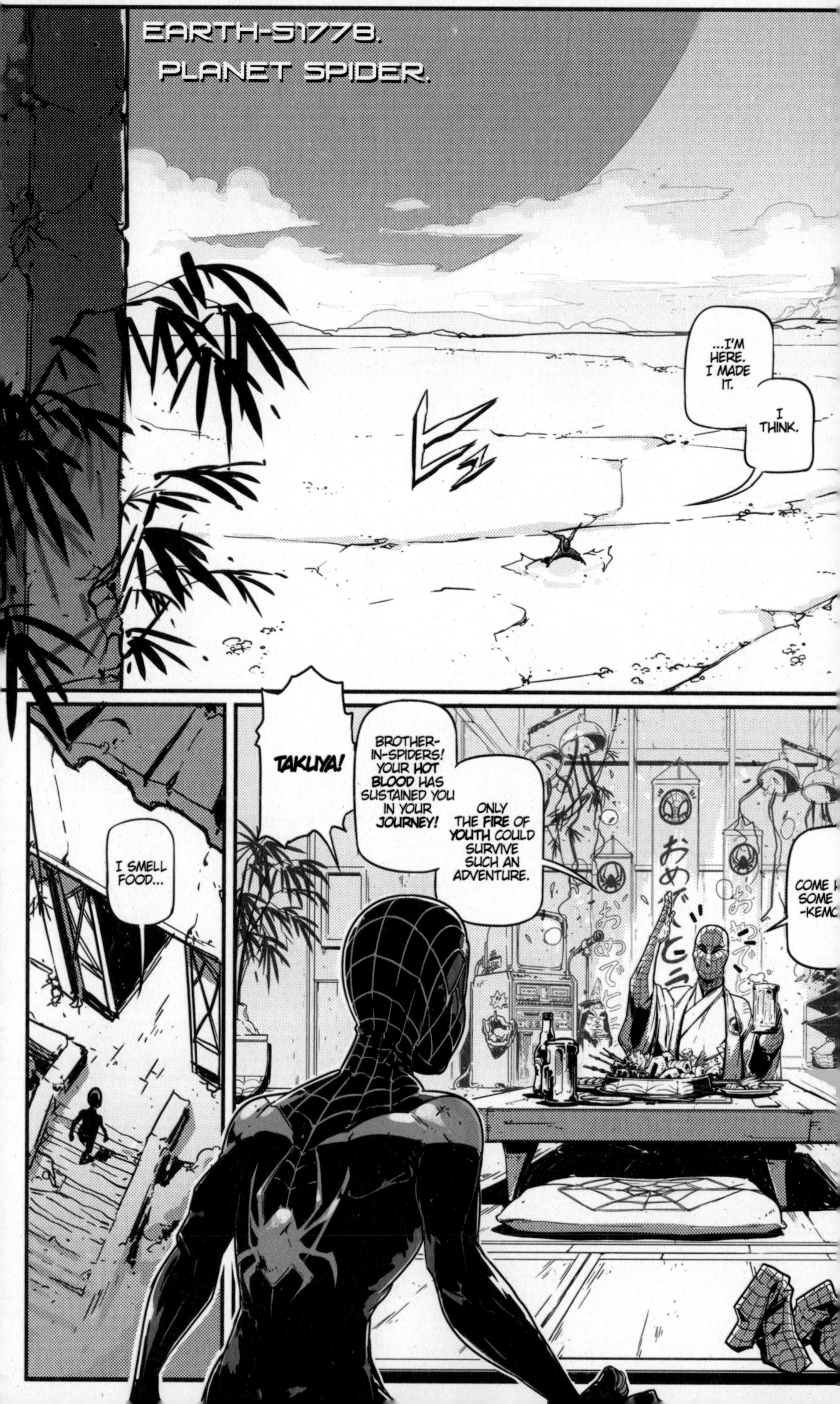
EARTH-51778.
PLANET SPIDER.
...I'M HERE. I MADE IT.
I THINK.
I SMELL FOOD...
TAKUYA!
BROTHER-IN-SPIDERS! YOUR HOT BLOOD HAS SUSTAINED YOU IN YOUR JOURNEY!
ONLY THE FIRE OF YOUTH COULD SURVIVE SUCH AN ADVENTURE.
COME I
SOME
-KEMC

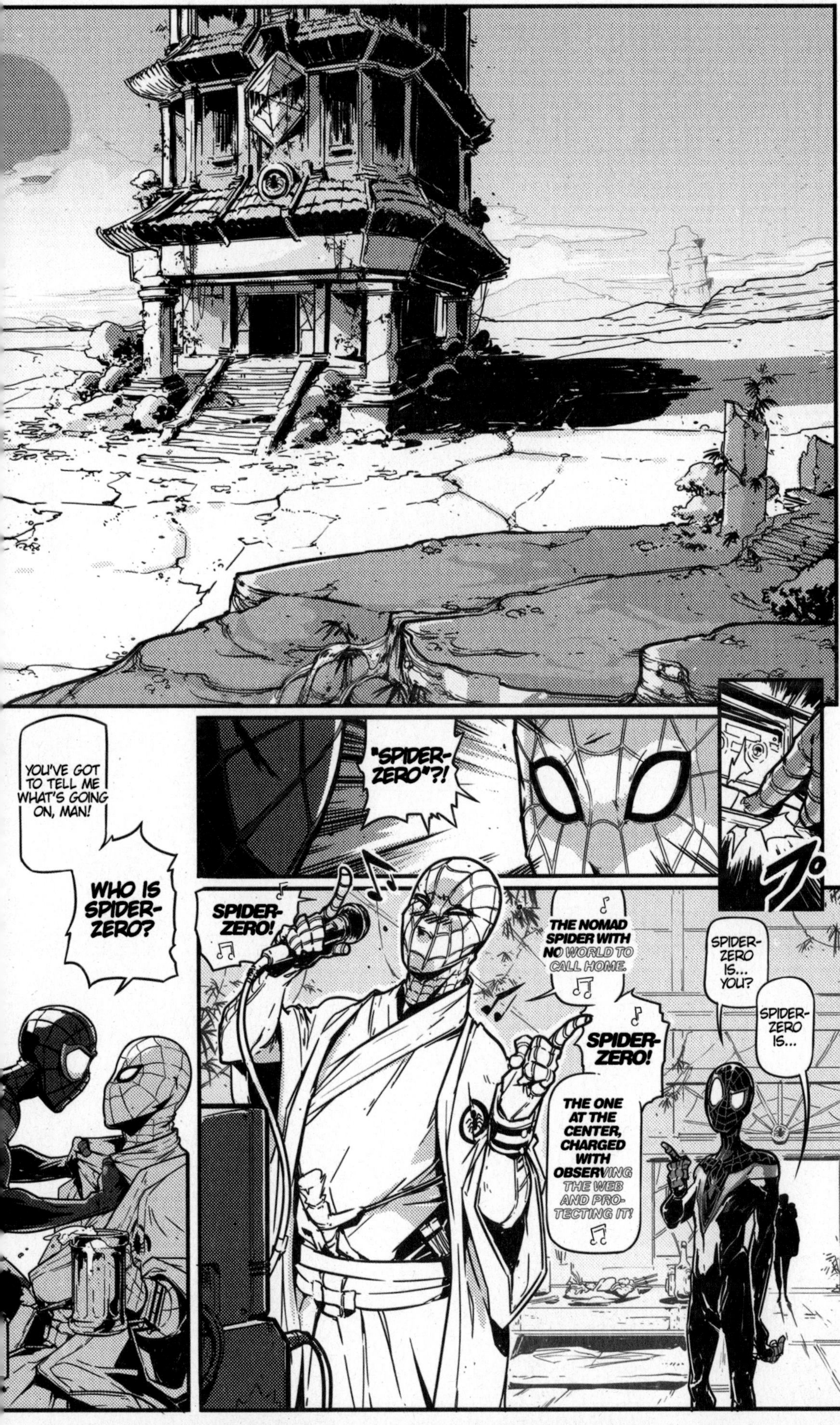
"SPIDER-ZERO"?!
YOU'VE GOT TO TELL ME WHAT'S GOING ON, MAN!
WHO IS SPIDER-ZERO?
SPIDER-ZERO!
THE NOMAD SPIDER WITH NO WORLD TO CALL HOME.
SPIDER-ZERO!
THE ONE AT THE CENTER, CHARGED WITH OBSERVING THE WEB AND PROTECTING IT!
SPIDER-ZERO IS... YOU?
SPIDER-ZERO IS...

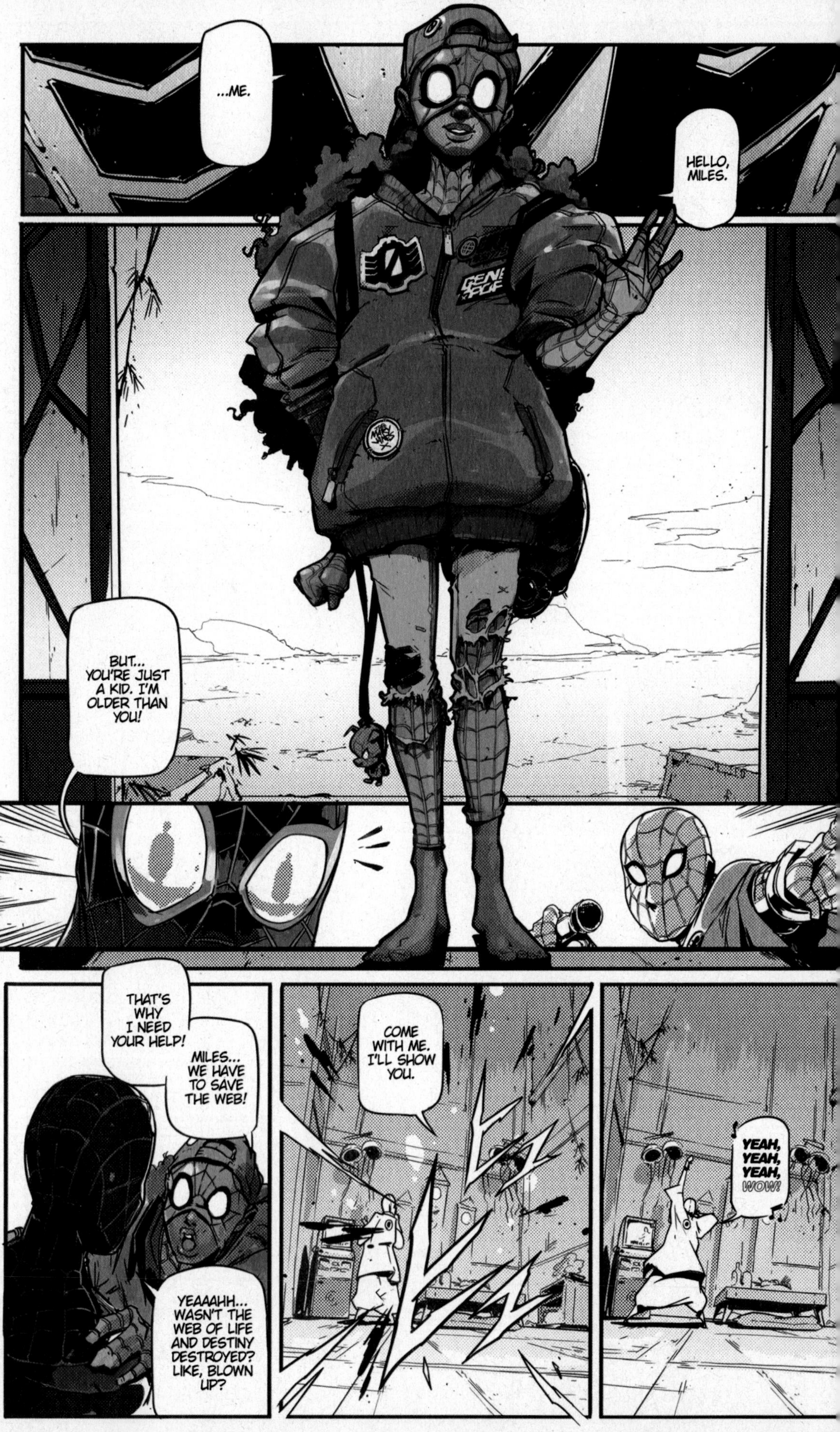
...ME.
HELLO, MILES.
BUT... YOU'RE JUST A KID. I'M OLDER THAN YOU!
THAT'S WHY I NEED YOUR HELP!
MILES... WE HAVE TO SAVE THE WEB!
YEAAAHH... WASN'T THE WEB OF LIFE AND DESTINY DESTROYED? LIKE, BLOWN UP?
COME WITH ME. I'LL SHOW YOU.
YEAH, YEAH, YEAH, WOW!

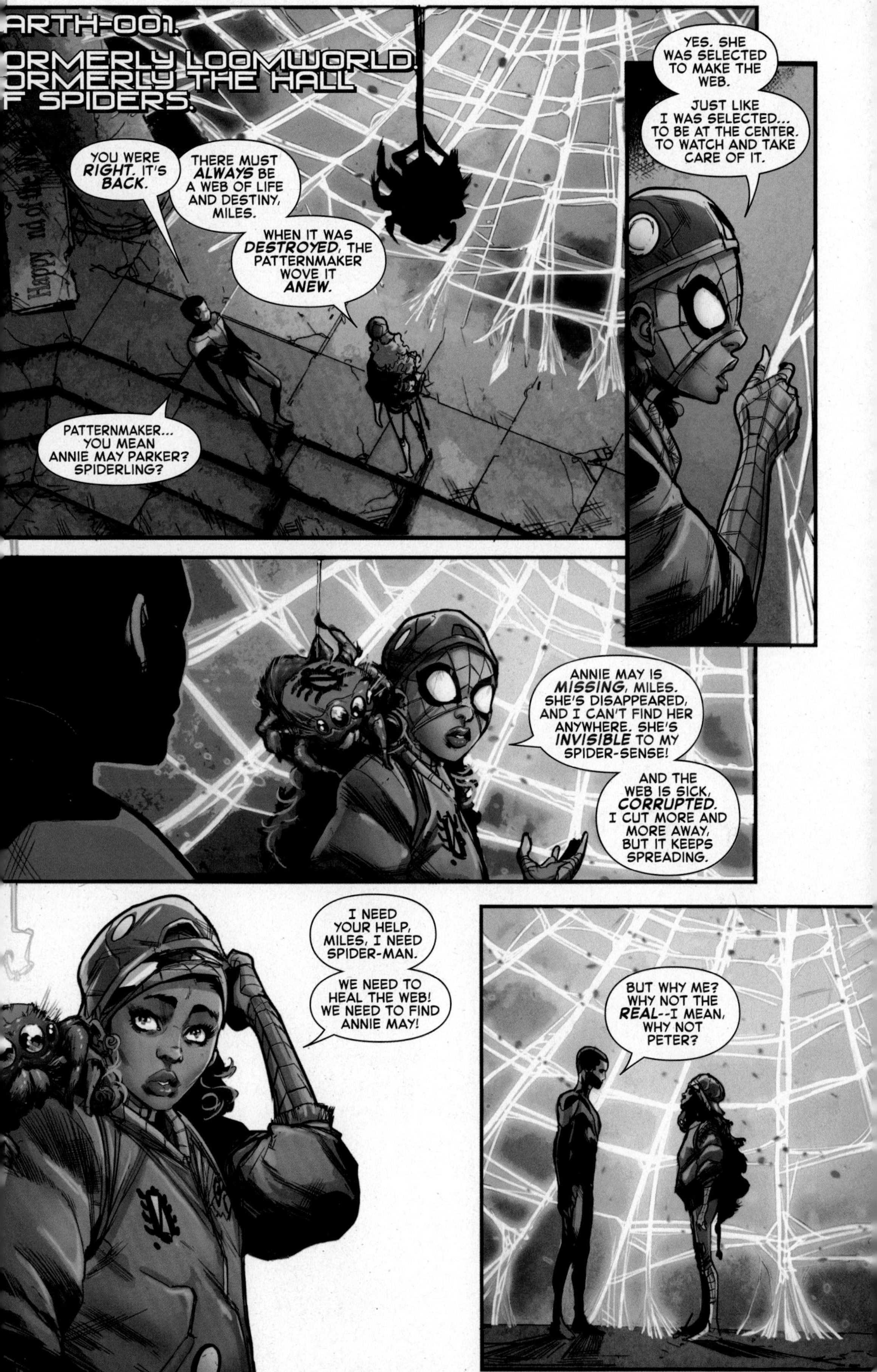
ARTH-001.
ORMERLY LOOMWORLD.
ORMERLY THE HALL
F SPIDERS.
YOU WERE RIGHT. IT'S BACK.
THERE MUST ALWAYS BE A WEB OF LIFE AND DESTINY, MILES.
WHEN IT WAS DESTROYED, THE PATTERNMAKER WOVE IT ANEW.
PATTERNMAKER... YOU MEAN ANNIE MAY PARKER? SPIDERLING?
YES. SHE WAS SELECTED TO MAKE THE WEB.
JUST LIKE I WAS SELECTED... TO BE AT THE CENTER. TO WATCH AND TAKE CARE OF IT.
ANNIE MAY IS MISSING, MILES. SHE'S DISAPPEARED, AND I CAN'T FIND HER ANYWHERE. SHE'S INVISIBLE TO MY SPIDER-SENSE!
AND THE WEB IS SICK, CORRUPTED. I CUT MORE AND MORE AWAY, BUT IT KEEPS SPREADING.
I NEED YOUR HELP, MILES, I NEED SPIDER-MAN.
WE NEED TO HEAL THE WEB! WE NEED TO FIND ANNIE MAY!
BUT WHY ME? WHY NOT THE REAL--I MEAN, WHY NOT PETER?

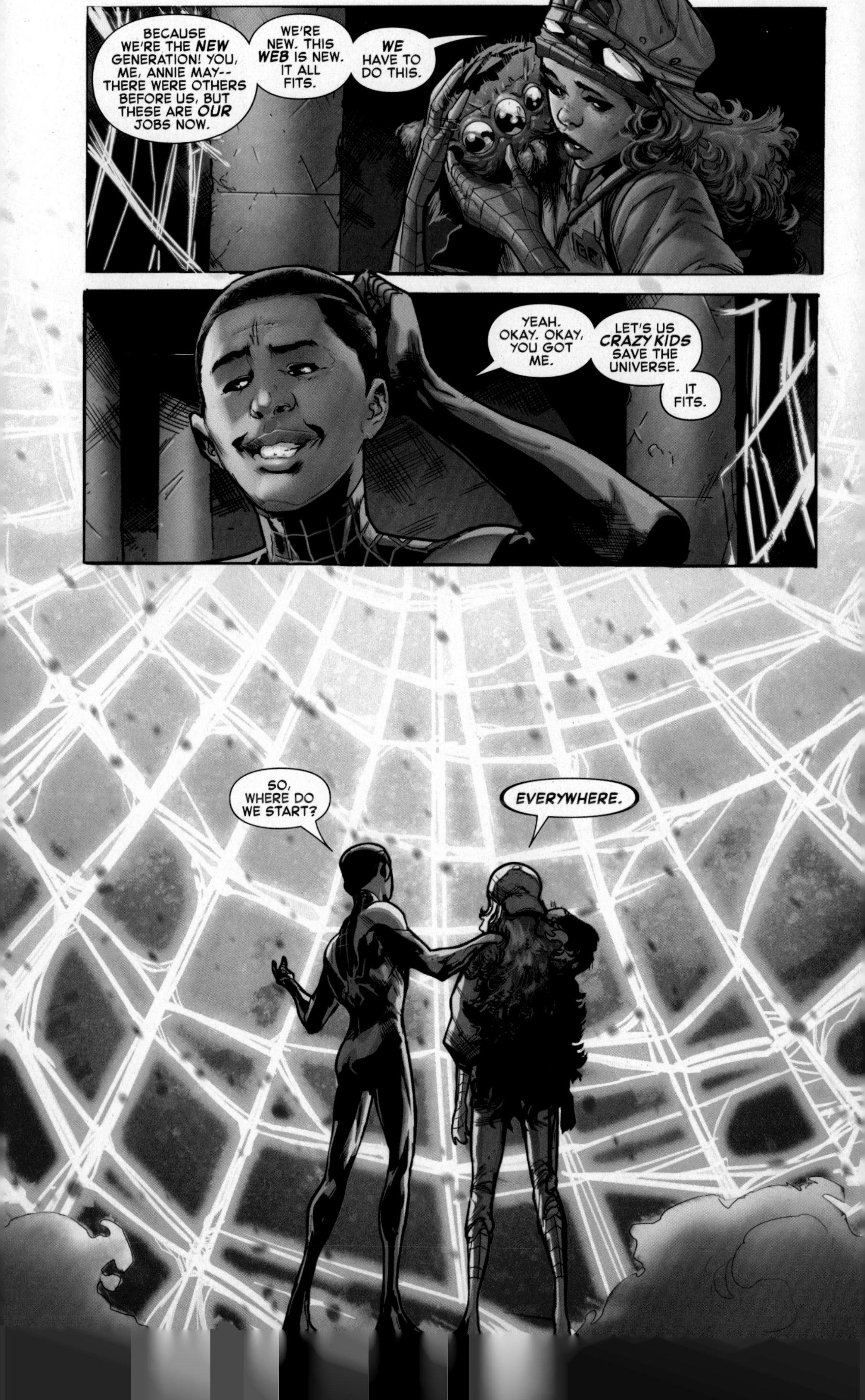

BECAUSE WE'RE THE NEW GENERATION! YOU, ME, ANNIE MAY-- THERE WERE OTHERS BEFORE US, BUT THESE ARE OUR JOBS NOW.
WE'RE NEW. THIS WEB IS NEW. IT ALL FITS.
WE HAVE TO DO THIS.
YEAH. OKAY. OKAY, YOU GOT ME.
LET'S US CRAZY KIDS SAVE THE UNIVERSE.
IT FITS.
SO, WHERE DO WE START?
EVERYWHERE.

SPIDER-VERSES

Welcome to the first issue of *Spider-Verse*! Whether you're a comic book fan, a *Spider-Man: Into the Spider-Verse* film fan or both, we're excited to explore the wild, wacky, sometimes scary and everything-in-between worlds of the Spider-Verse with you. Having read this first issue, you can see that we've assembled a vast team of amazingly talented artists from all corners of the Spider-Verse to help weave together Jed MacKay's epic story.

Many of you are probably already familiar with the hashtag "Spidersona" that launched around the release of *Spider-Man: Into the Spider-Verse*. We were just as impressed as you by everyone's talent and creativity, and so we reached out to some of you to create new Spidersona art especially for these issues. In each issue of *Spider-Verse* we're going to showcase three of these original pieces of Spidersona art by artists from around the globe. Keep reading to take a gander at our first three spectacular Spidersonas!

We've got an equally all-star team of writers and artists assembled for our upcoming issues, including Ryan North *(Unbeatable Squirrel Girl)* and Pere Pérez *(Uncanny X-Men)* for issue #2. Miles will be exploring even more exciting universes with other crazy Spider-People—some new, some familiar—all on the road to finding Spiderling and saving the Web of Life and Destiny. Our journey through the Spider-Verse is just getting started...

Also, we'd love to hear your thoughts on the series! E-mail us at SPIDEYOFFICE@MARVEL.COM. Please be sure to mark your e-mail "Okay to Print"!

--Nick, Kathleen & Martin

SPIDERSONA:
SPIDER-REQUIEM

Art & Text by COTTON VALENT
Thailand

Spider-Requiem's real name is Polymnia Swan—"Polymnia" also being the name of the Greek Muse of Dance. Her mask not only protects her identity but also conceals the scar on her face. Spider-Requiem is an excellent puppeteer who artfully stages her battles. In addition to the usual Spider-powers, she has the ability to control her handmade puppets in combat.

SPIDERSONA:
THE SPINSTER

Art & Text by ANTONIO DEMICO
France

By feeling the subtle vibrations on the webs she creates with her prehensile hair, the Spinster can hear any conversation no matter how far away it's taking place. Her design was inspired by noblewomen in the era of the French Revolution as well as the original Madame Web.

SPIDERSONA:
V

Art & Text by V-0-3
Poland

I love the whole cyberpunk genre, and since I'm also a huge fan of robots, I decided to combine all of it into a robo Spidersona! V lives in Kyoto in the year 2177. Her special power is connecting to the internet in order to apprehend people committing digital crimes.

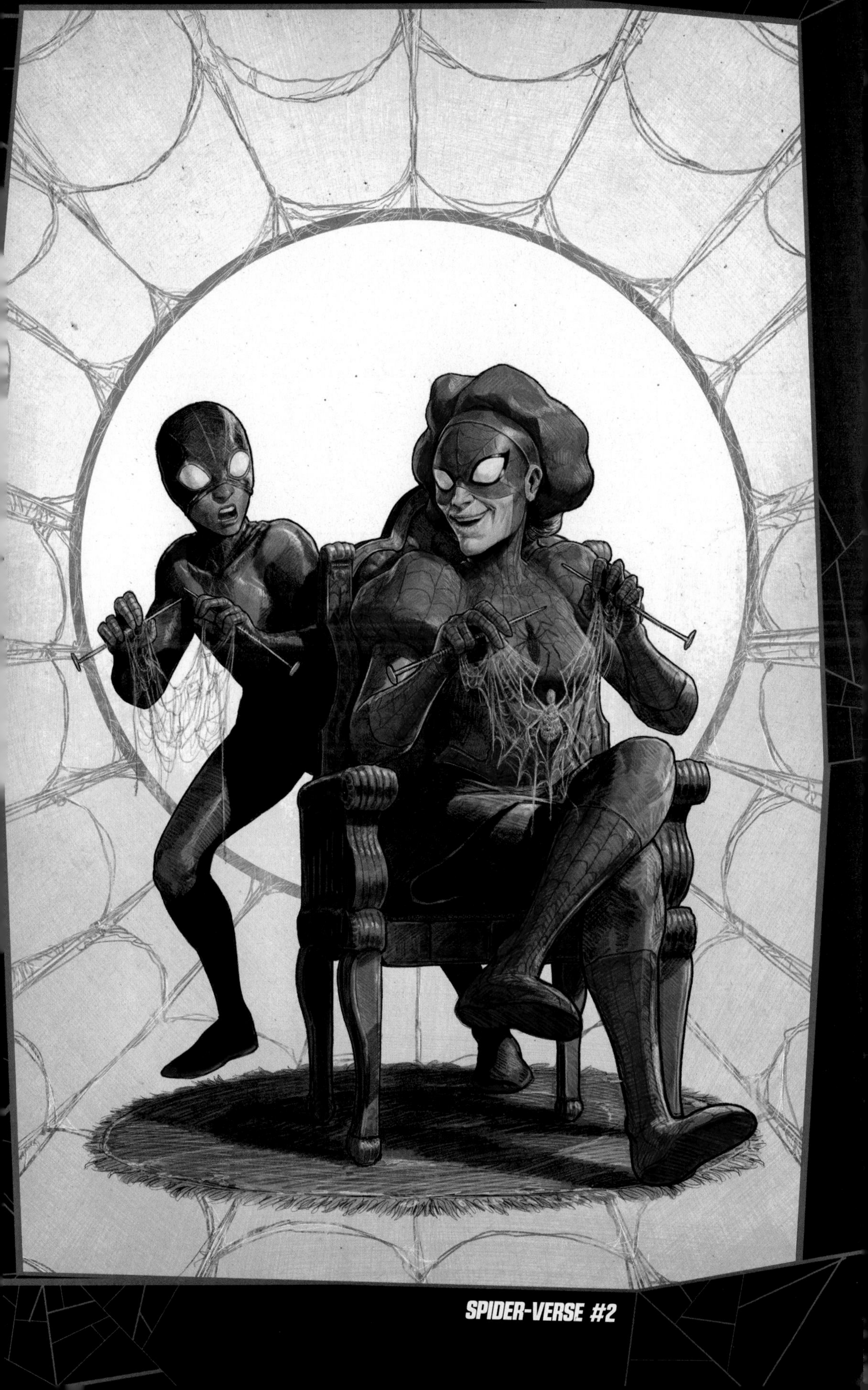

SPIDER-VERSE #2

BITTEN BY A RADIOACTIVE SPIDER, MAY PARKER GAINS ITS PROPORTIONAL ***SPEED***, ***STRENGTH***, AND ***AGILITY***! INITI USING HER POWERS ONLY TO PROTECT HER BRILLIANT BUT TIMID NEPHEW, PETER, EVERYTHING CHANGES WHEN SHE TENDS ***HIM*** DURING A ROBBERY INSTEAD OF CAPTURING THE ***CRIMINAL***--WHO GOES ON TO ALMOST ***KILL*** HER HUSBAND, BEN, T VERY NIGHT! MAY SWEARS TO USE HER POWERS NOT ONLY TO PROTECT HER NEPHEW, BUT THE ***WHOLE WORLD*** TOO. AR WITH THE FANTASTIC ***WEB-SHOOTERS*** PETER INVENTED, SHE FIGHTS FOR TRUTH AND JUSTICE AS...

THE SPECTACULAR SPIDER-MA'AM

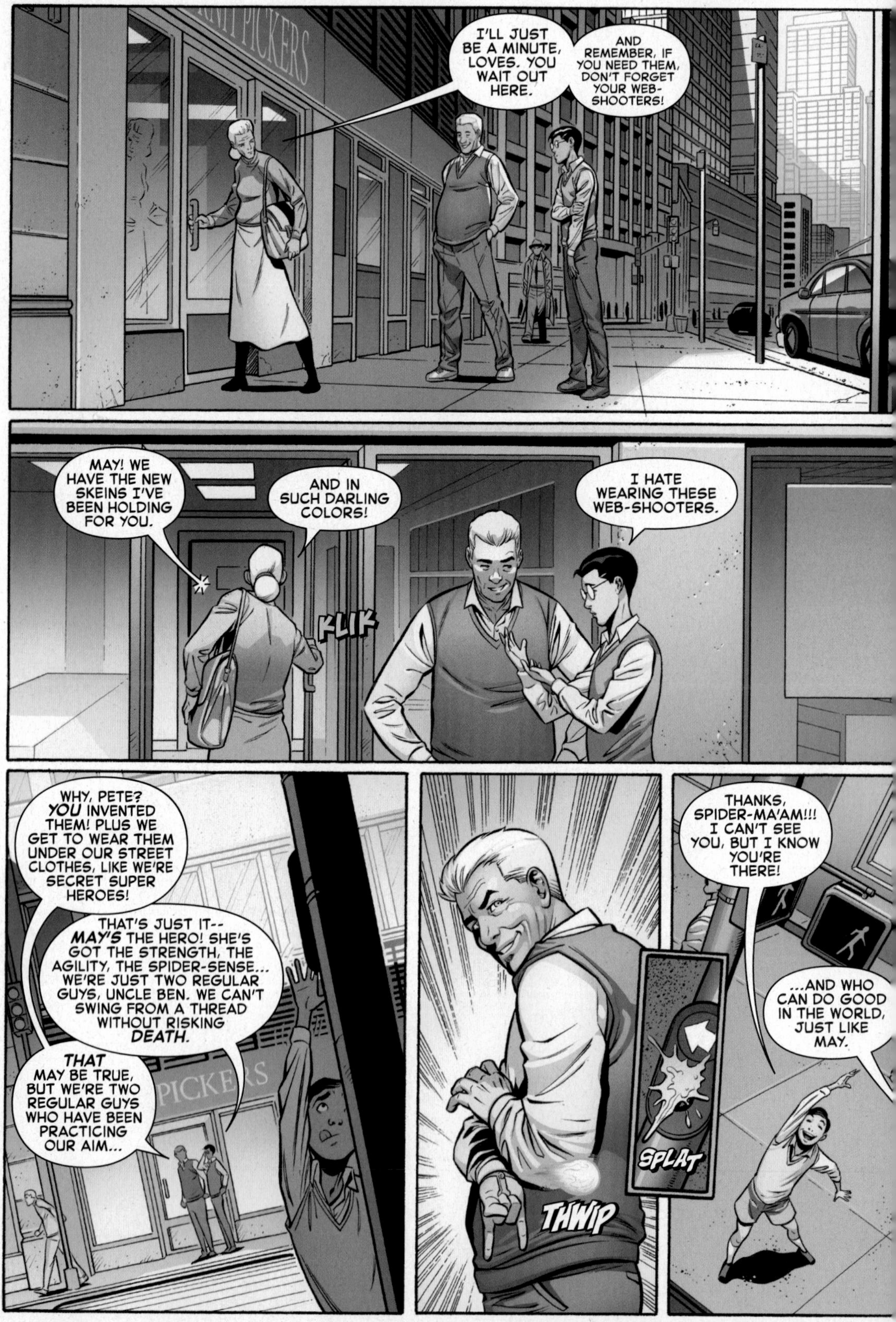

PICKERS
I'LL JUST BE A MINUTE, LOVES. YOU WAIT OUT HERE.
AND REMEMBER, IF YOU NEED THEM, DON'T FORGET YOUR WEB-SHOOTERS!
MAY! WE HAVE THE NEW SKEINS I'VE BEEN HOLDING FOR YOU.
AND IN SUCH DARLING COLORS!
KLIK
I HATE WEARING THESE WEB-SHOOTERS.
WHY, PETE? YOU INVENTED THEM! PLUS WE GET TO WEAR THEM UNDER OUR STREET CLOTHES, LIKE WE'RE SECRET SUPER HEROES!
THAT'S JUST IT-- MAY'S THE HERO! SHE'S GOT THE STRENGTH, THE AGILITY, THE SPIDER-SENSE... WE'RE JUST TWO REGULAR GUYS, UNCLE BEN. WE CAN'T SWING FROM A THREAD WITHOUT RISKING DEATH.
THAT MAY BE TRUE, BUT WE'RE TWO REGULAR GUYS WHO HAVE BEEN PRACTICING OUR AIM...
PICKERS
SPLAT
THWIP
THANKS, SPIDER-MA'AM!!! I CAN'T SEE YOU, BUT I KNOW YOU'RE THERE!
...AND WHO CAN DO GOOD IN THE WORLD, JUST LIKE MAY.

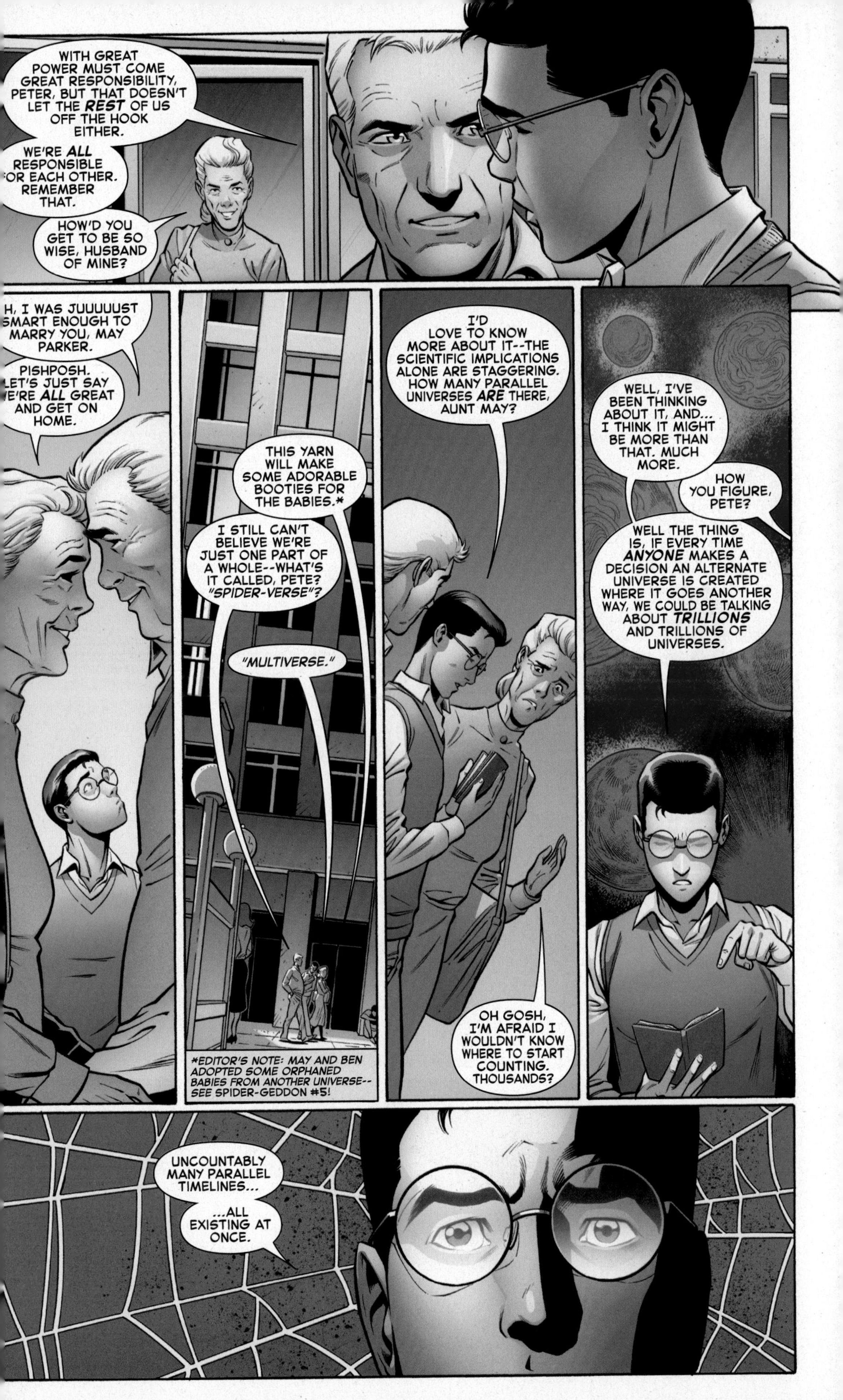

WITH GREAT POWER MUST COME GREAT RESPONSIBILITY, PETER, BUT THAT DOESN'T LET THE *REST* OF US OFF THE HOOK EITHER.
WE'RE *ALL* RESPONSIBLE FOR EACH OTHER. REMEMBER THAT.
HOW'D YOU GET TO BE SO WISE, HUSBAND OF MINE?
H, I WAS JUUUUUST SMART ENOUGH TO MARRY YOU, MAY PARKER.
PISHPOSH. LET'S JUST SAY WE'RE *ALL* GREAT AND GET ON HOME.
THIS YARN WILL MAKE SOME ADORABLE BOOTIES FOR THE BABIES.*
I STILL CAN'T BELIEVE WE'RE JUST ONE PART OF A WHOLE--WHAT'S IT CALLED, PETE? *"SPIDER-VERSE"?*
"MULTIVERSE."
*EDITOR'S NOTE: MAY AND BEN ADOPTED SOME ORPHANED BABIES FROM ANOTHER UNIVERSE-- SEE SPIDER-GEDDON #5!
I'D LOVE TO KNOW MORE ABOUT IT--THE SCIENTIFIC IMPLICATIONS ALONE ARE STAGGERING. HOW MANY PARALLEL UNIVERSES *ARE* THERE, AUNT MAY?
OH GOSH, I'M AFRAID I WOULDN'T KNOW WHERE TO START COUNTING. THOUSANDS?
WELL, I'VE BEEN THINKING ABOUT IT, AND... I THINK IT MIGHT BE MORE THAN THAT. MUCH MORE.
HOW YOU FIGURE, PETE?
WELL THE THING IS, IF EVERY TIME *ANYONE* MAKES A DECISION AN ALTERNATE UNIVERSE IS CREATED WHERE IT GOES ANOTHER WAY, WE COULD BE TALKING ABOUT *TRILLIONS* AND TRILLIONS OF UNIVERSES.
UNCOUNTABLY MANY PARALLEL TIMELINES...
...ALL EXISTING AT ONCE.

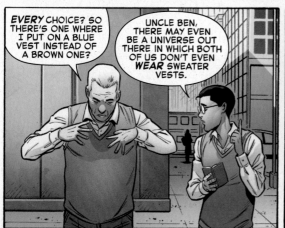

EVERY CHOICE? SO THERE'S ONE WHERE I PUT ON A BLUE VEST INSTEAD OF A BROWN ONE?

UNCLE BEN, THERE MAY EVEN BE A UNIVERSE OUT THERE IN WHICH BOTH OF US DON'T EVEN *WEAR* SWEATER VESTS.

PERISH THE THOUGHT.

IN FACT, NOW THAT I'M THINKING ABOUT IT, THAT ACTUALLY POINTS TO A CONCLUSION WE CAN DRAW: IF PARALLEL UNIVERSES *DO* PROLIFERATE AS I'M THEORIZING, THEN ANYTHING THAT *CAN* HAPPEN...*MUST* HAPPEN. IT'S INEVITABLE!

YOU HEAR THAT, BEN? OUR NEPHEW JUST CAME UP WITH PETER PARKER'S *FIRST LAW OF MULTIVERSES.*

AW HECK, AUNT MAY, I DON'T KNOW IF I'D CALL IT A *LAW*, AND I *CERTAINLY* WOULDN'T MAKE IT EPONYMOUS...

YOU DESERVE ALL THE CREDIT IN THE WORLD FOR YOUR SMARTS, LOVE, AND I WON'T LET *ANYONE* DENY YOU THAT, *ESPECIALLY* YOURSELF.

A UNIVERSE FOR EVERY POSSIBILITY...

IT'S A STAGGERING THOUGHT, AUNT MAY. HECK, THERE MAY EVEN BE ONE WHERE THE THREE OF US ARE *EVIL* AND DECIDE TO COME HERE TO KILL US JUST BECAUSE WE *CAN!*

I'M AFRAID I DON'T CARE FOR *THAT* IDEA AT ALL.

OH GOSH, MAY! I WAS JUST THINKING OF LOGICAL OPPOSITES, I DIDN'T *REALLY* MEAN WHAT I SAID, IT WAS JUST A JOKE AND--

PARDON THE INTERRUPTION, *NERDS...*

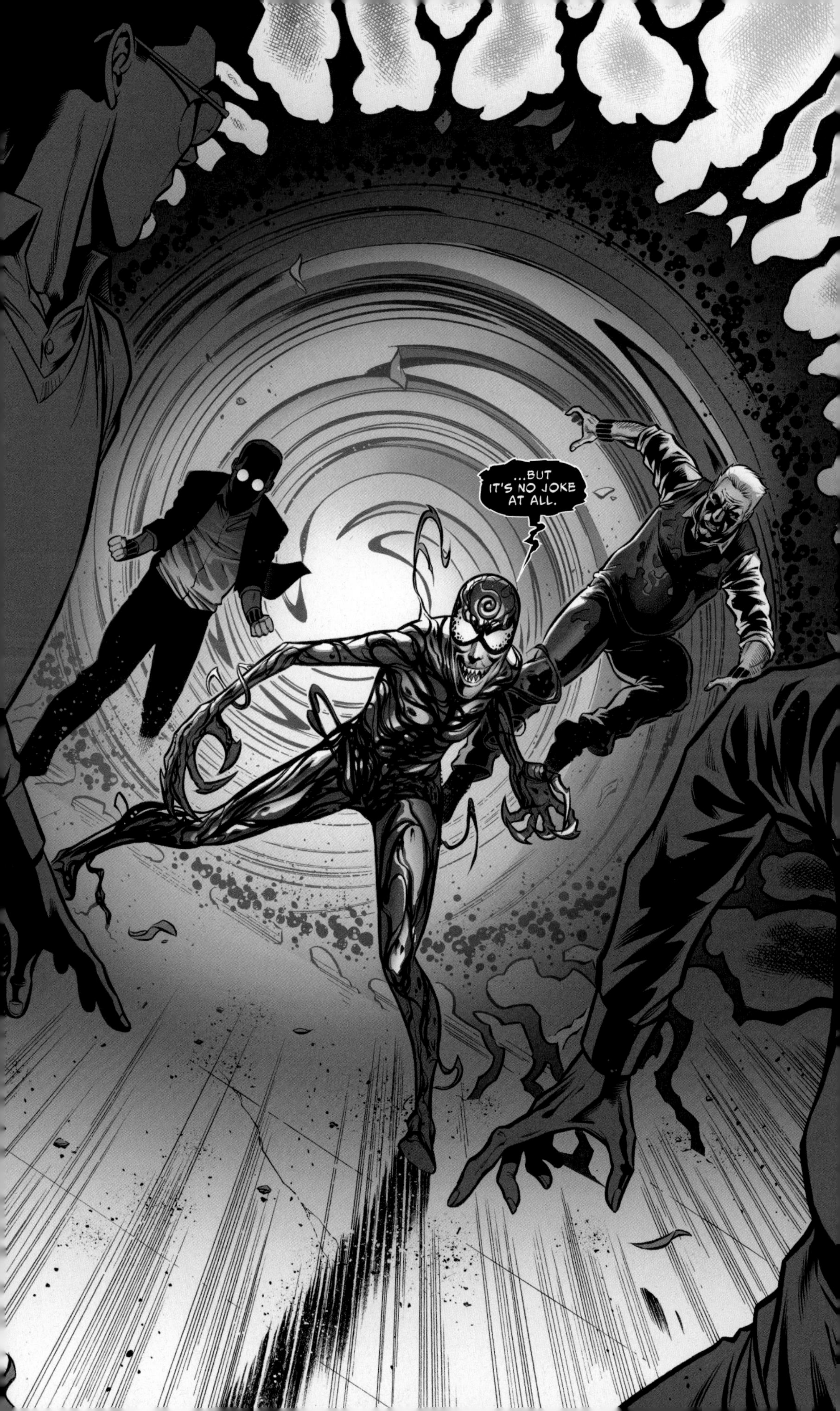
...BUT IT'S NO JOKE AT ALL.

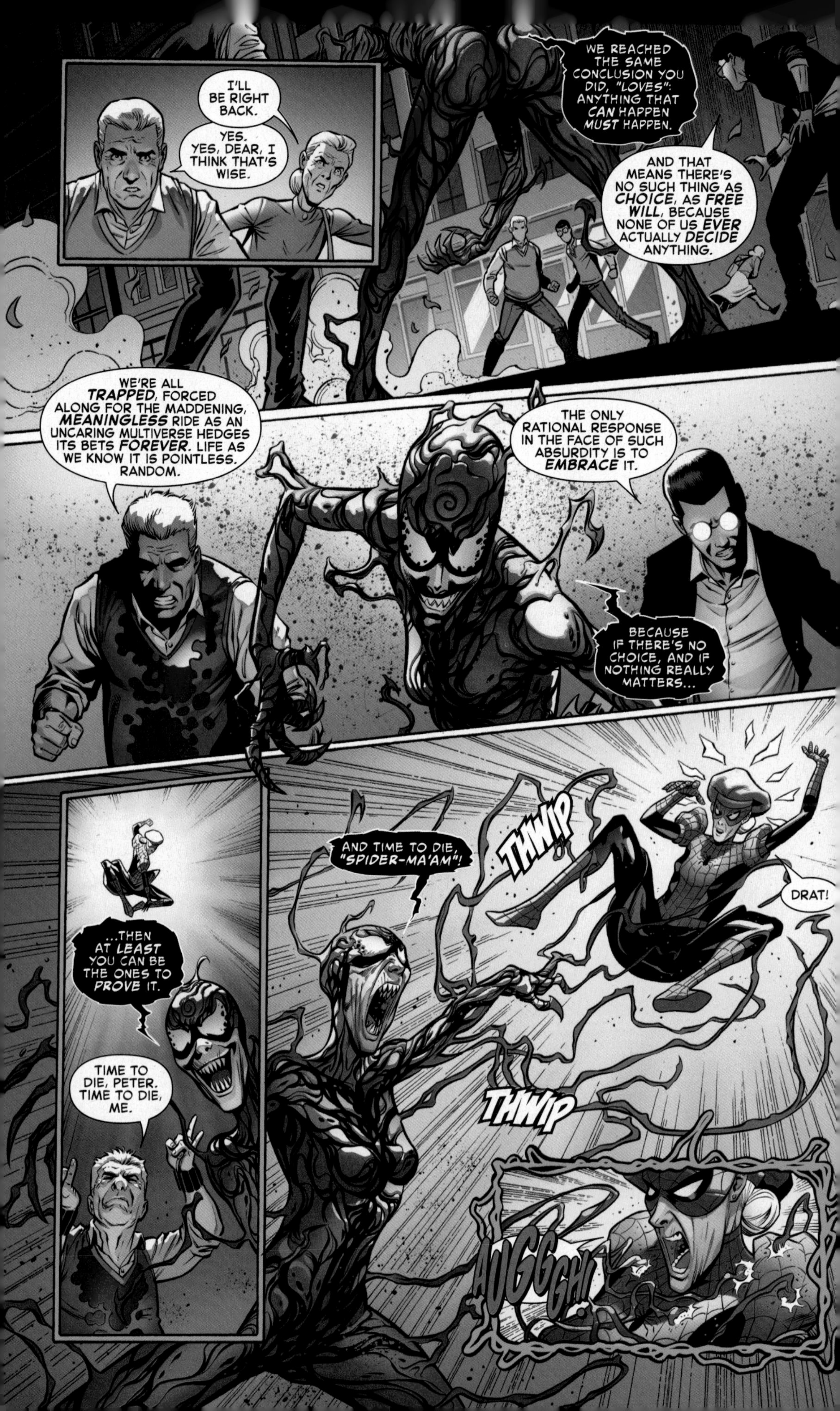

I'LL BE RIGHT BACK.
YES. YES, DEAR, I THINK THAT'S WISE.
WE REACHED THE SAME CONCLUSION YOU DID, "LOVES": ANYTHING THAT CAN HAPPEN MUST HAPPEN.
AND THAT MEANS THERE'S NO SUCH THING AS CHOICE, AS FREE WILL, BECAUSE NONE OF US EVER ACTUALLY DECIDE ANYTHING.
WE'RE ALL TRAPPED, FORCED ALONG FOR THE MADDENING, MEANINGLESS RIDE AS AN UNCARING MULTIVERSE HEDGES ITS BETS FOREVER. LIFE AS WE KNOW IT IS POINTLESS. RANDOM.
THE ONLY RATIONAL RESPONSE IN THE FACE OF SUCH ABSURDITY IS TO EMBRACE IT.
BECAUSE IF THERE'S NO CHOICE, AND IF NOTHING REALLY MATTERS...
...THEN AT LEAST YOU CAN BE THE ONES TO PROVE IT.
TIME TO DIE, PETER. TIME TO DIE, ME.
AND TIME TO DIE, "SPIDER-MA'AM"!
THWIP
DRAT!
THWIP
AUGGGH!

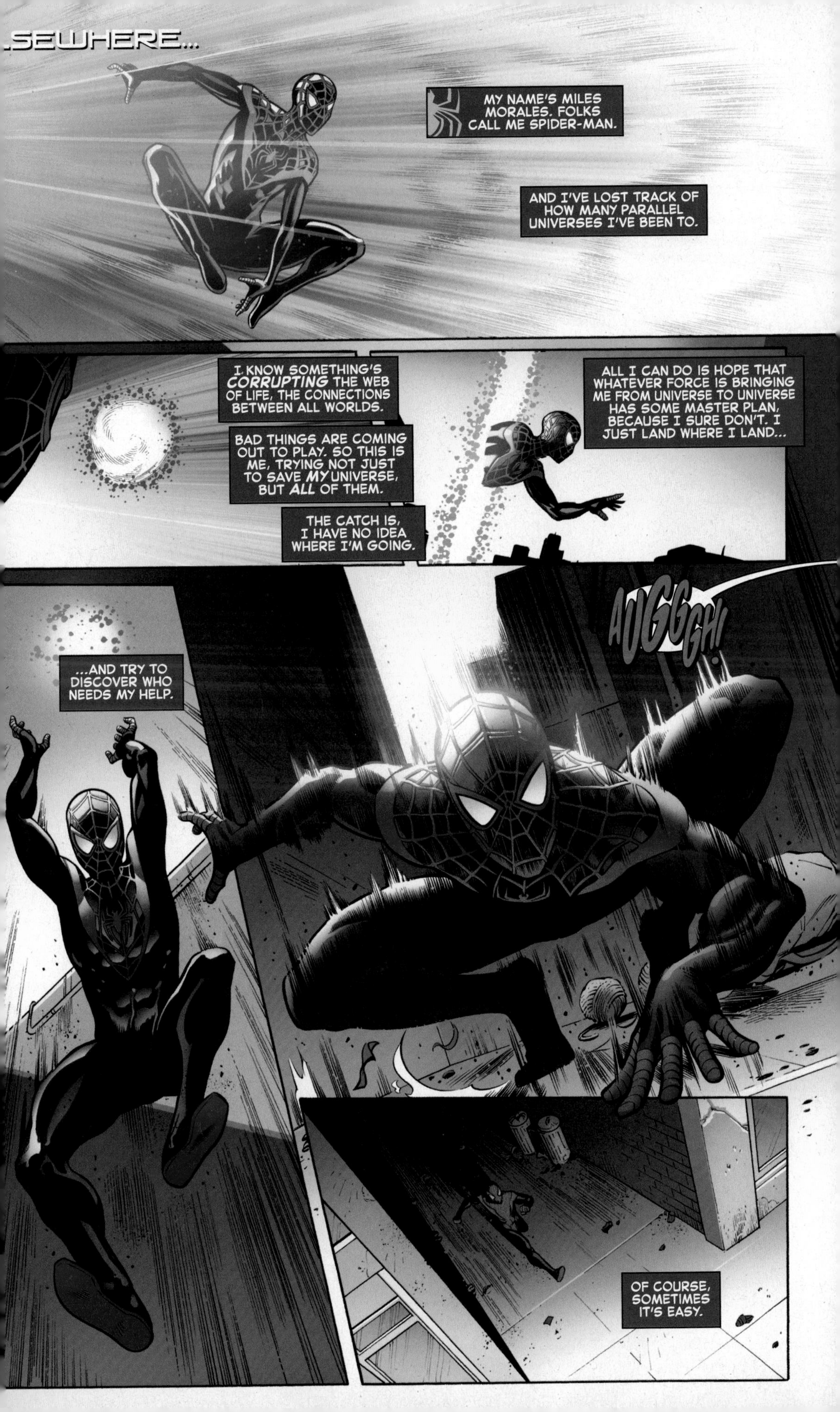

..SEWHERE...
MY NAME'S MILES MORALES. FOLKS CALL ME SPIDER-MAN.
AND I'VE LOST TRACK OF HOW MANY PARALLEL UNIVERSES I'VE BEEN TO.
I KNOW SOMETHING'S CORRUPTING THE WEB OF LIFE, THE CONNECTIONS BETWEEN ALL WORLDS.
BAD THINGS ARE COMING OUT TO PLAY. SO THIS IS ME, TRYING NOT JUST TO SAVE MY UNIVERSE, BUT ALL OF THEM.
THE CATCH IS, I HAVE NO IDEA WHERE I'M GOING.
ALL I CAN DO IS HOPE THAT WHATEVER FORCE IS BRINGING ME FROM UNIVERSE TO UNIVERSE HAS SOME MASTER PLAN, BECAUSE I SURE DON'T. I JUST LAND WHERE I LAND...
...AND TRY TO DISCOVER WHO NEEDS MY HELP.
AUGGGH!
OF COURSE, SOMETIMES IT'S EASY.

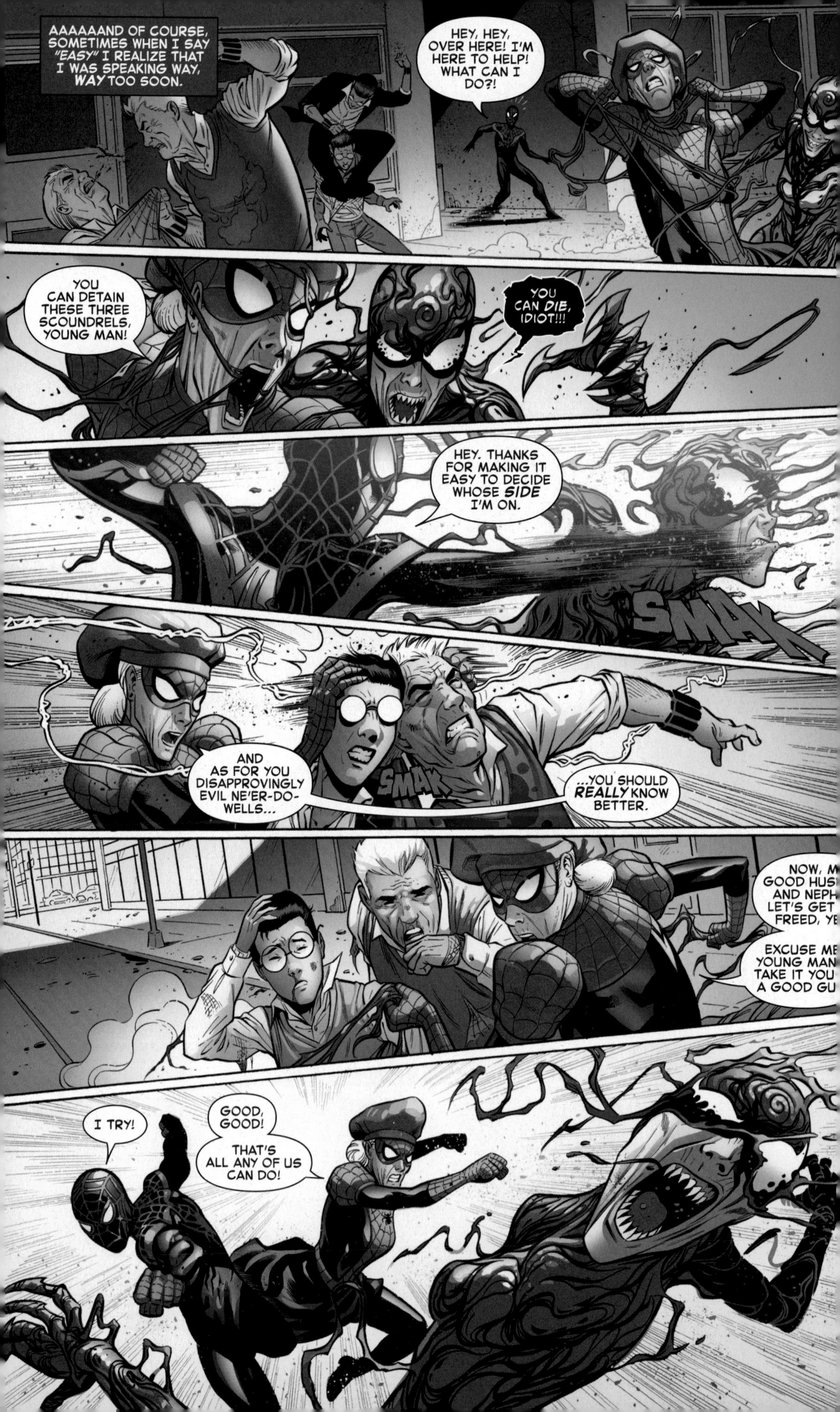
AAAAAAND OF COURSE, SOMETIMES WHEN I SAY "EASY" I REALIZE THAT I WAS SPEAKING WAY, WAY TOO SOON.
HEY, HEY, OVER HERE! I'M HERE TO HELP! WHAT CAN I DO?!
YOU CAN DETAIN THESE THREE SCOUNDRELS, YOUNG MAN!
YOU CAN DIE, IDIOT!!!
HEY. THANKS FOR MAKING IT EASY TO DECIDE WHOSE SIDE I'M ON.
SMAK
AND AS FOR YOU DISAPPROVINGLY EVIL NE'ER-DO-WELLS...
SMAK
...YOU SHOULD REALLY KNOW BETTER.
NOW, M GOOD HUS AND NEPH LET'S GET FREED, YE
EXCUSE ME YOUNG MAN TAKE IT YOU A GOOD GU
I TRY!
GOOD, GOOD!
THAT'S ALL ANY OF US CAN DO!

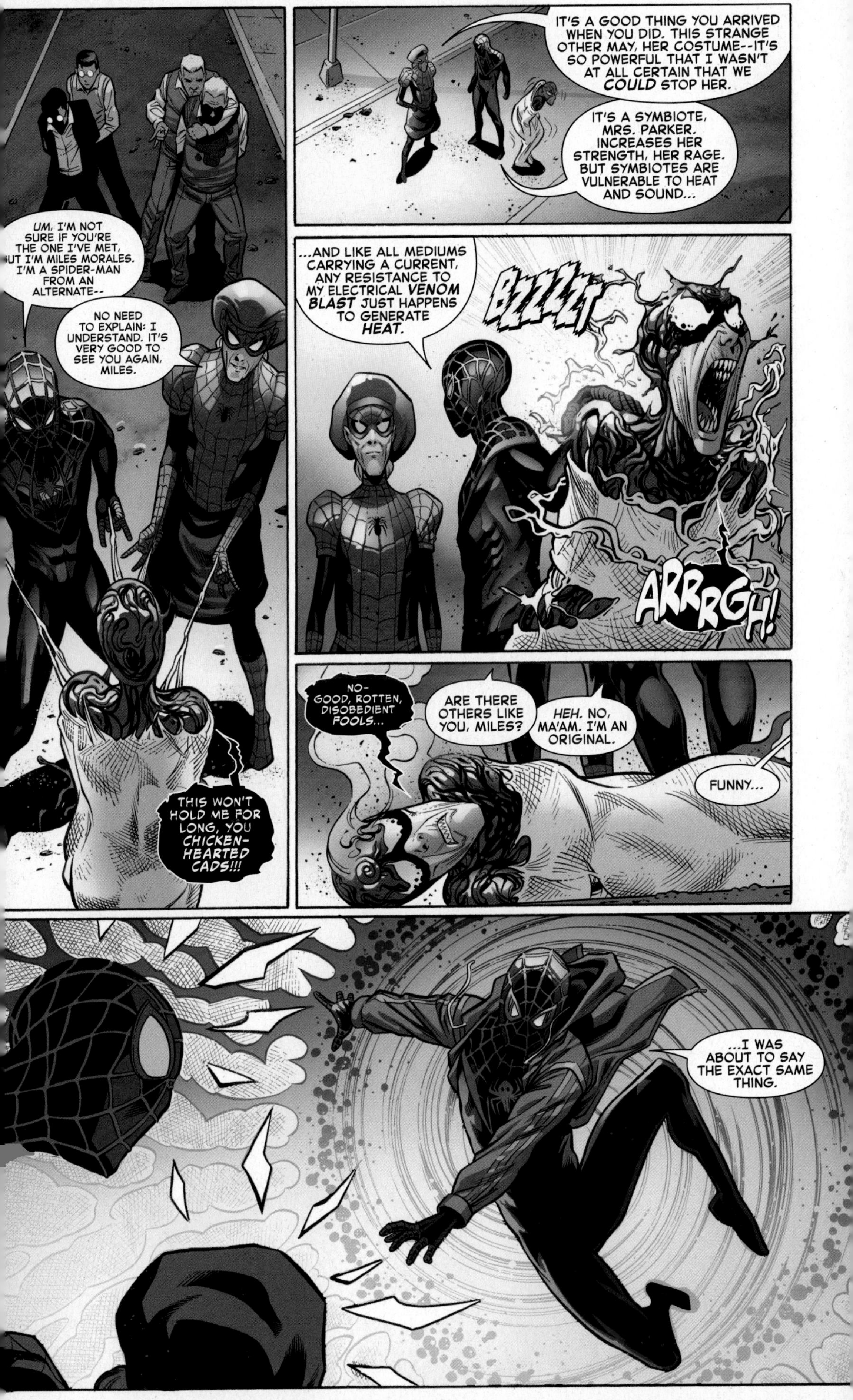
UM, I'M NOT SURE IF YOU'RE THE ONE I'VE MET, BUT I'M MILES MORALES. I'M A SPIDER-MAN FROM AN ALTERNATE--
NO NEED TO EXPLAIN: I UNDERSTAND. IT'S VERY GOOD TO SEE YOU AGAIN, MILES.
THIS WON'T HOLD ME FOR LONG, YOU CHICKEN-HEARTED CADS!!!
IT'S A GOOD THING YOU ARRIVED WHEN YOU DID. THIS STRANGE OTHER MAY, HER COSTUME--IT'S SO POWERFUL THAT I WASN'T AT ALL CERTAIN THAT WE COULD STOP HER.
IT'S A SYMBIOTE, MRS. PARKER. INCREASES HER STRENGTH, HER RAGE. BUT SYMBIOTES ARE VULNERABLE TO HEAT AND SOUND...
...AND LIKE ALL MEDIUMS CARRYING A CURRENT, ANY RESISTANCE TO MY ELECTRICAL VENOM BLAST JUST HAPPENS TO GENERATE HEAT.
BZZZZT
ARRRGH!
NO-GOOD, ROTTEN, DISOBEDIENT FOOLS...
ARE THERE OTHERS LIKE YOU, MILES?
HEH. NO, MA'AM. I'M AN ORIGINAL.
FUNNY...
...I WAS ABOUT TO SAY THE EXACT SAME THING.

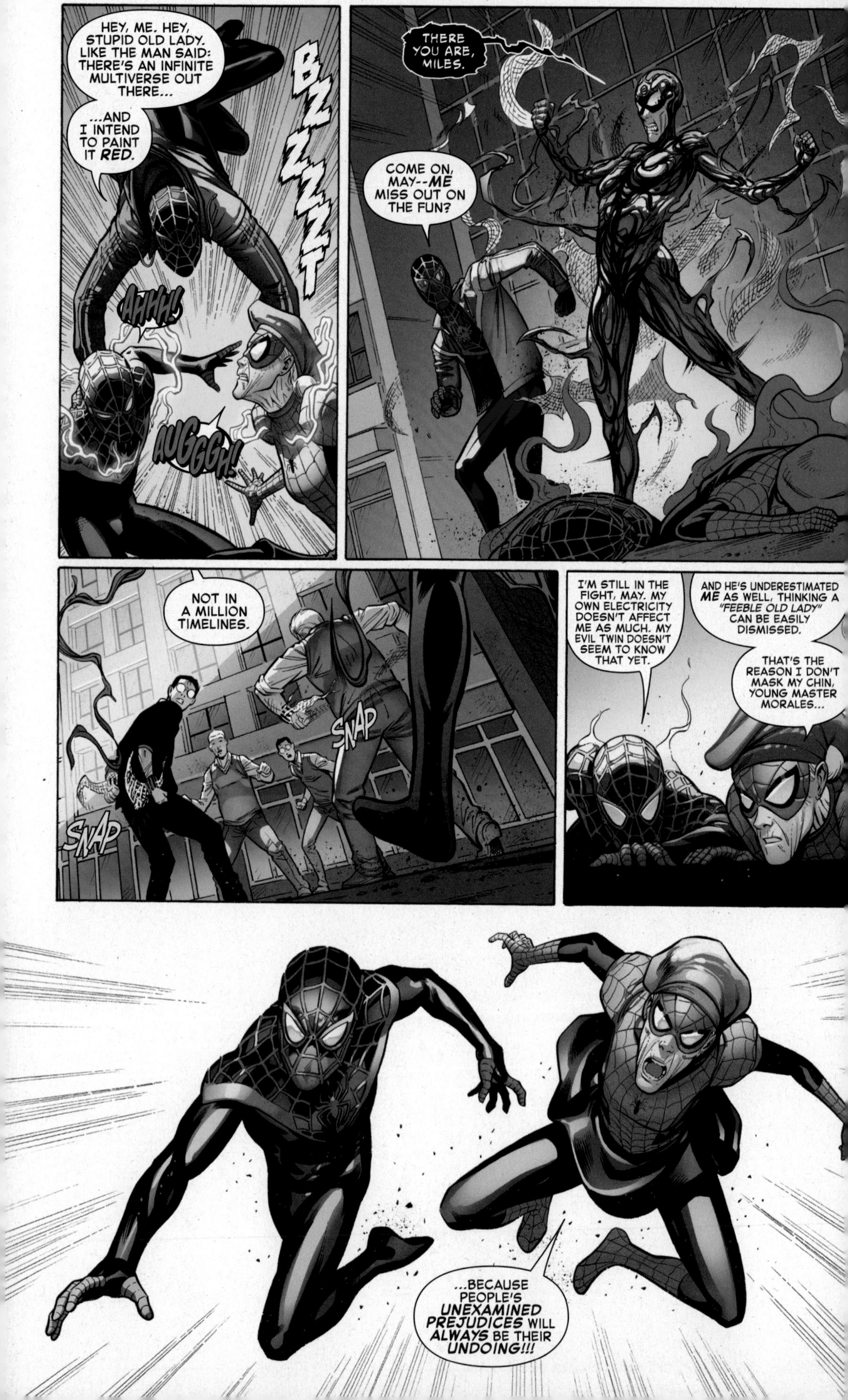
HEY, ME. HEY, STUPID OLD LADY. LIKE THE MAN SAID: THERE'S AN INFINITE MULTIVERSE OUT THERE...
...AND I INTEND TO PAINT IT RED.
BZZZZZT
AHHH!
AUGGGH!
THERE YOU ARE, MILES.
COME ON, MAY--ME MISS OUT ON THE FUN?
NOT IN A MILLION TIMELINES.
SNAP
SNAP
I'M STILL IN THE FIGHT, MAY. MY OWN ELECTRICITY DOESN'T AFFECT ME AS MUCH. MY EVIL TWIN DOESN'T SEEM TO KNOW THAT YET.
AND HE'S UNDERESTIMATED ME AS WELL, THINKING A "FEEBLE OLD LADY" CAN BE EASILY DISMISSED.
THAT'S THE REASON I DON'T MASK MY CHIN, YOUNG MASTER MORALES...
...BECAUSE PEOPLE'S UNEXAMINED PREJUDICES WILL ALWAYS BE THEIR UNDOING!!!

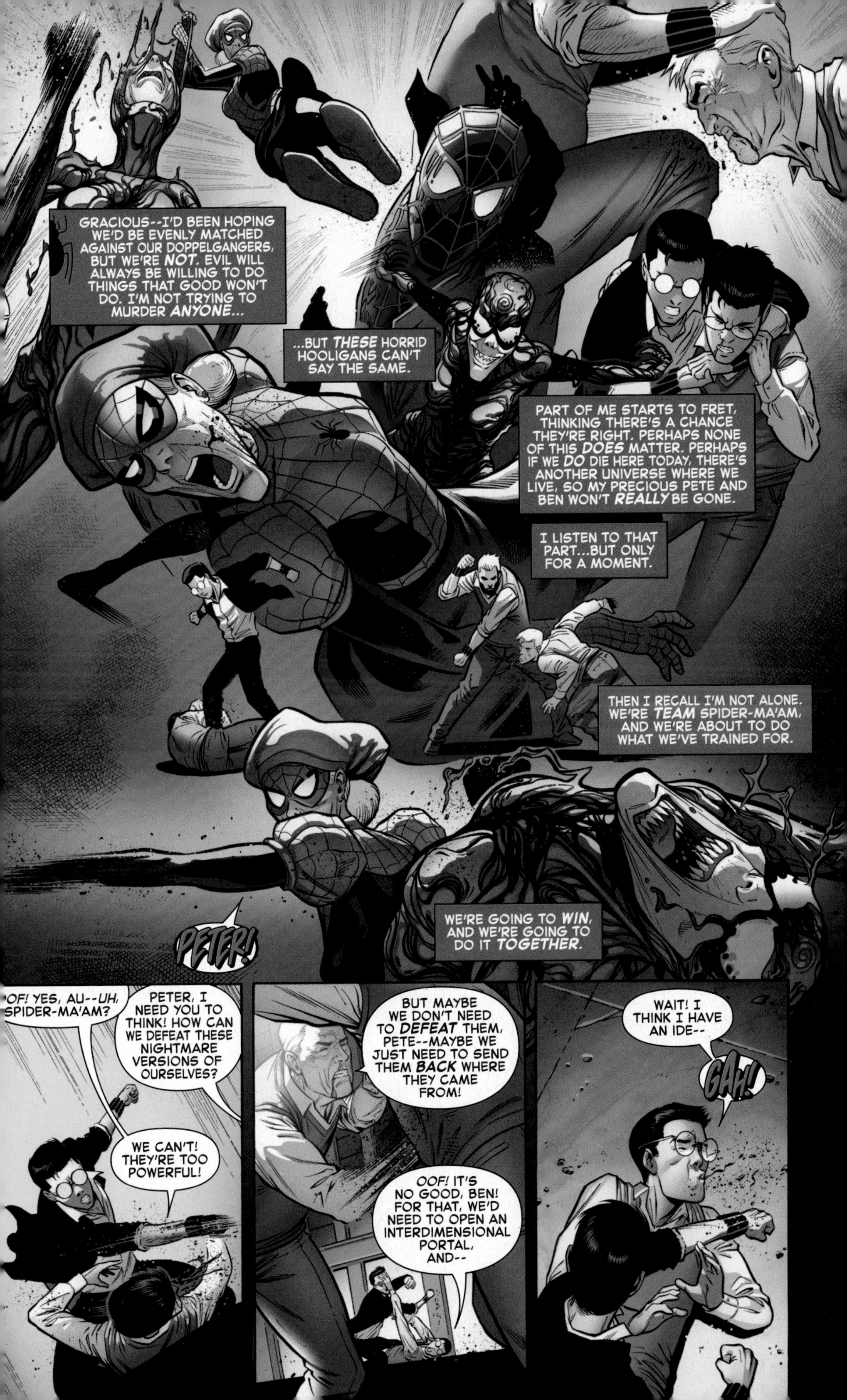
GRACIOUS--I'D BEEN HOPING WE'D BE EVENLY MATCHED AGAINST OUR DOPPELGANGERS, BUT WE'RE NOT. EVIL WILL ALWAYS BE WILLING TO DO THINGS THAT GOOD WON'T DO. I'M NOT TRYING TO MURDER ANYONE...
...BUT THESE HORRID HOOLIGANS CAN'T SAY THE SAME.
PART OF ME STARTS TO FRET, THINKING THERE'S A CHANCE THEY'RE RIGHT. PERHAPS NONE OF THIS DOES MATTER. PERHAPS IF WE DO DIE HERE TODAY, THERE'S ANOTHER UNIVERSE WHERE WE LIVE, SO MY PRECIOUS PETE AND BEN WON'T REALLY BE GONE.
I LISTEN TO THAT PART...BUT ONLY FOR A MOMENT.
THEN I RECALL I'M NOT ALONE. WE'RE TEAM SPIDER-MA'AM, AND WE'RE ABOUT TO DO WHAT WE'VE TRAINED FOR.
PETER!
WE'RE GOING TO WIN, AND WE'RE GOING TO DO IT TOGETHER.
PETER, I NEED YOU TO THINK! HOW CAN WE DEFEAT THESE NIGHTMARE VERSIONS OF OURSELVES?
OOF! YES, AU--UH, SPIDER-MA'AM?
WE CAN'T! THEY'RE TOO POWERFUL!
BUT MAYBE WE DON'T NEED TO DEFEAT THEM, PETE--MAYBE WE JUST NEED TO SEND THEM BACK WHERE THEY CAME FROM!
OOF! IT'S NO GOOD, BEN! FOR THAT, WE'D NEED TO OPEN AN INTERDIMENSIONAL PORTAL, AND--
WAIT! I THINK I HAVE AN IDE--
GAH!

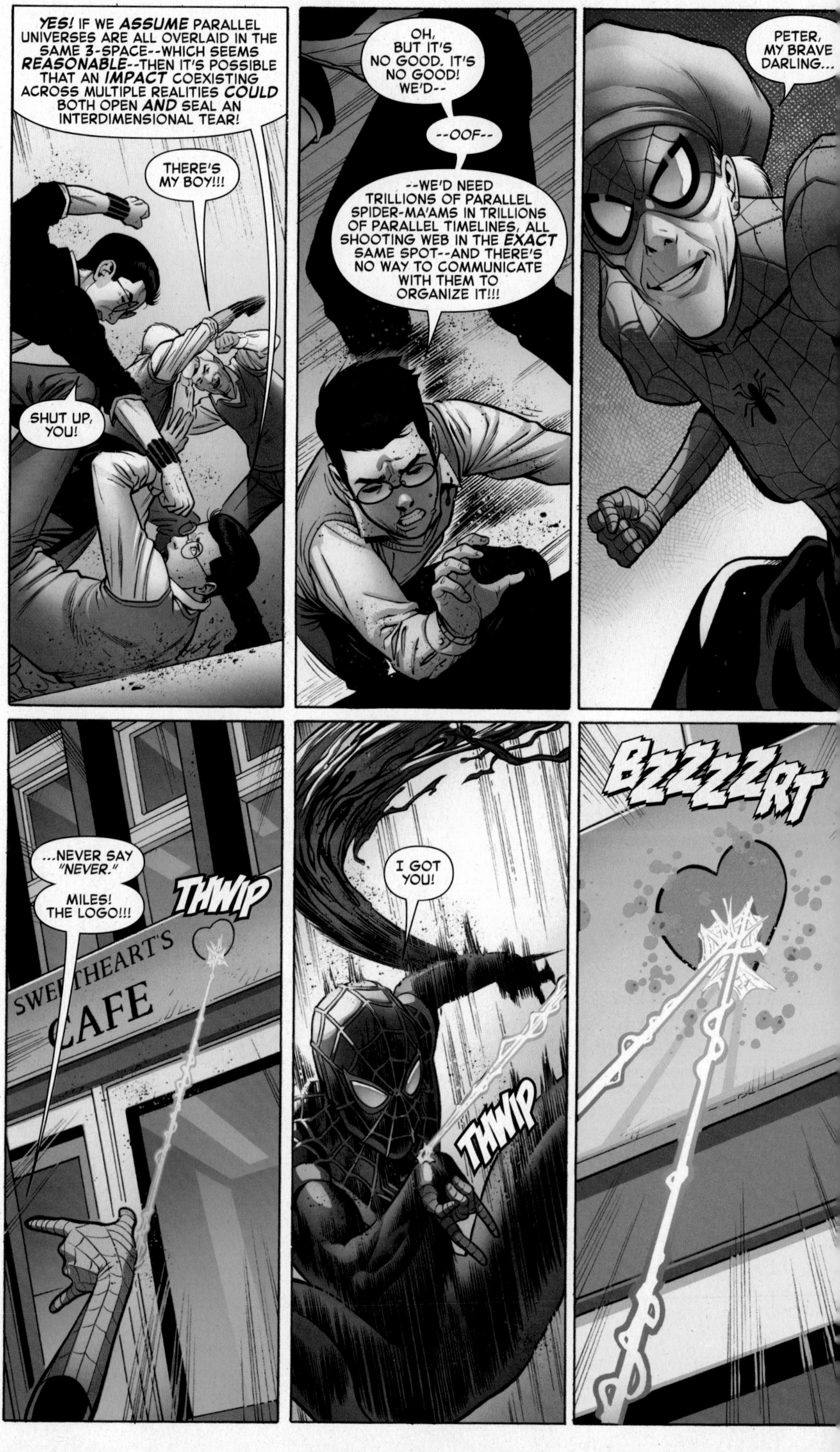

YES! IF WE ASSUME PARALLEL UNIVERSES ARE ALL OVERLAID IN THE SAME 3-SPACE--WHICH SEEMS REASONABLE--THEN IT'S POSSIBLE THAT AN IMPACT COEXISTING ACROSS MULTIPLE REALITIES COULD BOTH OPEN AND SEAL AN INTERDIMENSIONAL TEAR!
THERE'S MY BOY!!!
SHUT UP, YOU!
OH, BUT IT'S NO GOOD. IT'S NO GOOD! WE'D--
--OOF--
--WE'D NEED TRILLIONS OF PARALLEL SPIDER-MA'AMS IN TRILLIONS OF PARALLEL TIMELINES, ALL SHOOTING WEB IN THE EXACT SAME SPOT--AND THERE'S NO WAY TO COMMUNICATE WITH THEM TO ORGANIZE IT!!!
PETER, MY BRAVE DARLING...
...NEVER SAY "NEVER."
MILES! THE LOGO!!!
THWIP
CAFE
I GOT YOU!
THWIP
BZZZZZRT

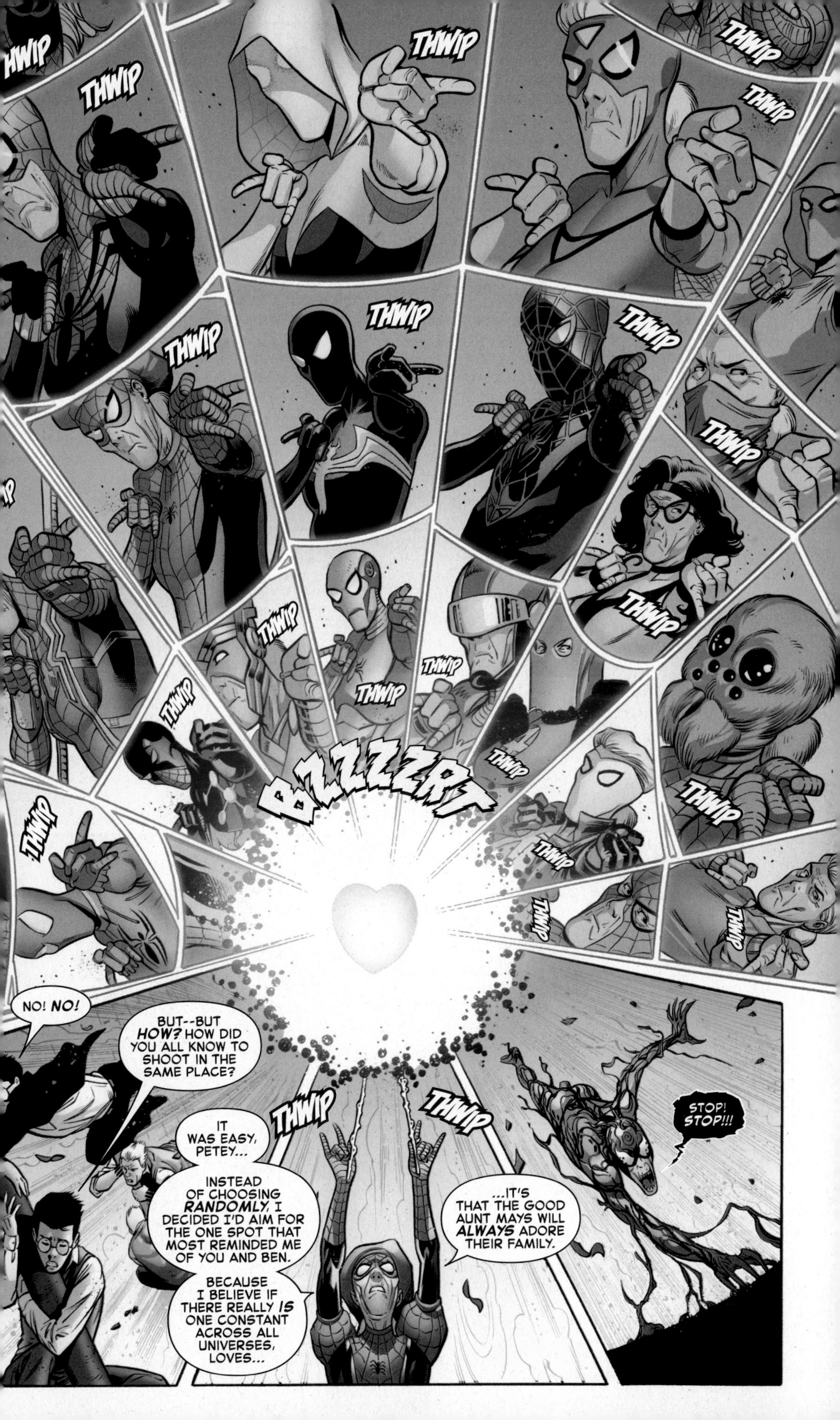
THWIP
THWIP
THWIP
THWIP
THWIP
THWIP
THWIP
THWIP
THWIP
THWIP
THWIP
THWIP
THWIP
THWIP
THWIP
THWIP
THWIP
THWIP
THWIP
THWIP
BZZZZZRT
NO! NO!
BUT--BUT HOW? HOW DID YOU ALL KNOW TO SHOOT IN THE SAME PLACE?
THWIP
THWIP
IT WAS EASY, PETEY...
INSTEAD OF CHOOSING RANDOMLY, I DECIDED I'D AIM FOR THE ONE SPOT THAT MOST REMINDED ME OF YOU AND BEN.
BECAUSE I BELIEVE IF THERE REALLY IS ONE CONSTANT ACROSS ALL UNIVERSES, LOVES...
...IT'S THAT THE GOOD AUNT MAYS WILL ALWAYS ADORE THEIR FAMILY.
STOP! STOP!!!

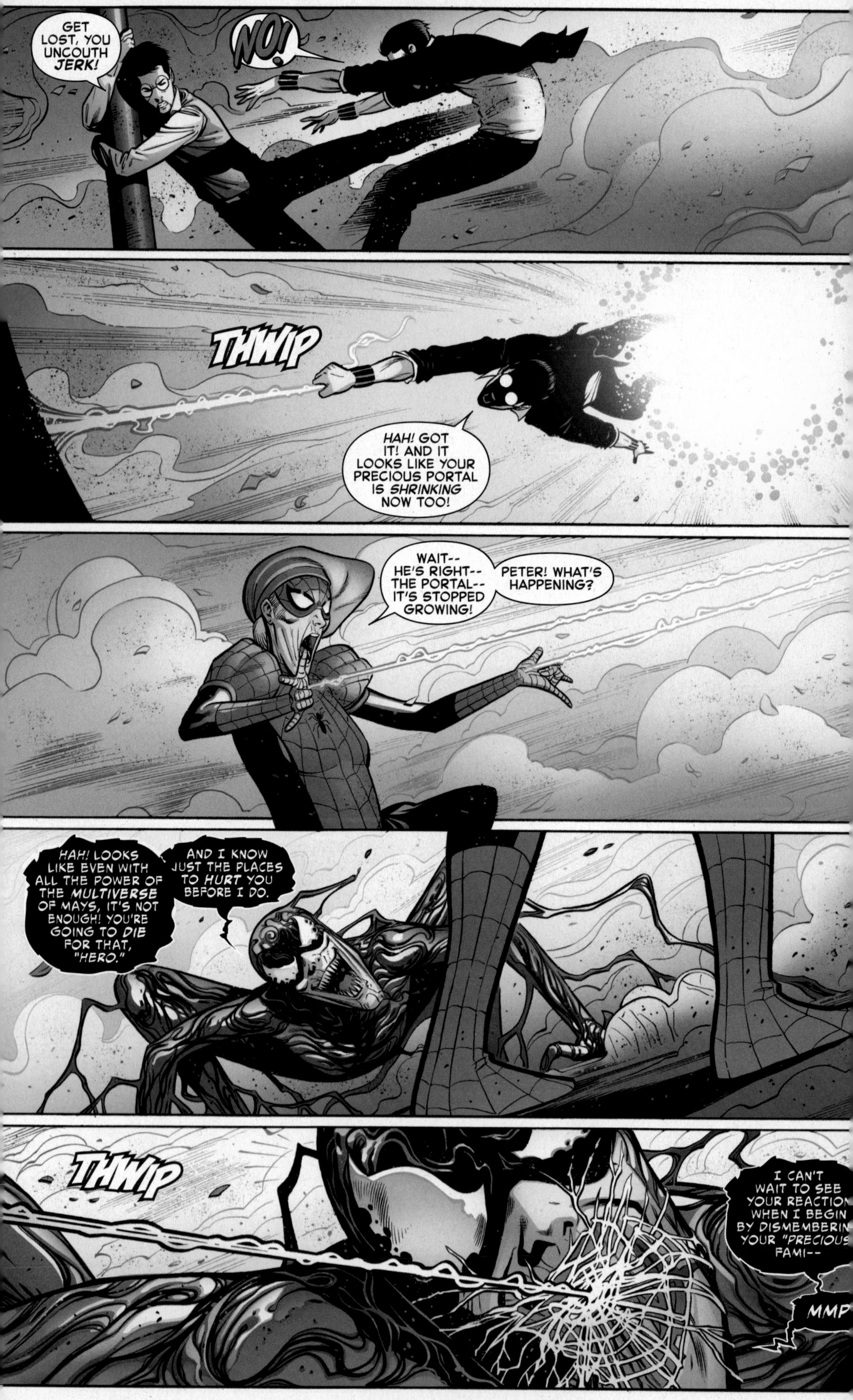
GET LOST, YOU UNCOUTH JERK!
NO!
THWIP
HAH! GOT IT! AND IT LOOKS LIKE YOUR PRECIOUS PORTAL IS SHRINKING NOW TOO!
WAIT-- HE'S RIGHT-- THE PORTAL-- IT'S STOPPED GROWING!
PETER! WHAT'S HAPPENING?
HAH! LOOKS LIKE EVEN WITH ALL THE POWER OF THE MULTIVERSE OF MAYS, IT'S NOT ENOUGH! YOU'RE GOING TO DIE FOR THAT, "HERO."
AND I KNOW JUST THE PLACES TO HURT YOU BEFORE I DO.
THWIP
I CAN'T WAIT TO SEE YOUR REACTION WHEN I BEGIN BY DISMEMBERIN YOUR "PRECIOUS FAMI--
MMP

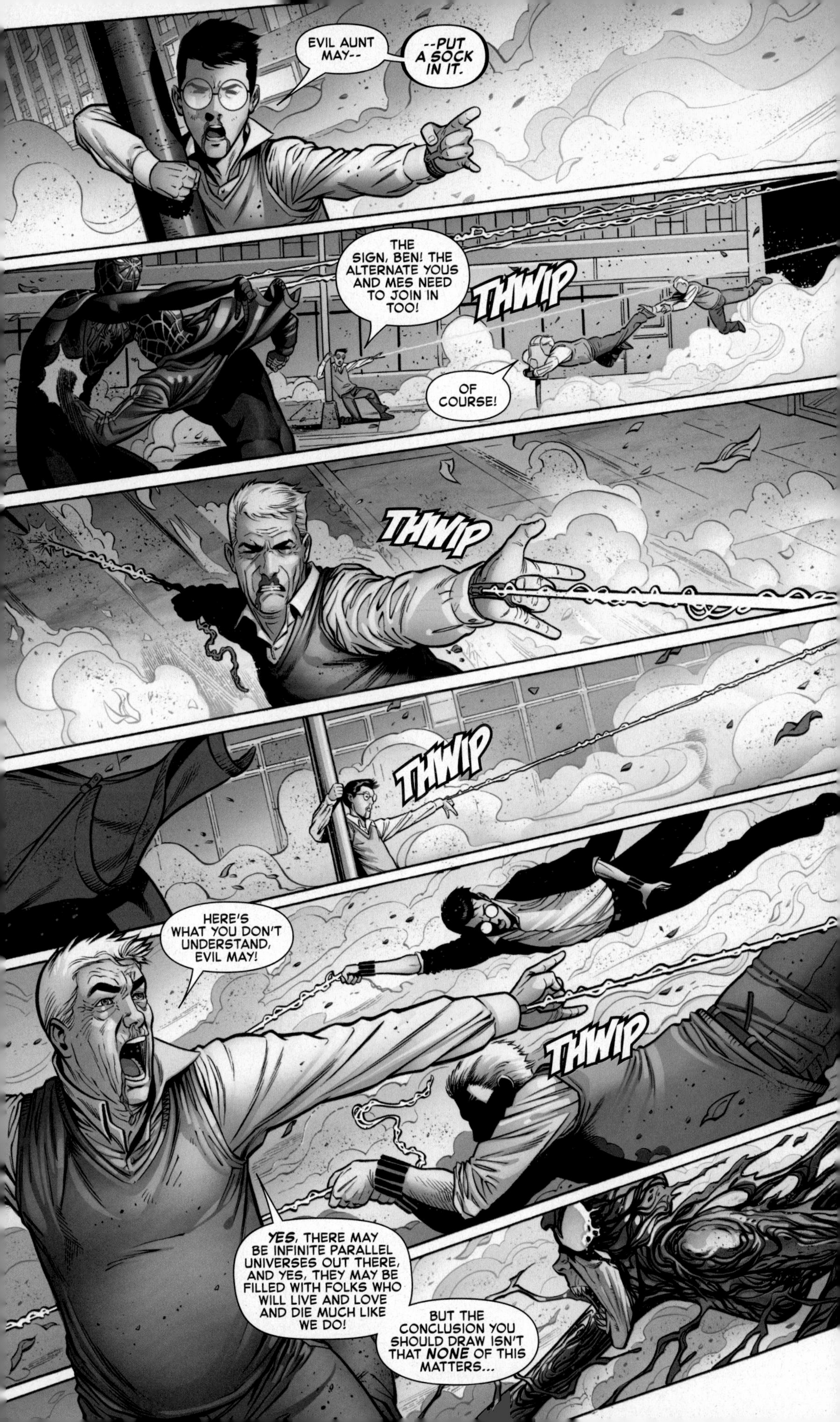
EVIL AUNT MAY--
--PUT A SOCK IN IT.
THE SIGN, BEN! THE ALTERNATE YOUS AND MES NEED TO JOIN IN TOO!
THWIP
OF COURSE!
THWIP
THWIP
HERE'S WHAT YOU DON'T UNDERSTAND, EVIL MAY!
THWIP
YES, THERE MAY BE INFINITE PARALLEL UNIVERSES OUT THERE, AND YES, THEY MAY BE FILLED WITH FOLKS WHO WILL LIVE AND LOVE AND DIE MUCH LIKE WE DO!
BUT THE CONCLUSION YOU SHOULD DRAW ISN'T THAT NONE OF THIS MATTERS...

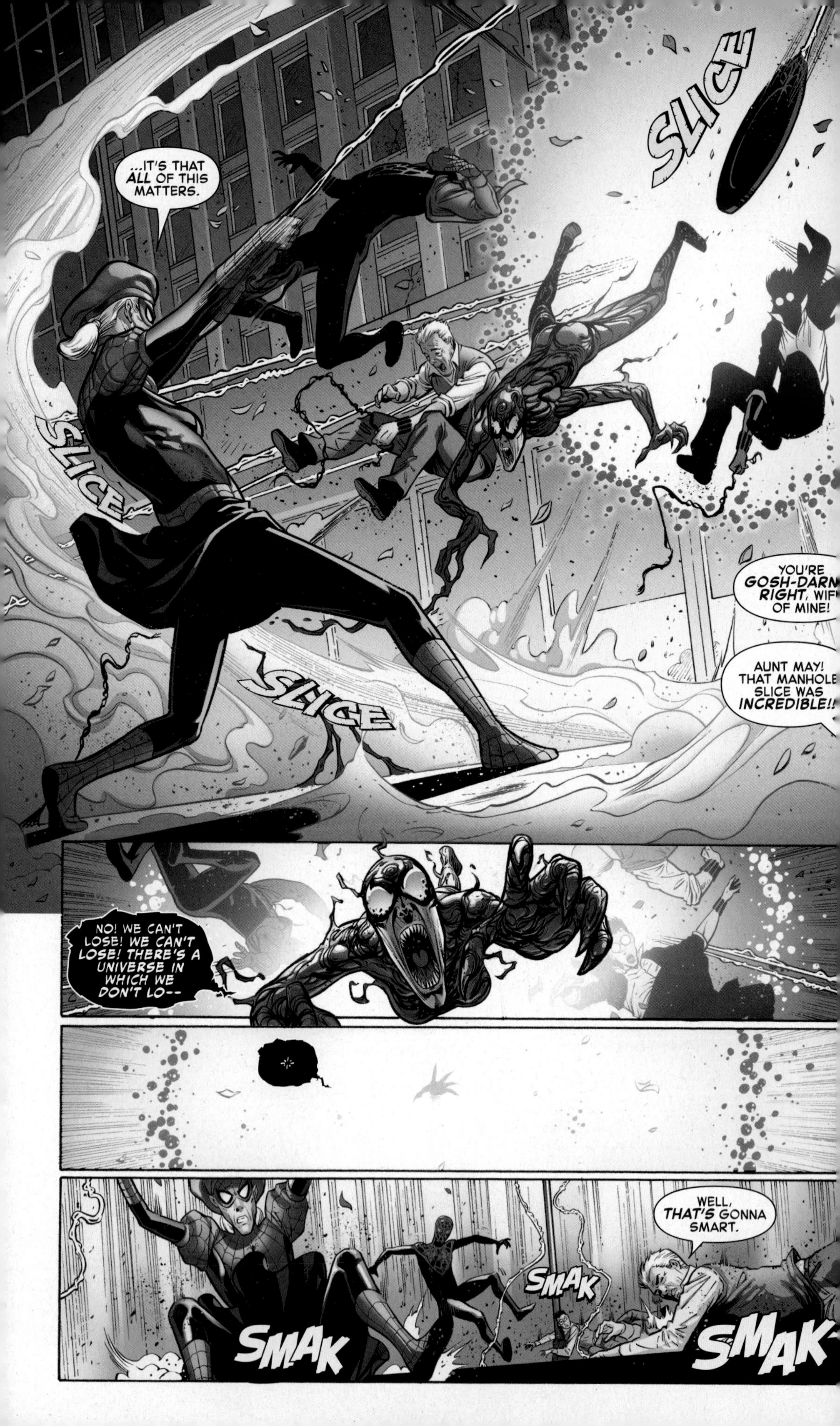

...IT'S THAT ALL OF THIS MATTERS.
SLICE
SLICE
SLICE
YOU'RE GOSH-DARN RIGHT, WIFE OF MINE!
AUNT MAY! THAT MANHOLE SLICE WAS INCREDIBLE!!
NO! WE CAN'T LOSE! WE CAN'T LOSE! THERE'S A UNIVERSE IN WHICH WE DON'T LO--
WELL, THAT'S GONNA SMART.
SMAK
SMAK
SMAK

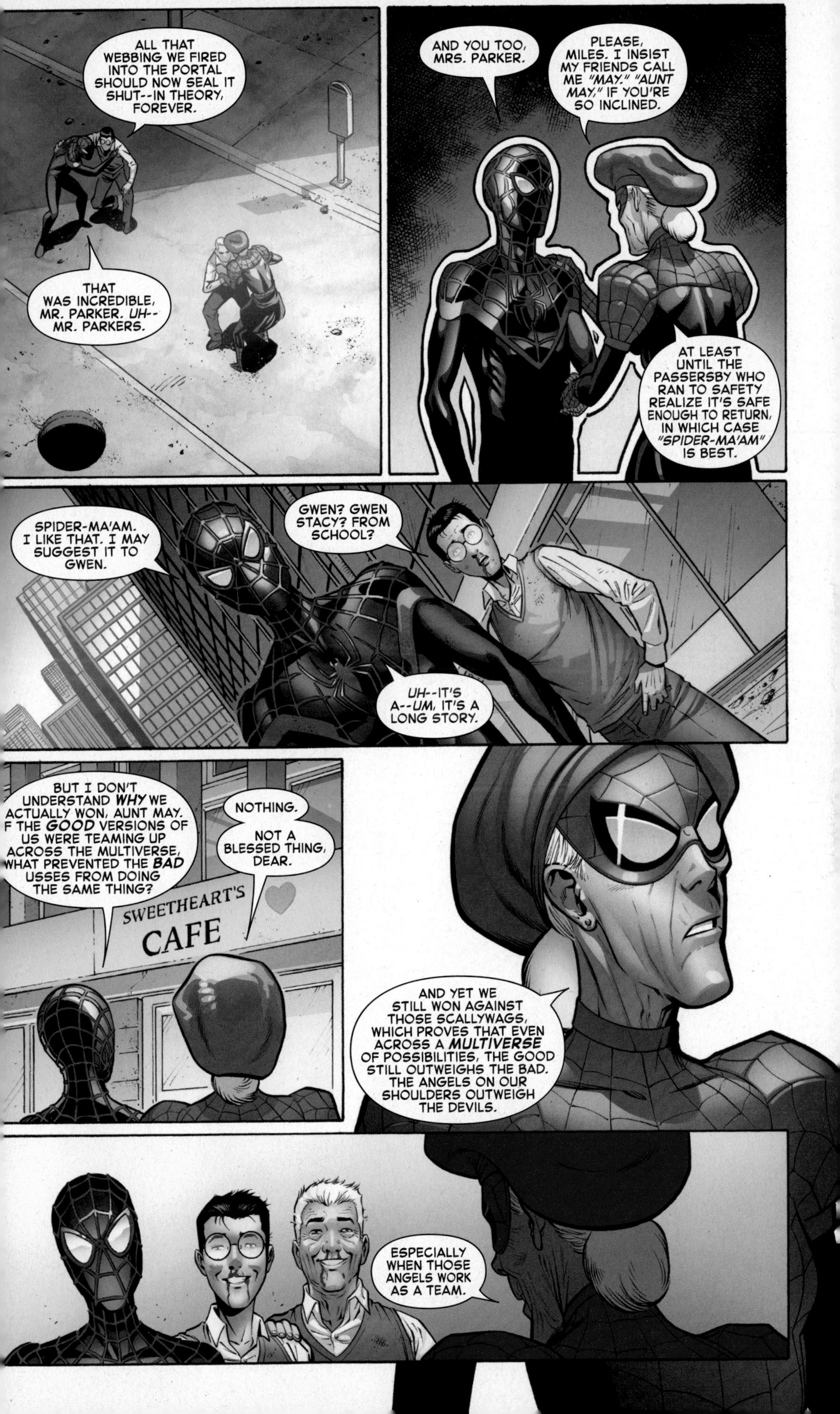
ALL THAT WEBBING WE FIRED INTO THE PORTAL SHOULD NOW SEAL IT SHUT--IN THEORY, FOREVER.
THAT WAS INCREDIBLE, MR. PARKER. UH-- MR. PARKERS.
AND YOU TOO, MRS. PARKER.
PLEASE, MILES. I INSIST MY FRIENDS CALL ME "MAY." "AUNT MAY," IF YOU'RE SO INCLINED.
AT LEAST UNTIL THE PASSERSBY WHO RAN TO SAFETY REALIZE IT'S SAFE ENOUGH TO RETURN, IN WHICH CASE "SPIDER-MA'AM" IS BEST.
SPIDER-MA'AM. I LIKE THAT. I MAY SUGGEST IT TO GWEN.
GWEN? GWEN STACY? FROM SCHOOL?
UH--IT'S A--UM, IT'S A LONG STORY.
BUT I DON'T UNDERSTAND WHY WE ACTUALLY WON, AUNT MAY. F THE GOOD VERSIONS OF US WERE TEAMING UP ACROSS THE MULTIVERSE, WHAT PREVENTED THE BAD USSES FROM DOING THE SAME THING?
NOTHING.
NOT A BLESSED THING, DEAR.
SWEETHEART'S CAFE
AND YET WE STILL WON AGAINST THOSE SCALLYWAGS, WHICH PROVES THAT EVEN ACROSS A MULTIVERSE OF POSSIBILITIES, THE GOOD STILL OUTWEIGHS THE BAD. THE ANGELS ON OUR SHOULDERS OUTWEIGH THE DEVILS.
ESPECIALLY WHEN THOSE ANGELS WORK AS A TEAM.

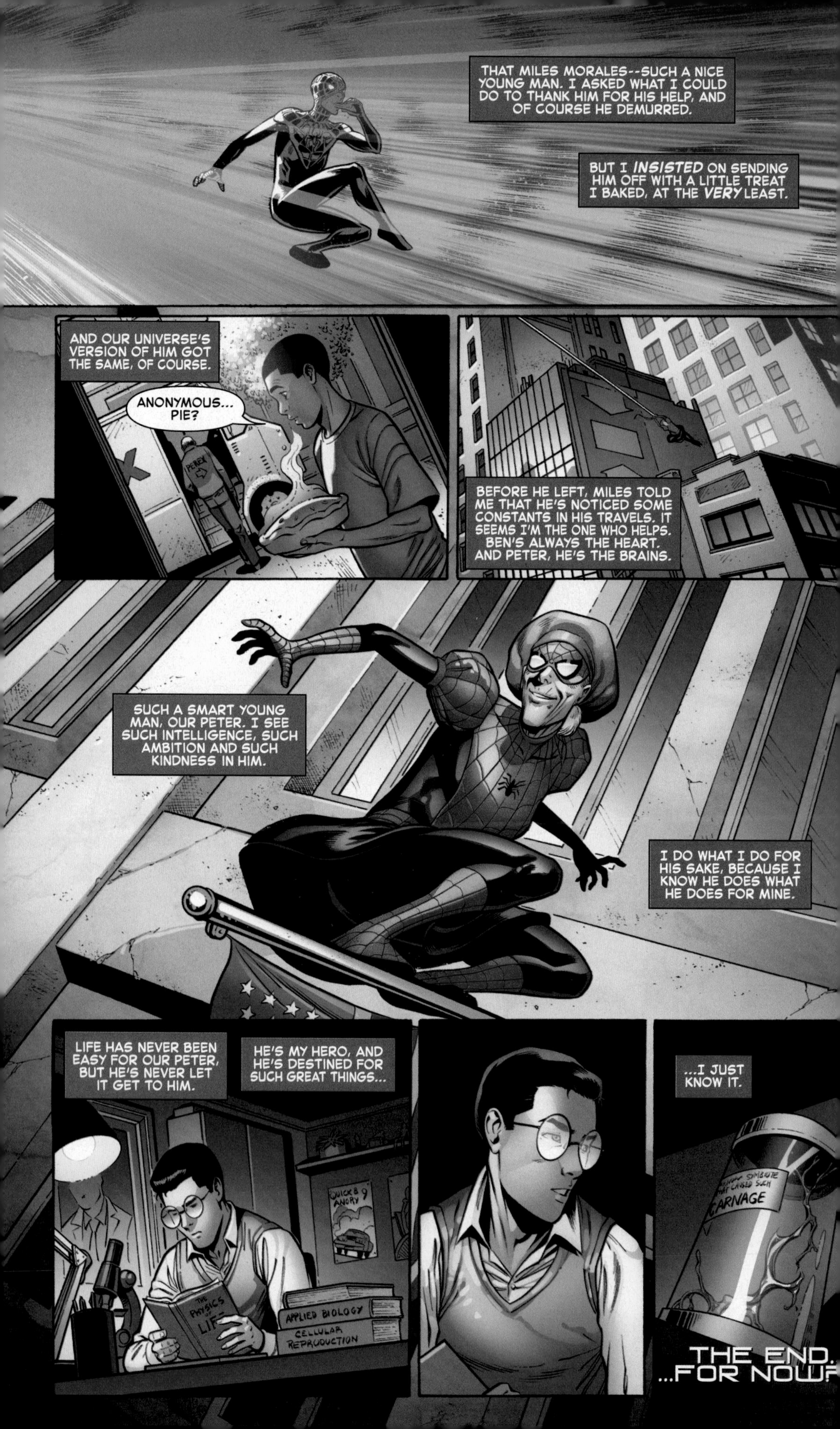

THAT MILES MORALES--SUCH A NICE YOUNG MAN. I ASKED WHAT I COULD DO TO THANK HIM FOR HIS HELP, AND OF COURSE HE DEMURRED.
BUT I *INSISTED* ON SENDING HIM OFF WITH A LITTLE TREAT I BAKED, AT THE *VERY* LEAST.
AND OUR UNIVERSE'S VERSION OF HIM GOT THE SAME, OF COURSE.
ANONYMOUS... PIE?
BEFORE HE LEFT, MILES TOLD ME THAT HE'S NOTICED SOME CONSTANTS IN HIS TRAVELS. IT SEEMS I'M THE ONE WHO HELPS. BEN'S ALWAYS THE HEART. AND PETER, HE'S THE BRAINS.
SUCH A SMART YOUNG MAN, OUR PETER. I SEE SUCH INTELLIGENCE, SUCH AMBITION AND SUCH KINDNESS IN HIM.
I DO WHAT I DO FOR HIS SAKE, BECAUSE I KNOW HE DOES WHAT HE DOES FOR MINE.
LIFE HAS NEVER BEEN EASY FOR OUR PETER, BUT HE'S NEVER LET IT GET TO HIM.
HE'S MY HERO, AND HE'S DESTINED FOR SUCH GREAT THINGS...
THE PHYSICS OF LIFE
APPLIED BIOLOGY
CELLULAR REPRODUCTION
...I JUST KNOW IT.
CARNAGE
THE END. ...FOR NOW!

SPIDERSONA:
SPIDAIR

Art & Text by DICE SHIMI
France

Spidair was bitten by a spider created in a space laboratory. As a result, he has very thick skin that protects him from extreme temperatures. He can also make his whole body glow so bright that his enemies are blinded!

SPIDERSONA:
SEA-SPIDER

Art & Text by JAMES GIFFORD
United Kingdom

1700s Spain. On land, he is a renowned nobleman. On the seven seas, he travels aboard the infamous brigantine ship the Aracne. Sea-Spider's powers include water-breathing, sharpshooting and a perfect sense of balance. His hook and grappling pistols are excellent tools with which to traverse ships and make his escape when needed!

SPIDERSONA:
SPIDER-STING

Art & Text by TORI APIRADEE
United States

Spider-Sting gets his name from the acidic properties of his webs, which can erode materials like concrete and brick. Neon green is one of my favorite colors, so I decided to center the design on the color and its associations, such as radioactivity and acid.

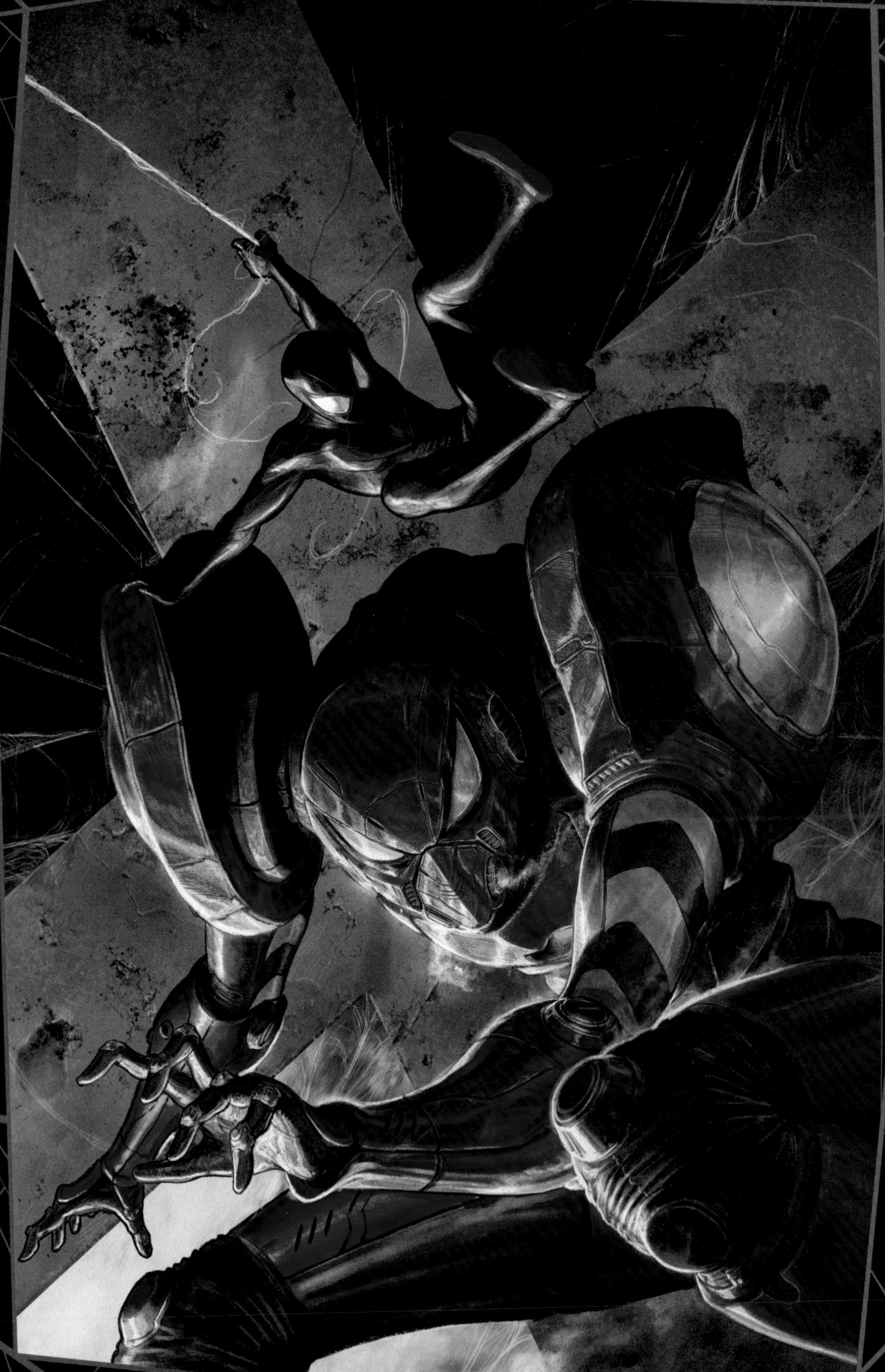

SPIDER-VERSE #3

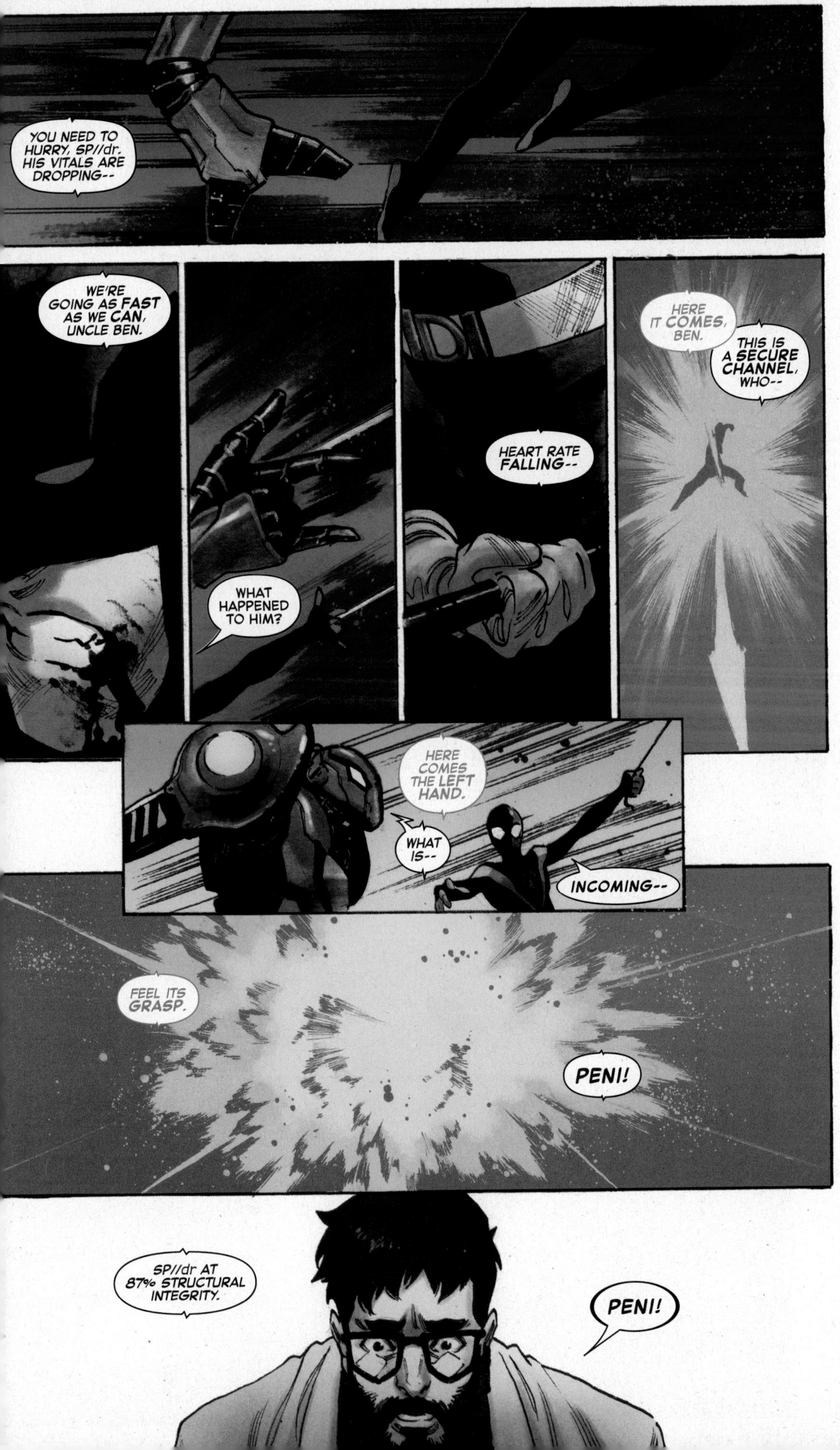
YOU NEED TO HURRY, SP//dr. HIS VITALS ARE DROPPING--
WE'RE GOING AS FAST AS WE CAN, UNCLE BEN.
WHAT HAPPENED TO HIM?
HEART RATE FALLING--
HERE IT COMES, BEN.
THIS IS A SECURE CHANNEL, WHO--
HERE COMES THE LEFT HAND.
WHAT IS--
INCOMING--
FEEL ITS GRASP.
PENI!
SP//dr AT 87% STRUCTURAL INTEGRITY.
PENI!

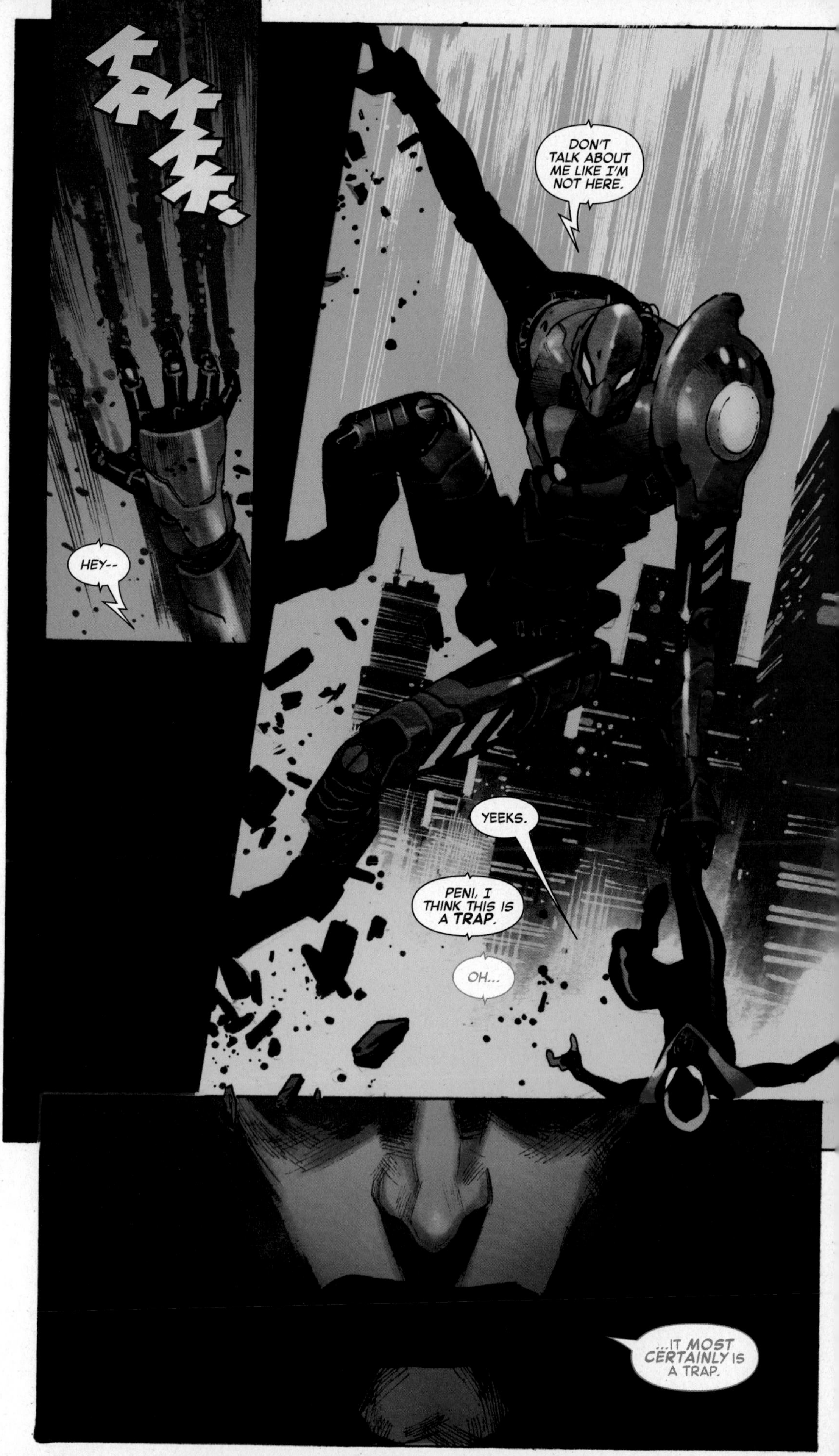
HEY--
DON'T TALK ABOUT ME LIKE I'M NOT HERE.
YEEKS.
PENI, I THINK THIS IS A *TRAP*.
OH...
...IT *MOST CERTAINLY* IS A TRAP.

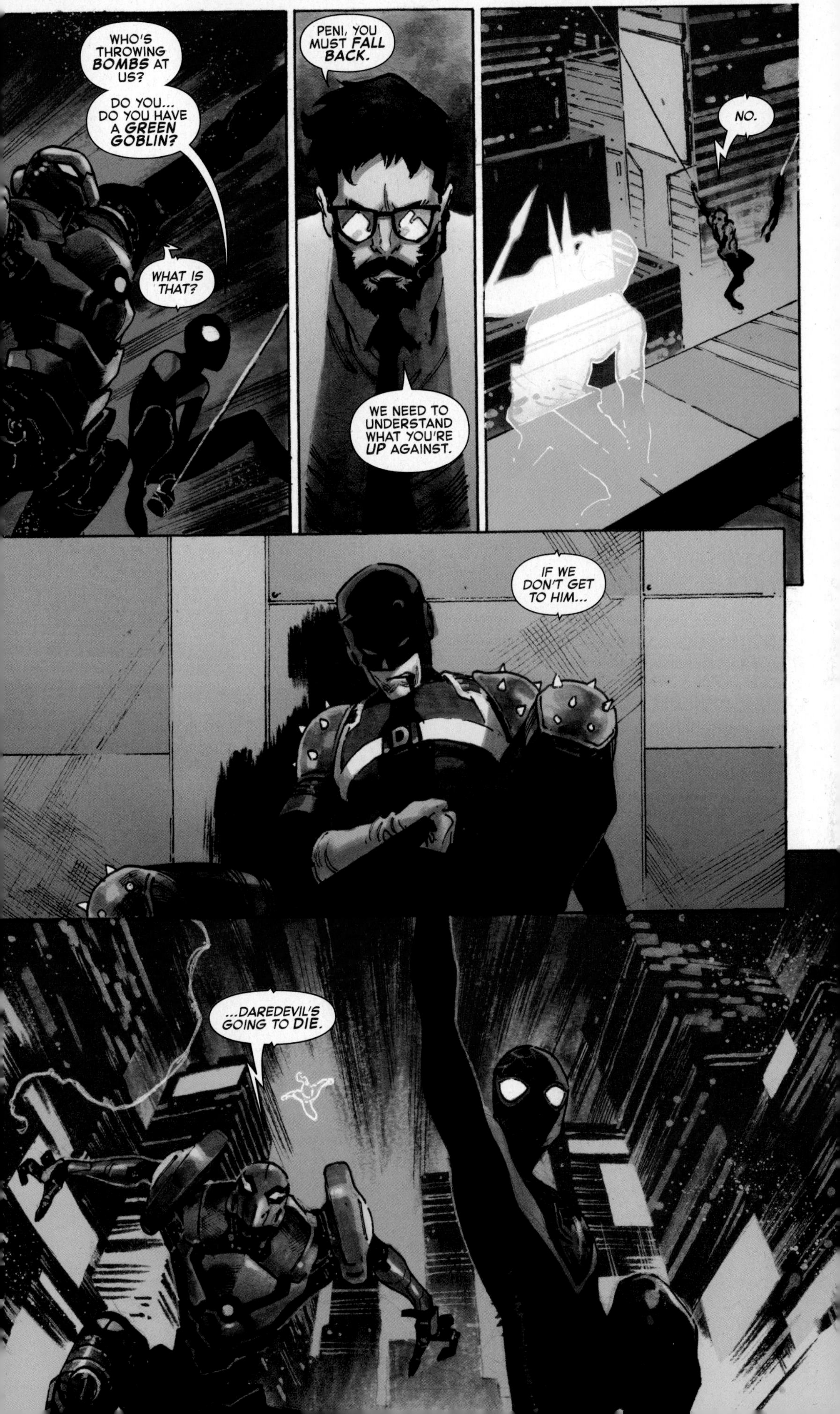
WHO'S THROWING BOMBS AT US?
DO YOU... DO YOU HAVE A GREEN GOBLIN?
WHAT IS THAT?
PENI, YOU MUST FALL BACK.
WE NEED TO UNDERSTAND WHAT YOU'RE UP AGAINST.
NO.
IF WE DON'T GET TO HIM...
...DAREDEVIL'S GOING TO DIE.

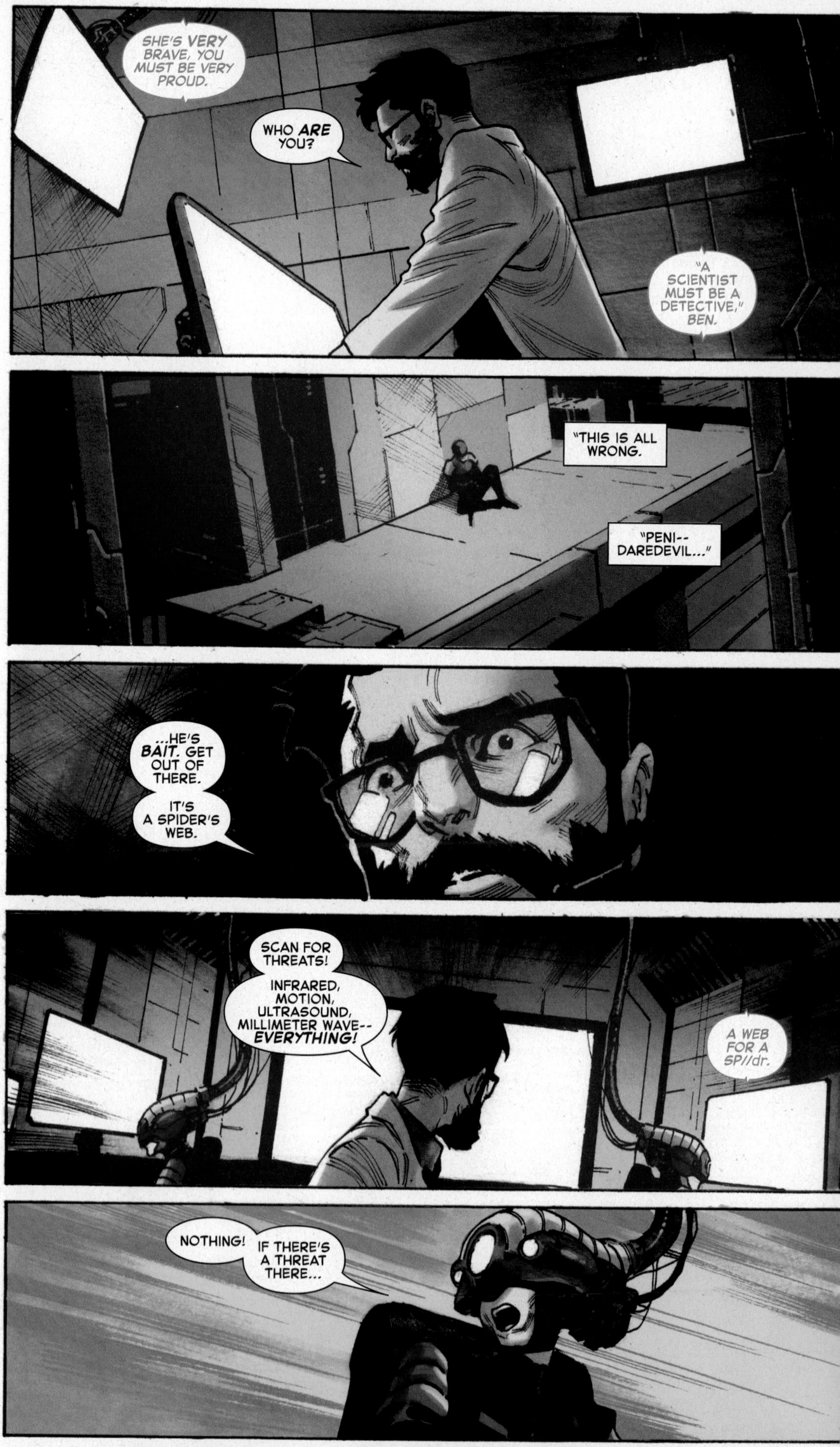
SHE'S VERY BRAVE, YOU MUST BE VERY PROUD.
WHO ARE YOU?
"A SCIENTIST MUST BE A DETECTIVE," BEN.
"THIS IS ALL WRONG.
"PENI-- DAREDEVIL..."
...HE'S BAIT. GET OUT OF THERE.
IT'S A SPIDER'S WEB.
SCAN FOR THREATS!
INFRARED, MOTION, ULTRASOUND, MILLIMETER WAVE-- EVERYTHING!
A WEB FOR A SP//dr.
NOTHING!
IF THERE'S A THREAT THERE...

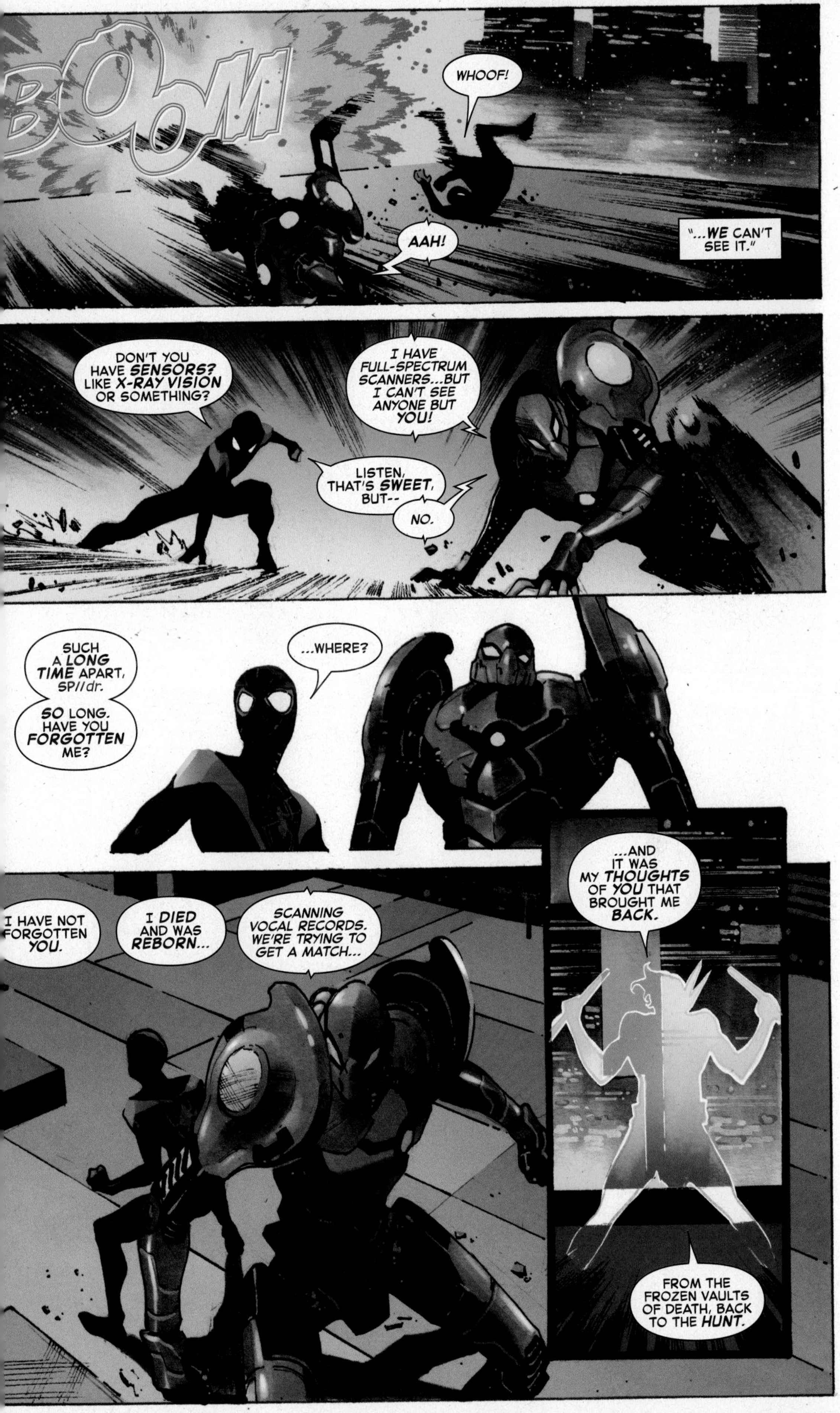
BOOM
WHOOF!
AAH!
"...WE CAN'T SEE IT."
DON'T YOU HAVE SENSORS? LIKE X-RAY VISION OR SOMETHING?
I HAVE FULL-SPECTRUM SCANNERS...BUT I CAN'T SEE ANYONE BUT YOU!
LISTEN, THAT'S SWEET, BUT--
NO.
SUCH A LONG TIME APART, SP//dr.
SO LONG. HAVE YOU FORGOTTEN ME?
...WHERE?
I HAVE NOT FORGOTTEN YOU.
I DIED AND WAS REBORN...
SCANNING VOCAL RECORDS. WE'RE TRYING TO GET A MATCH...
...AND IT WAS MY THOUGHTS OF YOU THAT BROUGHT ME BACK.
FROM THE FROZEN VAULTS OF DEATH, BACK TO THE HUNT.

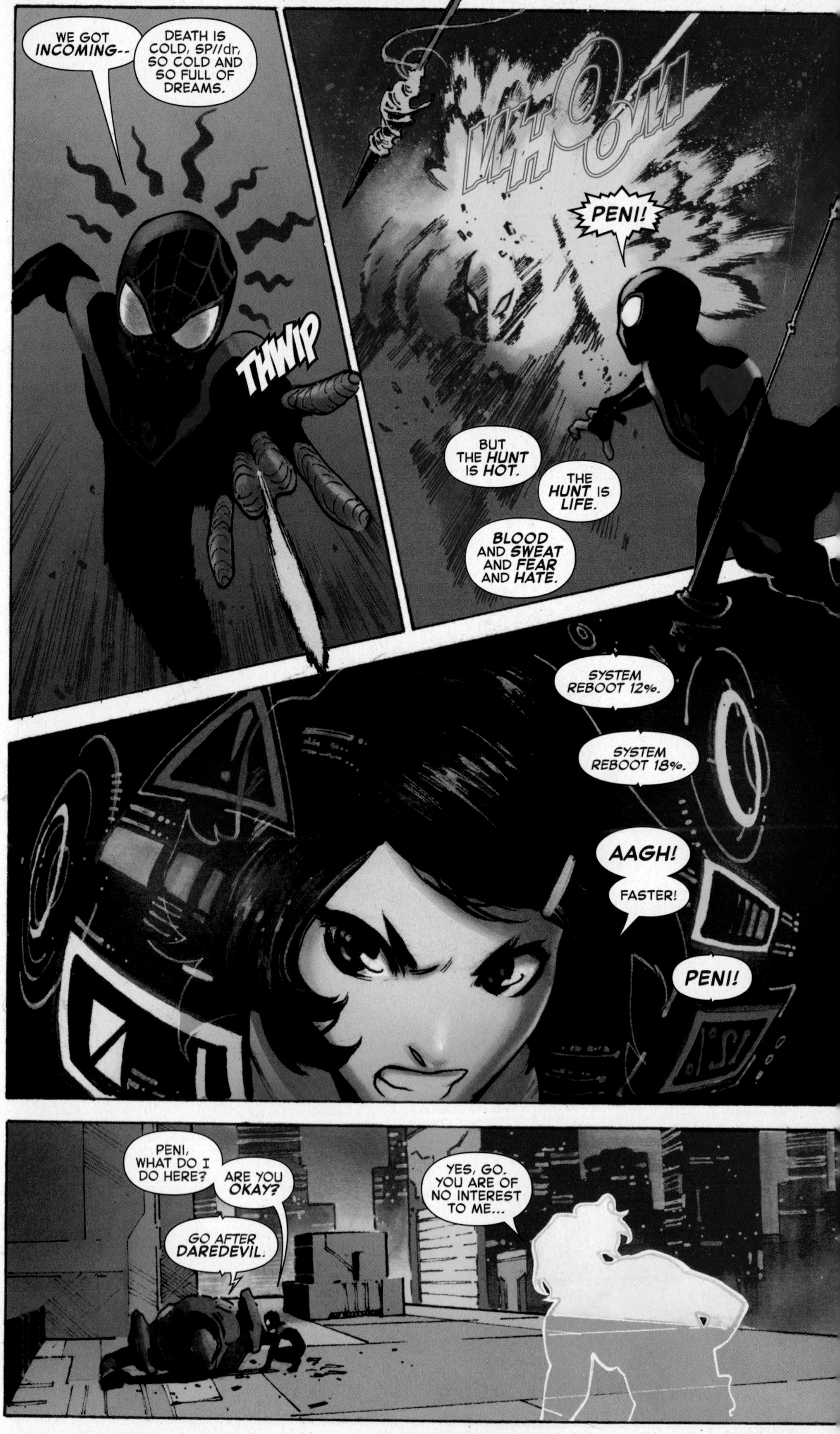
WE GOT INCOMING--
DEATH IS COLD, SP//dr, SO COLD AND SO FULL OF DREAMS.
THWIP
WHOOM
PENI!
BUT THE HUNT IS HOT.
THE HUNT IS LIFE.
BLOOD AND SWEAT AND FEAR AND HATE.
SYSTEM REBOOT 12%.
SYSTEM REBOOT 18%.
AAGH!
FASTER!
PENI!
PENI, WHAT DO I DO HERE?
ARE YOU OKAY?
GO AFTER DAREDEVIL.
YES, GO. YOU ARE OF NO INTEREST TO ME...

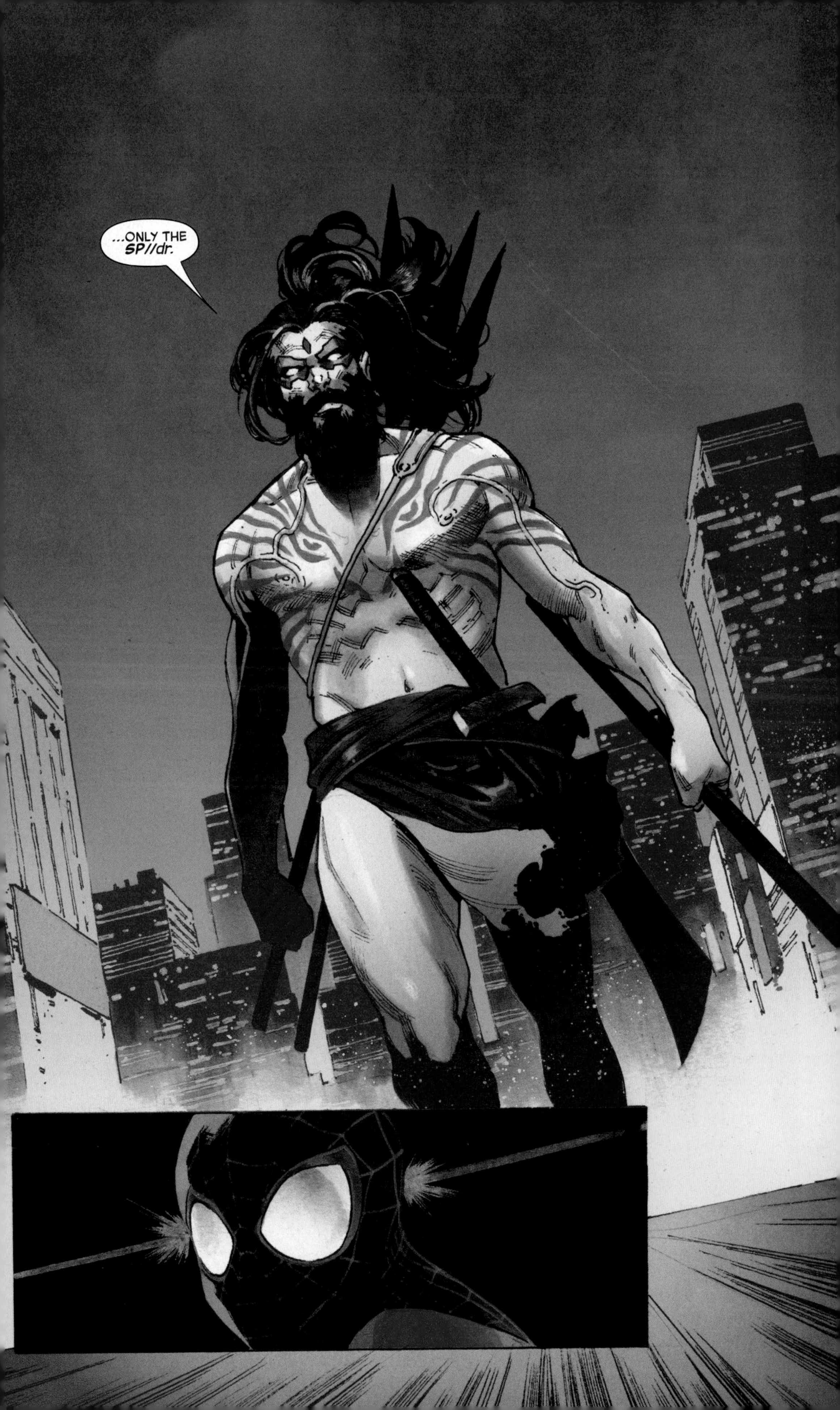
...ONLY THE SP//dr.

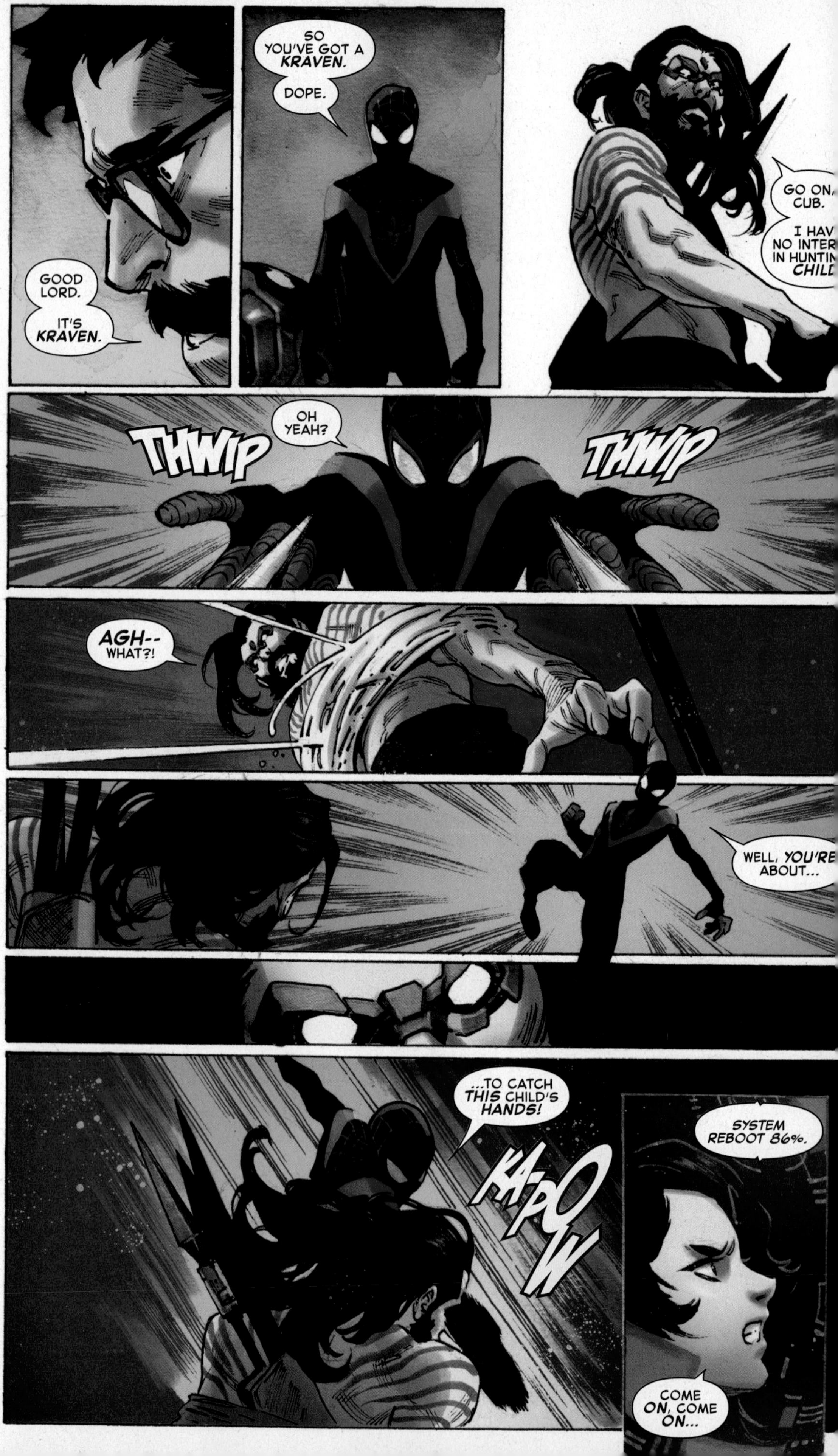

GOOD LORD.
IT'S KRAVEN.
SO YOU'VE GOT A KRAVEN.
DOPE.
GO ON, CUB.
I HAV NO INTER IN HUNTIN CHILD
OH YEAH?
THWIP
THWIP
AGH-- WHAT?!
WELL, YOU'RE ABOUT...
...TO CATCH THIS CHILD'S HANDS!
KA-POW
SYSTEM REBOOT 86%.
COME ON, COME ON...

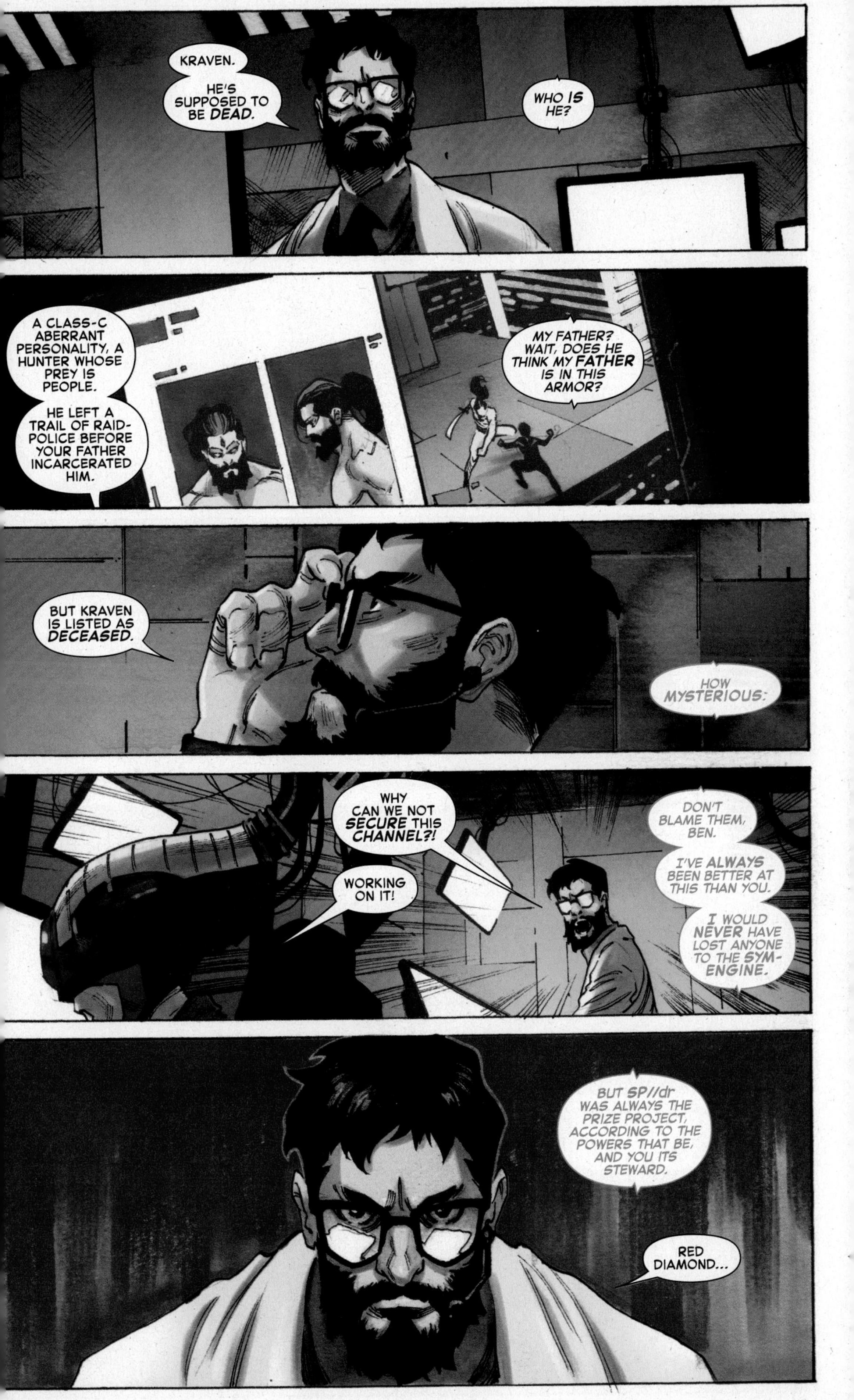
KRAVEN.
HE'S SUPPOSED TO BE DEAD.
WHO IS HE?
A CLASS-C ABERRANT PERSONALITY, A HUNTER WHOSE PREY IS PEOPLE.
HE LEFT A TRAIL OF RAID-POLICE BEFORE YOUR FATHER INCARCERATED HIM.
MY FATHER? WAIT, DOES HE THINK MY FATHER IS IN THIS ARMOR?
BUT KRAVEN IS LISTED AS DECEASED.
HOW MYSTERIOUS.
WHY CAN WE NOT SECURE THIS CHANNEL?!
WORKING ON IT!
DON'T BLAME THEM, BEN.
I'VE ALWAYS BEEN BETTER AT THIS THAN YOU.
I WOULD NEVER HAVE LOST ANYONE TO THE SYM-ENGINE.
BUT SP//dr WAS ALWAYS THE PRIZE PROJECT, ACCORDING TO THE POWERS THAT BE, AND YOU ITS STEWARD.
RED DIAMOND...

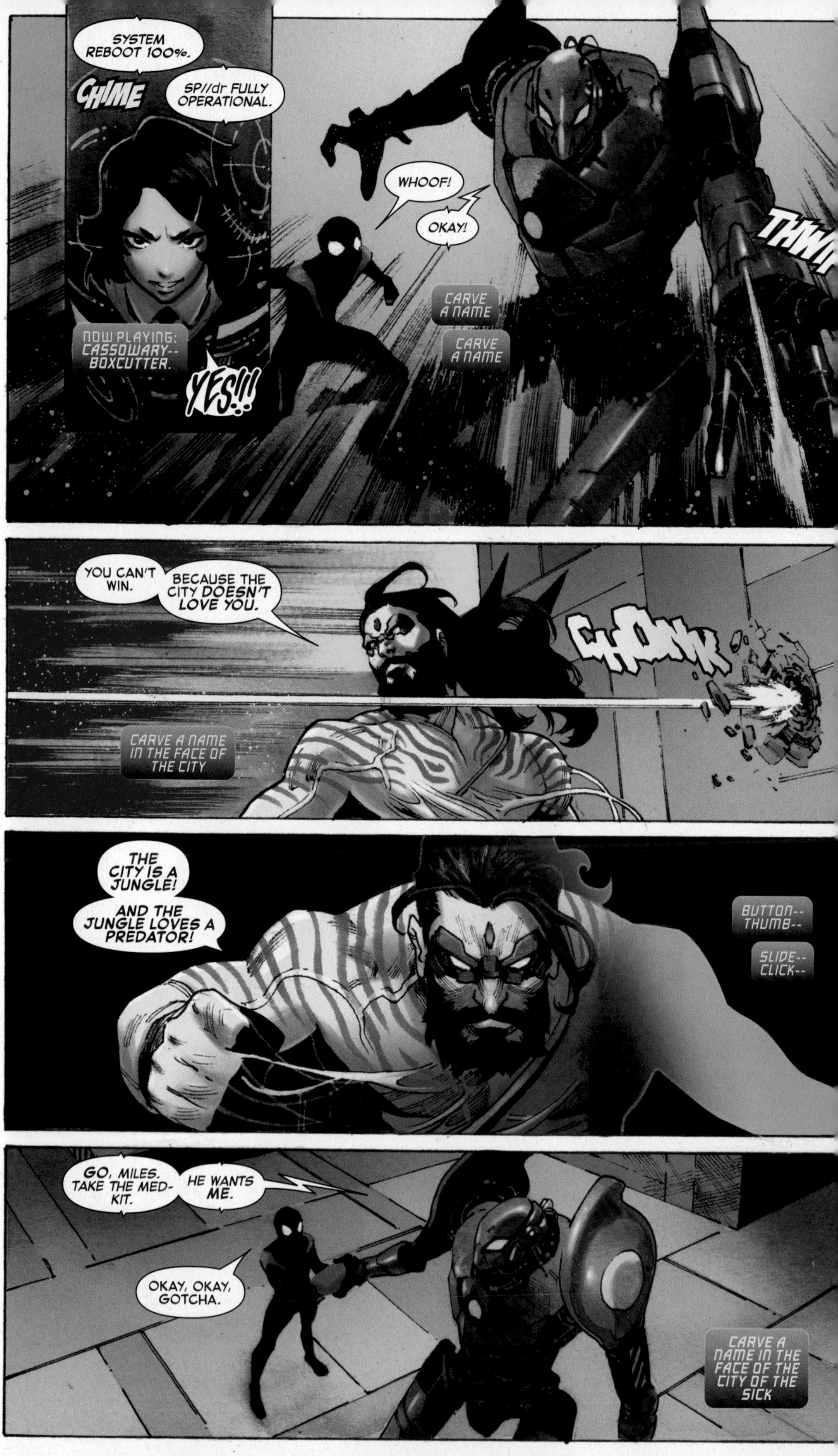
SYSTEM REBOOT 100%.
CHIME
SP//dr FULLY OPERATIONAL.
NOW PLAYING: CASSOWARY-- BOXCUTTER.
YES!!!
WHOOF!
OKAY!
CARVE A NAME
CARVE A NAME
YOU CAN'T WIN.
BECAUSE THE CITY DOESN'T LOVE YOU.
CHOMK
CARVE A NAME IN THE FACE OF THE CITY
THE CITY IS A JUNGLE!
AND THE JUNGLE LOVES A PREDATOR!
BUTTON-- THUMB--
SLIDE-- CLICK--
GO, MILES. TAKE THE MED-KIT.
HE WANTS ME.
OKAY, OKAY, GOTCHA.
CARVE A NAME IN THE FACE OF THE CITY OF THE SICK

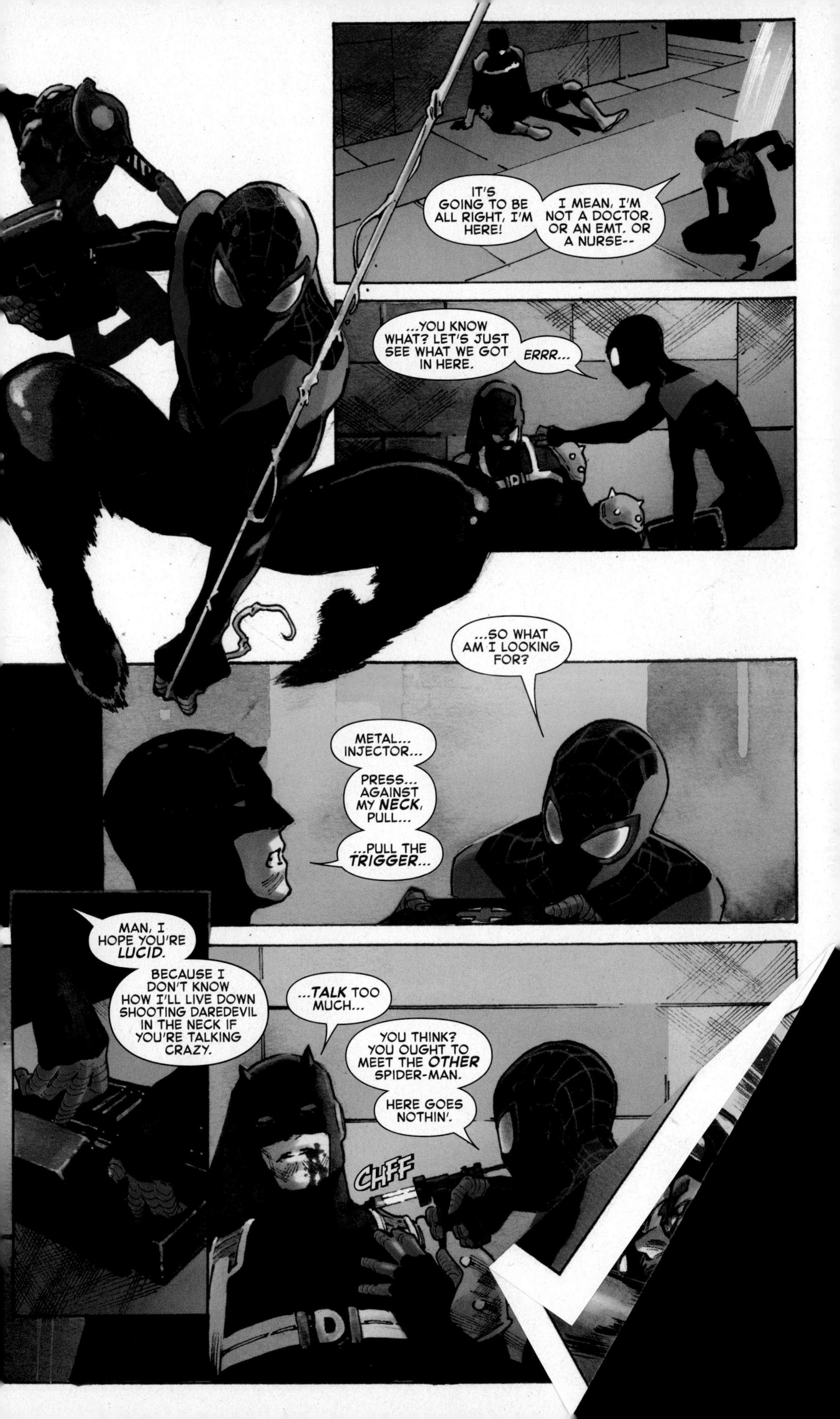
IT'S GOING TO BE ALL RIGHT, I'M HERE!
I MEAN, I'M NOT A DOCTOR. OR AN EMT. OR A NURSE--
...YOU KNOW WHAT? LET'S JUST SEE WHAT WE GOT IN HERE.
ERRR...
...SO WHAT AM I LOOKING FOR?
METAL... INJECTOR...
PRESS... AGAINST MY NECK, PULL...
...PULL THE TRIGGER...
MAN, I HOPE YOU'RE LUCID.
BECAUSE I DON'T KNOW HOW I'LL LIVE DOWN SHOOTING DAREDEVIL IN THE NECK IF YOU'RE TALKING CRAZY.
...TALK TOO MUCH...
YOU THINK? YOU OUGHT TO MEET THE OTHER SPIDER-MAN.
HERE GOES NOTHIN'.
CHFF

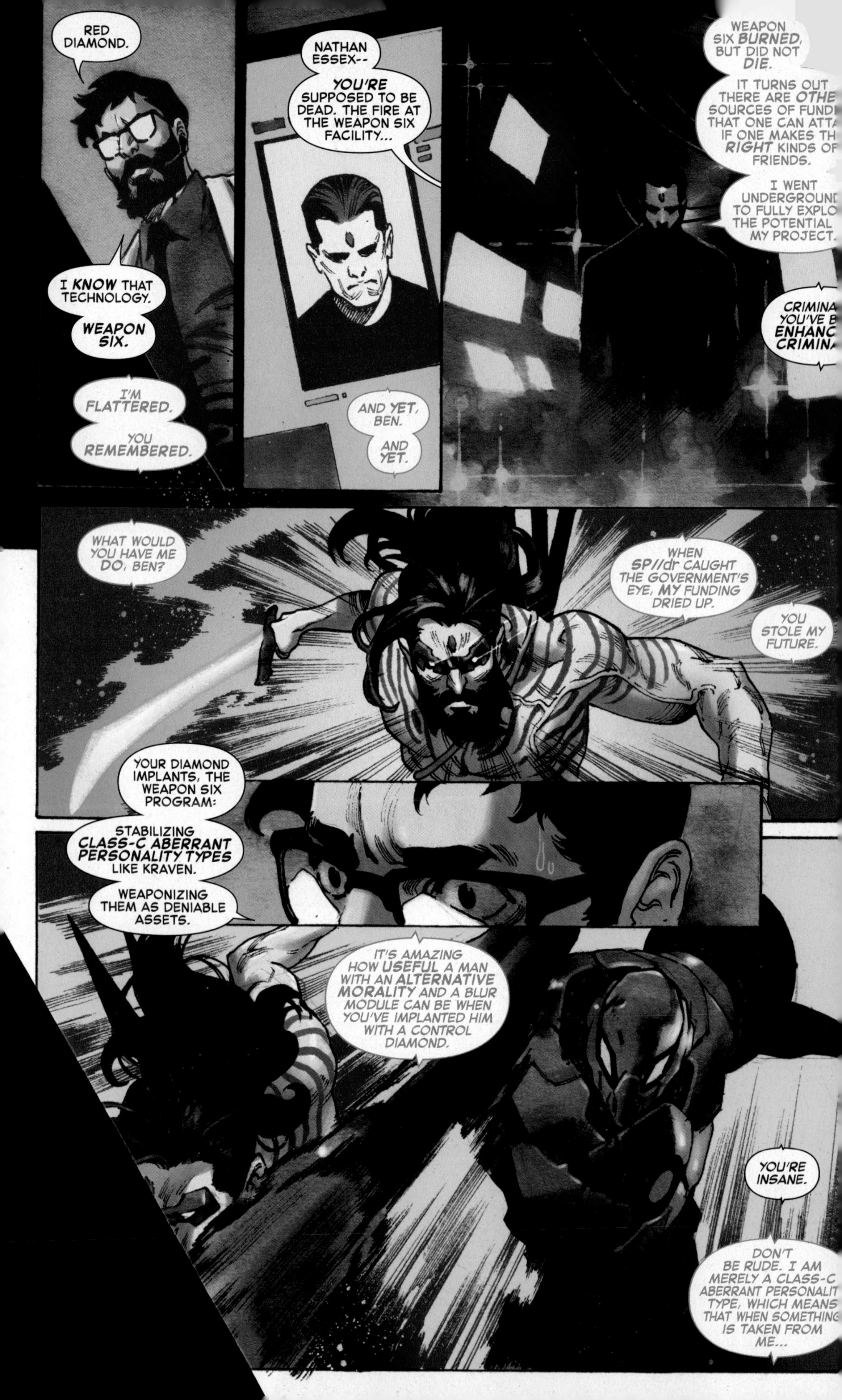
RED DIAMOND.
I KNOW THAT TECHNOLOGY.
WEAPON SIX.
I'M FLATTERED.
YOU REMEMBERED.
NATHAN ESSEX--
YOU'RE SUPPOSED TO BE DEAD. THE FIRE AT THE WEAPON SIX FACILITY...
AND YET, BEN.
AND YET.
WEAPON SIX BURNED, BUT DID NOT DIE.
WHAT WOULD YOU HAVE ME DO, BEN?
WHEN SP//dr CAUGHT THE GOVERNMENT'S EYE, MY FUNDING DRIED UP.
YOU STOLE MY FUTURE.
YOUR DIAMOND IMPLANTS, THE WEAPON SIX PROGRAM:
STABILIZING CLASS-C ABERRANT PERSONALITY TYPES LIKE KRAVEN.
WEAPONIZING THEM AS DENIABLE ASSETS.
IT'S AMAZING HOW USEFUL A MAN WITH AN ALTERNATIVE MORALITY AND A BLUR MODULE CAN BE WHEN YOU'VE IMPLANTED HIM WITH A CONTROL DIAMOND.
YOU'RE INSANE.

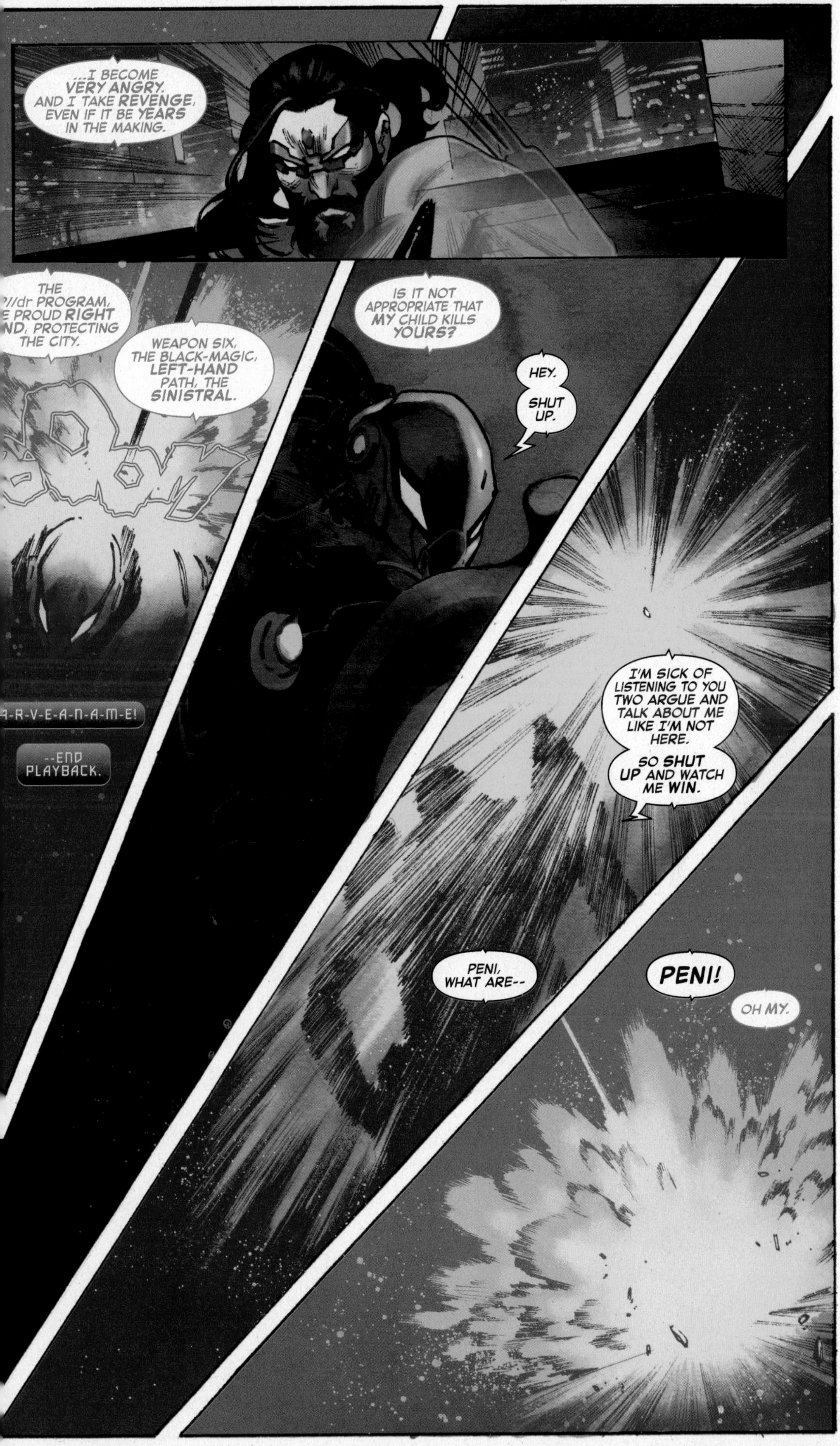
...I BECOME VERY ANGRY. AND I TAKE REVENGE, EVEN IF IT BE YEARS IN THE MAKING.
THE P//dr PROGRAM, E PROUD RIGHT ND, PROTECTING THE CITY.
WEAPON SIX, THE BLACK-MAGIC, LEFT-HAND PATH, THE SINISTRAL.
IS IT NOT APPROPRIATE THAT MY CHILD KILLS YOURS?
HEY.
SHUT UP.
A-R-V-E-A-N-A-M-E!
--END PLAYBACK.
I'M SICK OF LISTENING TO YOU TWO ARGUE AND TALK ABOUT ME LIKE I'M NOT HERE.
SO SHUT UP AND WATCH ME WIN.
PENI, WHAT ARE--
PENI!
OH MY.

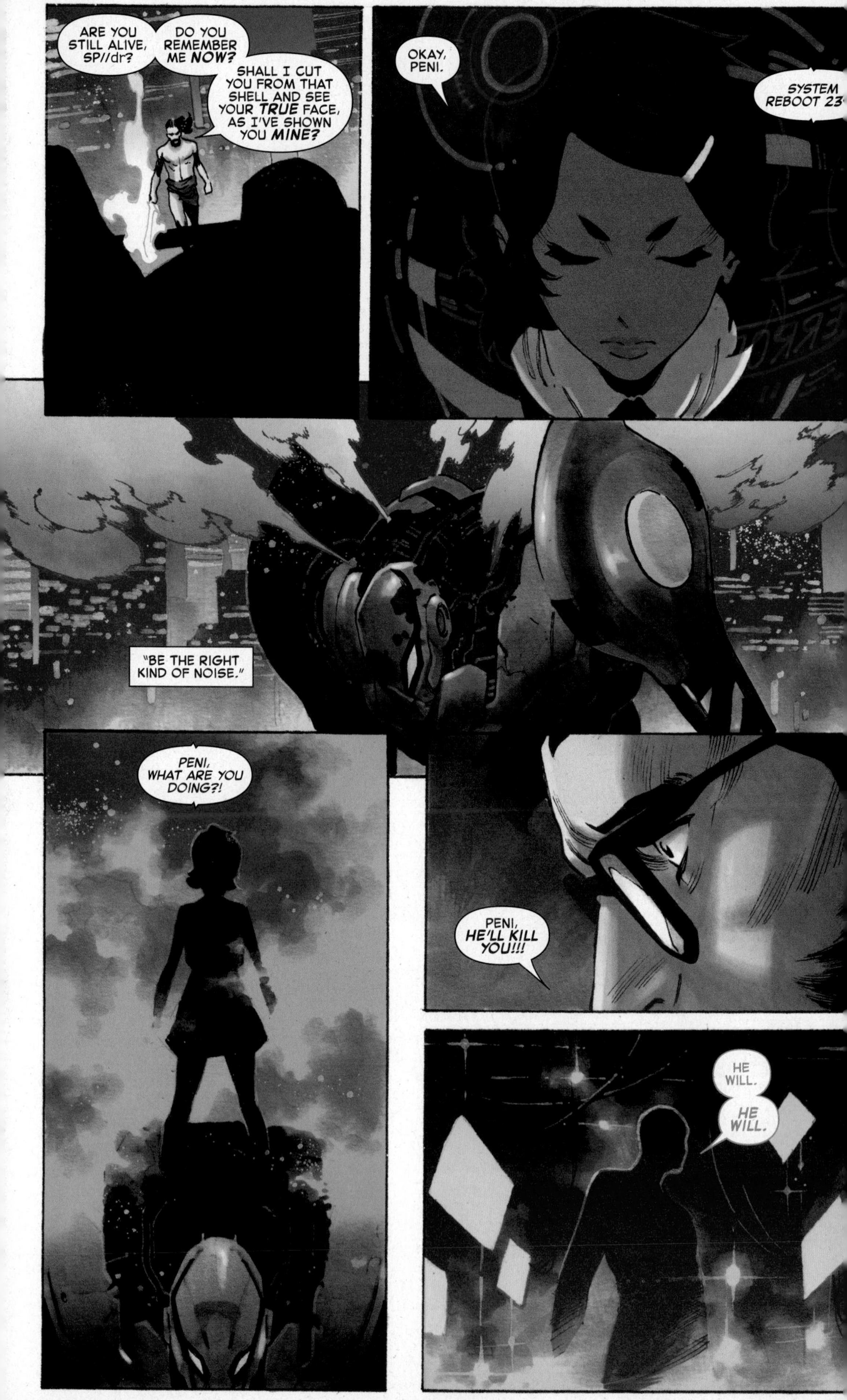
ARE YOU STILL ALIVE, SP//dr?
DO YOU REMEMBER ME NOW?
SHALL I CUT YOU FROM THAT SHELL AND SEE YOUR TRUE FACE, AS I'VE SHOWN YOU MINE?
OKAY, PENI.
SYSTEM REBOOT 23
"BE THE RIGHT KIND OF NOISE."
PENI, WHAT ARE YOU DOING?!
PENI, HE'LL KILL YOU!!!
HE WILL.
HE WILL.

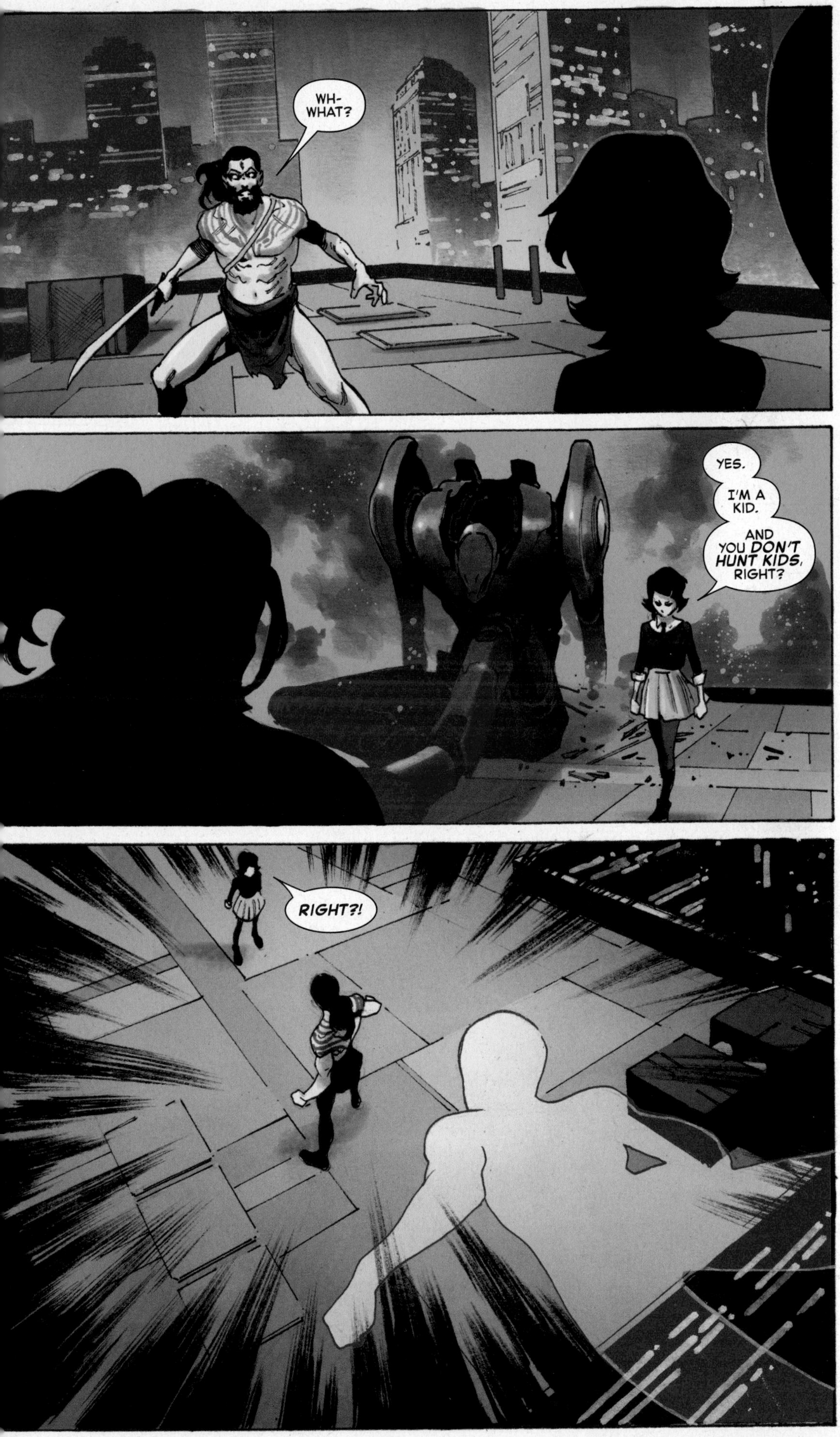
WH-
WHAT?
YES.
I'M A KID.
AND YOU DON'T HUNT KIDS, RIGHT?
RIGHT?!

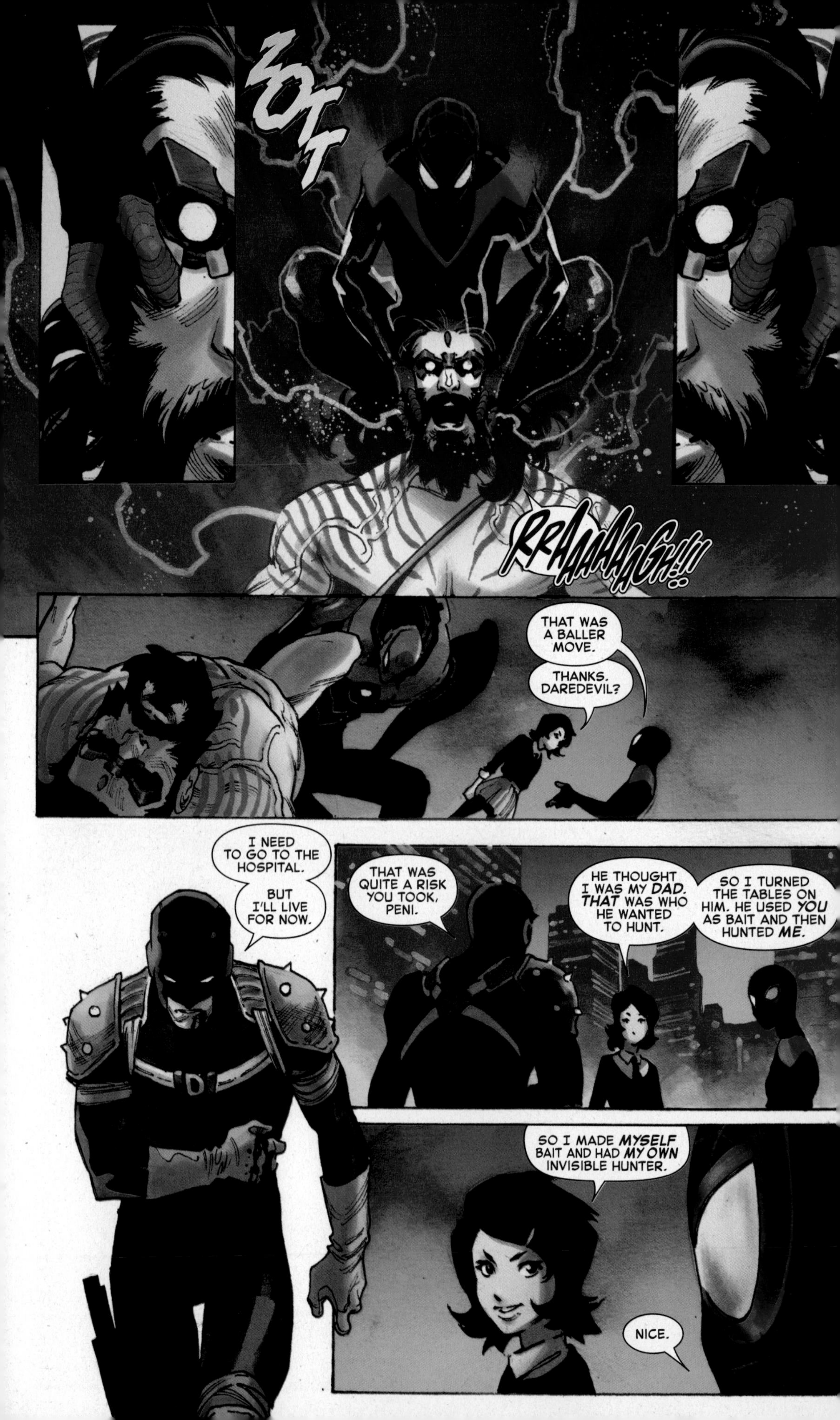
ZOTT
RRAAAAAAGH!!!
THAT WAS A BALLER MOVE.
THANKS. DAREDEVIL?
I NEED TO GO TO THE HOSPITAL.
BUT I'LL LIVE FOR NOW.
THAT WAS QUITE A RISK YOU TOOK, PENI.
HE THOUGHT I WAS MY DAD. THAT WAS WHO HE WANTED TO HUNT.
SO I TURNED THE TABLES ON HIM. HE USED YOU AS BAIT AND THEN HUNTED ME.
SO I MADE MYSELF BAIT AND HAD MY OWN INVISIBLE HUNTER.
NICE.

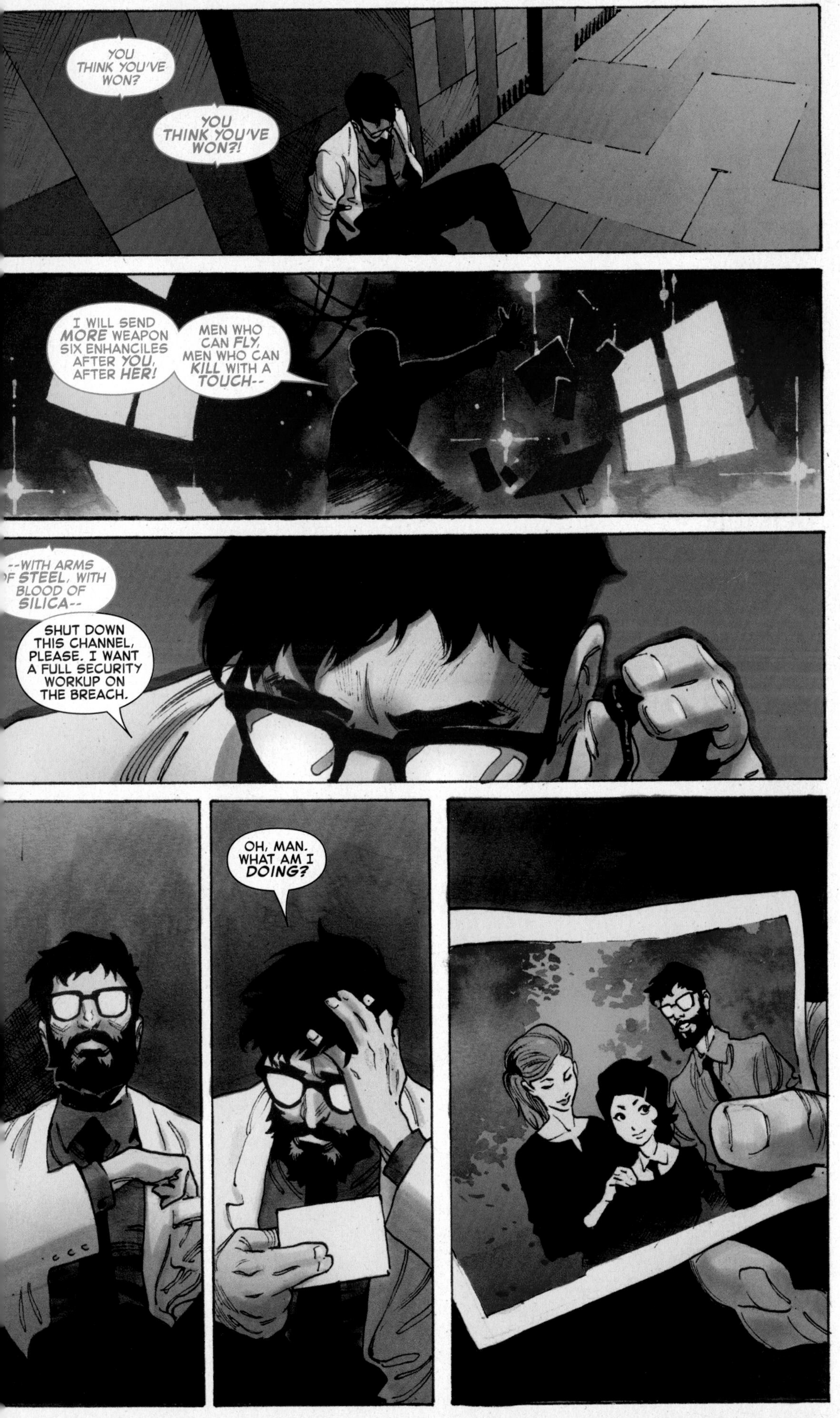
YOU THINK YOU'VE WON?
YOU THINK YOU'VE WON?!
I WILL SEND MORE WEAPON SIX ENHANCILES AFTER YOU, AFTER HER!
MEN WHO CAN FLY, MEN WHO CAN KILL WITH A TOUCH--
--WITH ARMS OF STEEL, WITH BLOOD OF SILICA--
SHUT DOWN THIS CHANNEL, PLEASE. I WANT A FULL SECURITY WORKUP ON THE BREACH.
OH, MAN. WHAT AM I DOING?

SPIDERSONA:
SUN-SPIDER

Art & Text by DAYNA BRODER
United States

As a disabled person, I almost never get to see any disabled super heroes. I wanted to create someone like me: an ambulatory wheelchair user, who can still kick butt in her own modified way. Sun-Spider is hyper-flexible, though this does have drawbacks since it means she requires extra stability, and

SPIDERSONA:
GARDEN-SPIDER

Art & Text by ALYSSA RAGNI
United States

Petunia Parker, A.K.A. the Garden-Spider, was shrunk down to the size of a bug. She now spends her days caring for her plants, swinging from flowers the size of skyscrapers and keeping buds safe from the Aphid and his crew of sinister insects. All in all, it's not so bad being small—living inside her old watering can has been pretty cozy!

SPIDERSONA:
WHITE WIDOW

Art & Text by CARLY HENSON
United States

White Widow, A.K.A. Venice Doadi, lives in a future timeline and possesses the ability to coat both her webs and her clawed gloves with toxins she secretes from her skin at will. Two of my biggest inspirations were the peacock spider and the black widow—I wanted her to have an eye-catching appearance that reiterates her lethal ability.

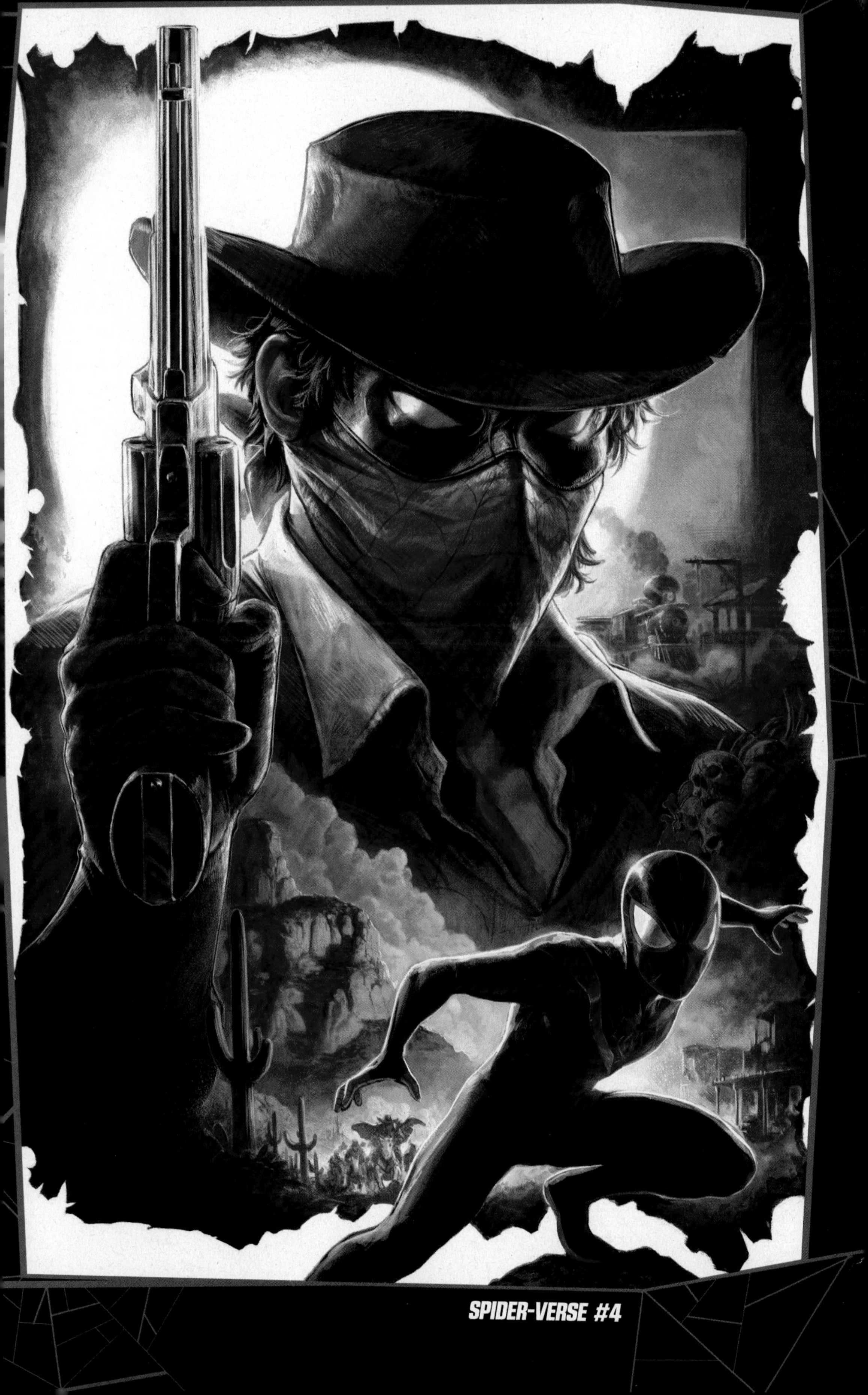

SPIDER-VERSE #4

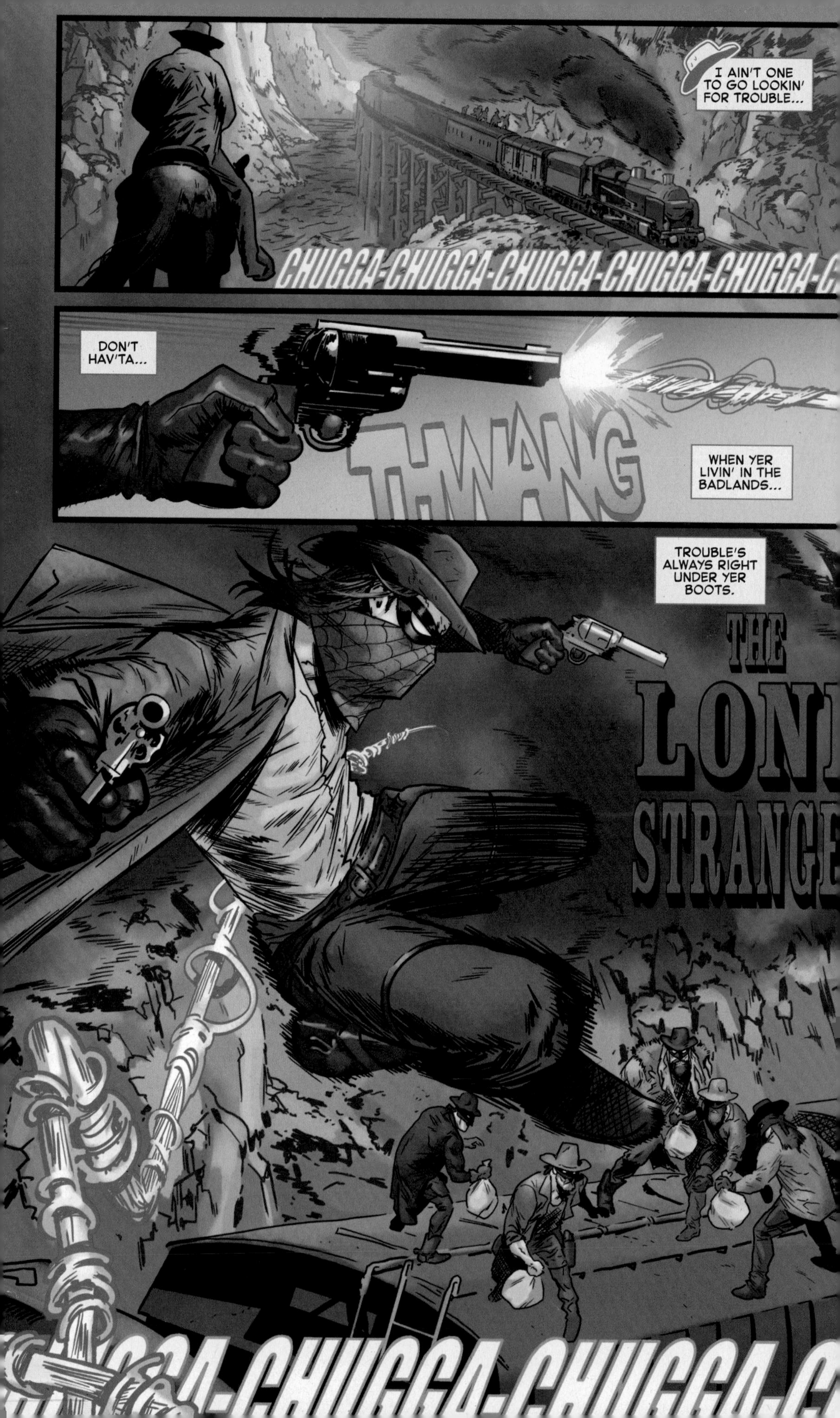
I AIN'T ONE TO GO LOOKIN' FOR TROUBLE...
CHUGGA-CHUGGA-CHUGGA-CHUGGA-CHUGGA-
DON'T HAV'TA...
THWANG
WHEN YER LIVIN' IN THE BADLANDS...
TROUBLE'S ALWAYS RIGHT UNDER YER BOOTS.
THE LONE STRANGE
-CHUGGA-CHUGGA-

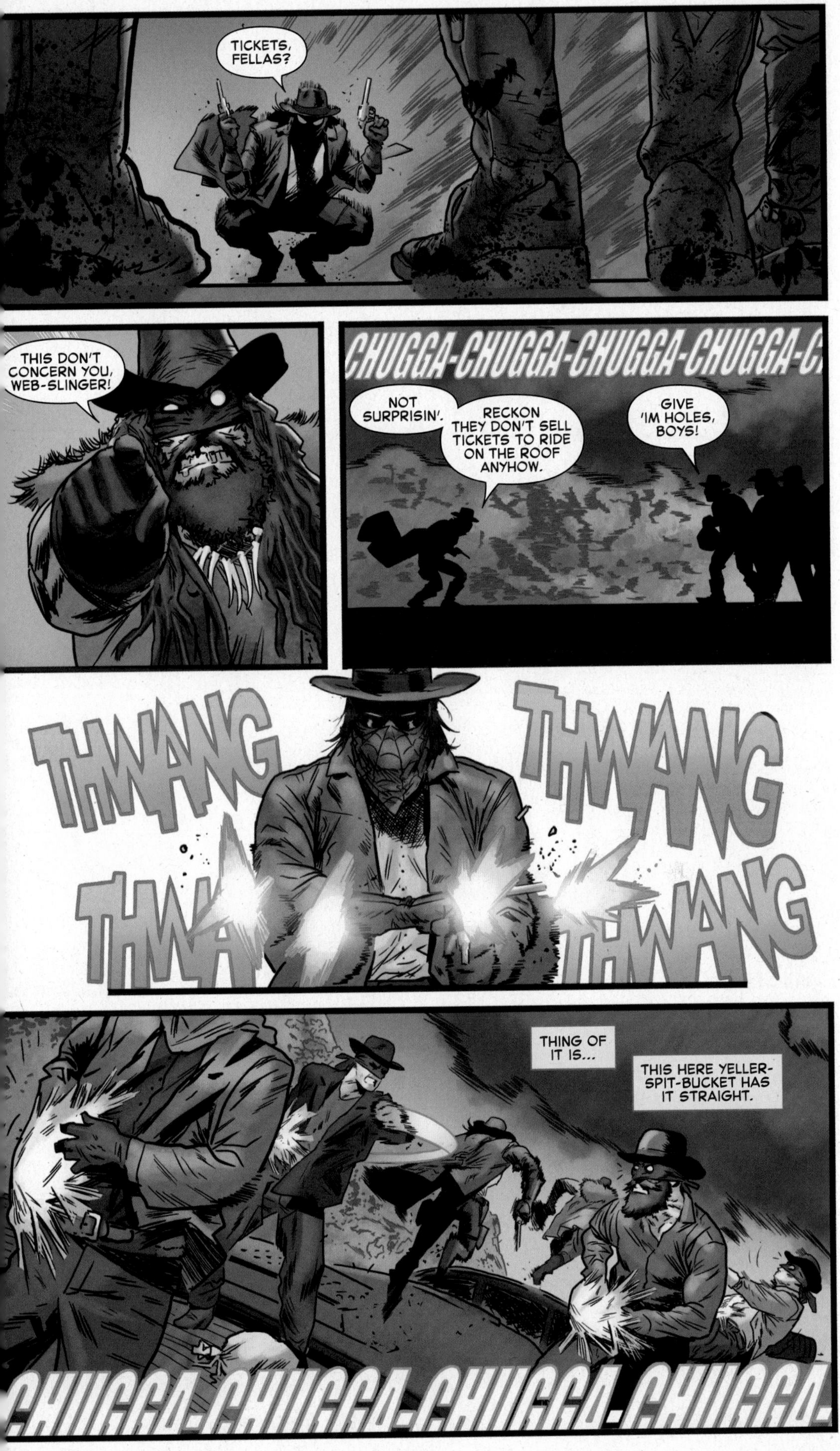
TICKETS, FELLAS?
THIS DON'T CONCERN YOU, WEB-SLINGER!
CHUGGA-CHUGGA-CHUGGA-CHUGGA-
NOT SURPRISIN'.
RECKON THEY DON'T SELL TICKETS TO RIDE ON THE ROOF ANYHOW.
GIVE 'IM HOLES, BOYS!
THWANG
THWANG
THWANG
THWANG
THING OF IT IS...
THIS HERE YELLER-SPIT-BUCKET HAS IT STRAIGHT.
CHUGGA-CHUGGA-CHUGGA-CHUGGA-

THIS **DON'T** CONCERN ME.

BUT I MADE MYSELF A PROMISE A LONG TIME AGO.

IN A WORLD FULL UP ON EVIL...

CHUGGA-CHUGGA-CHUGGA-CHUGGA-CHUGGA-CHUGGA-CHUGGA-CHUGG

I AIM TO DO A LITTLE GOOD.

THUNK

HOLD IT RIGHT THERE, ITSY BITSY.

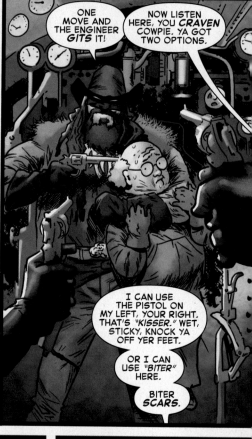

ONE MOVE AND THE ENGINEER **GITS** IT!

NOW LISTEN HERE, YOU **CRAVEN** COWPIE. YA GOT TWO OPTIONS.

I CAN USE THE PISTOL ON MY LEFT, YOUR RIGHT. THAT'S "KISSER." WET, STICKY, KNOCK YA OFF YER FEET.

OR I CAN USE "BITER" HERE.

BITER **SCARS.**

UUHNG!

FIRST RULE OF TRAIN ROBBIN':

FAMILIARIZE YERSELF WITH EMERGENCY EXITS!

THRO

KRAK

ADIOS, WEB-SLIN--

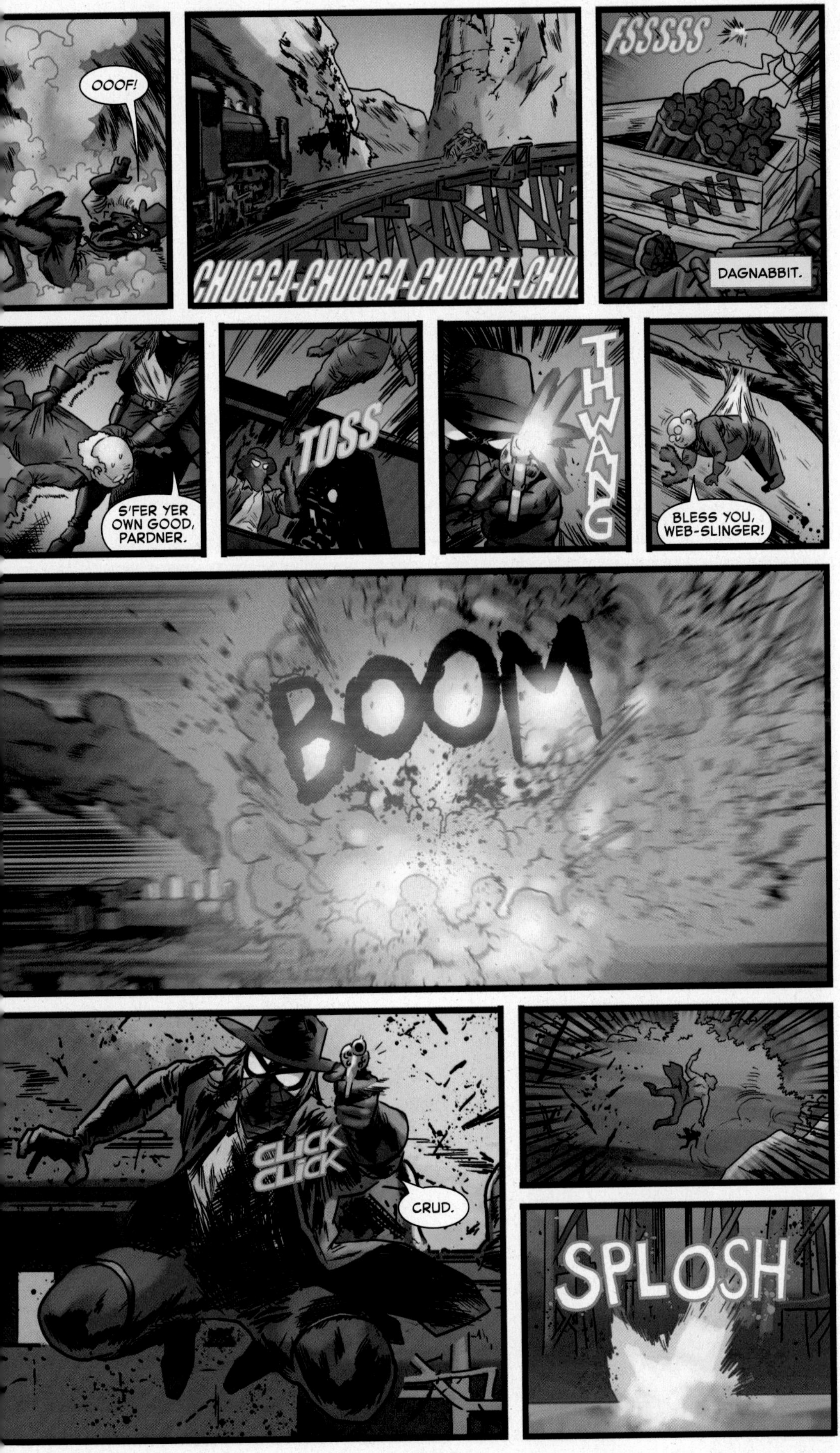
OOOF!
CHUGGA-CHUGGA-CHUGGA-CHU
FSSSSS
TNT
DAGNABBIT.
S'FER YER OWN GOOD, PARDNER.
TOSS
THWANG
BLESS YOU, WEB-SLINGER!
BOOM
CLICK CLICK
CRUD.
SPLOSH

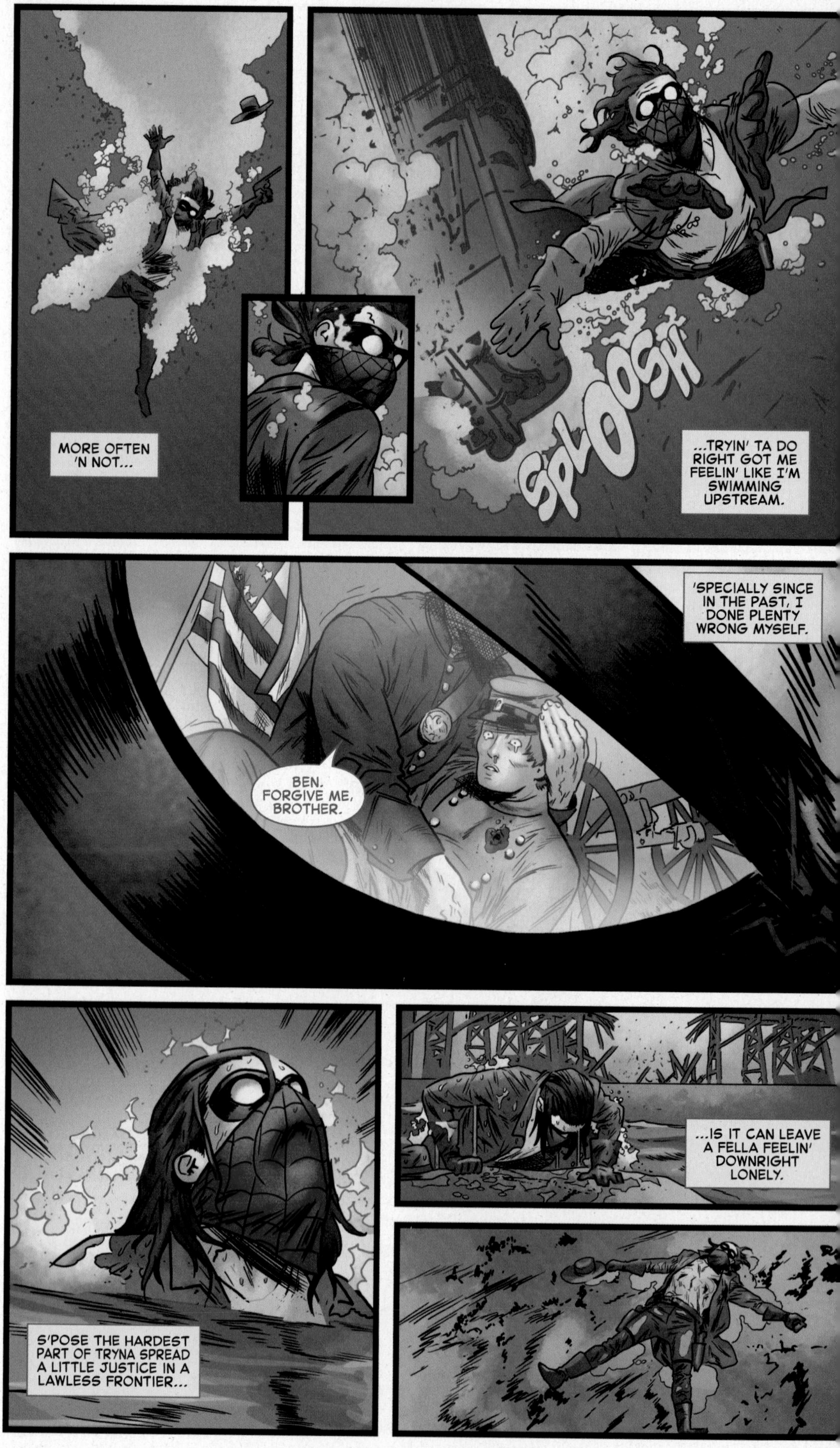
MORE OFTEN 'N NOT...
SPLOOSH
...TRYIN' TA DO RIGHT GOT ME FEELIN' LIKE I'M SWIMMING UPSTREAM.
'SPECIALLY SINCE IN THE PAST, I DONE PLENTY WRONG MYSELF.
BEN. FORGIVE ME, BROTHER.
S'POSE THE HARDEST PART OF TRYNA SPREAD A LITTLE JUSTICE IN A LAWLESS FRONTIER...
...IS IT CAN LEAVE A FELLA FEELIN' DOWNRIGHT LONELY.

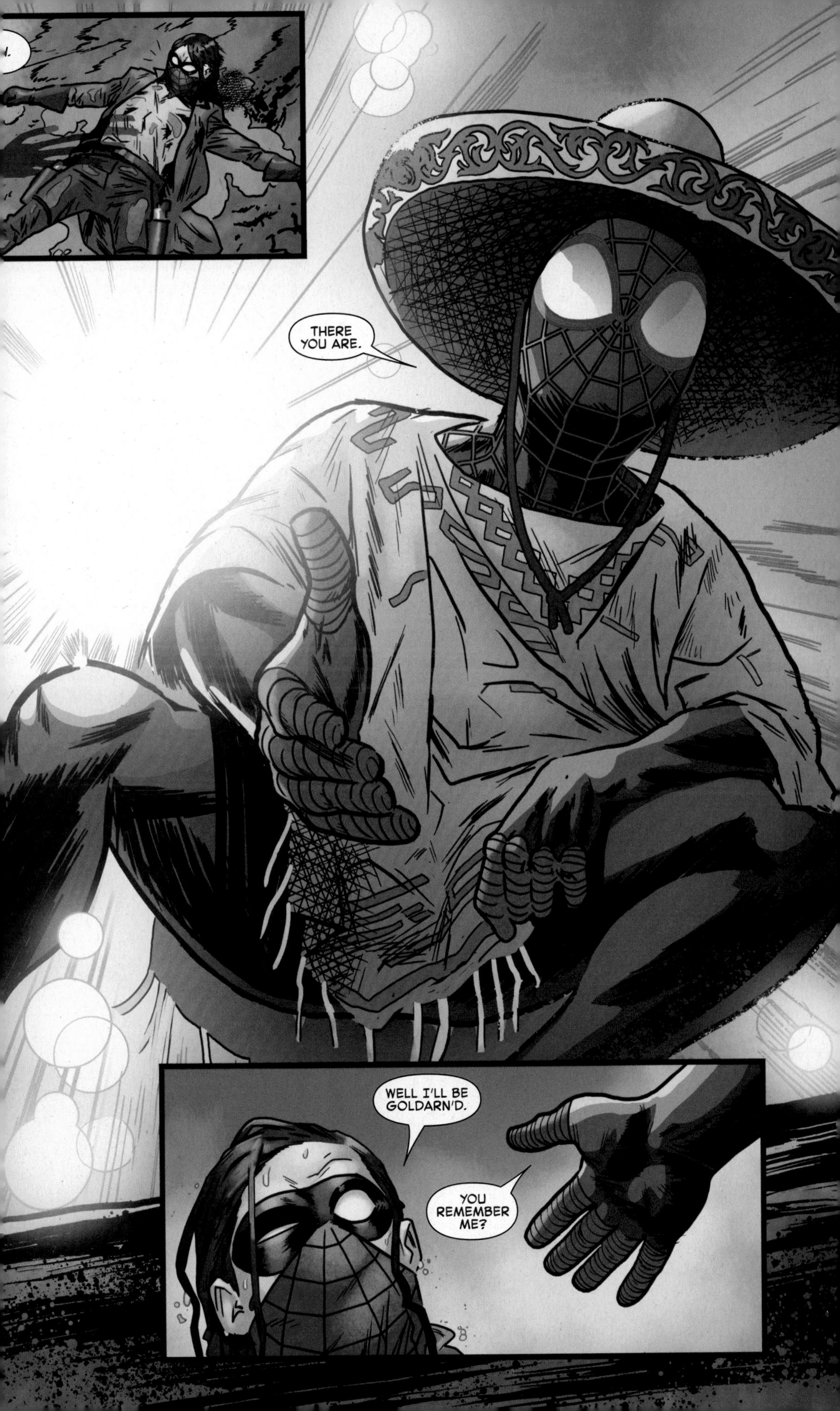
THERE YOU ARE.
WELL I'LL BE GOLDARN'D.
YOU REMEMBER ME?

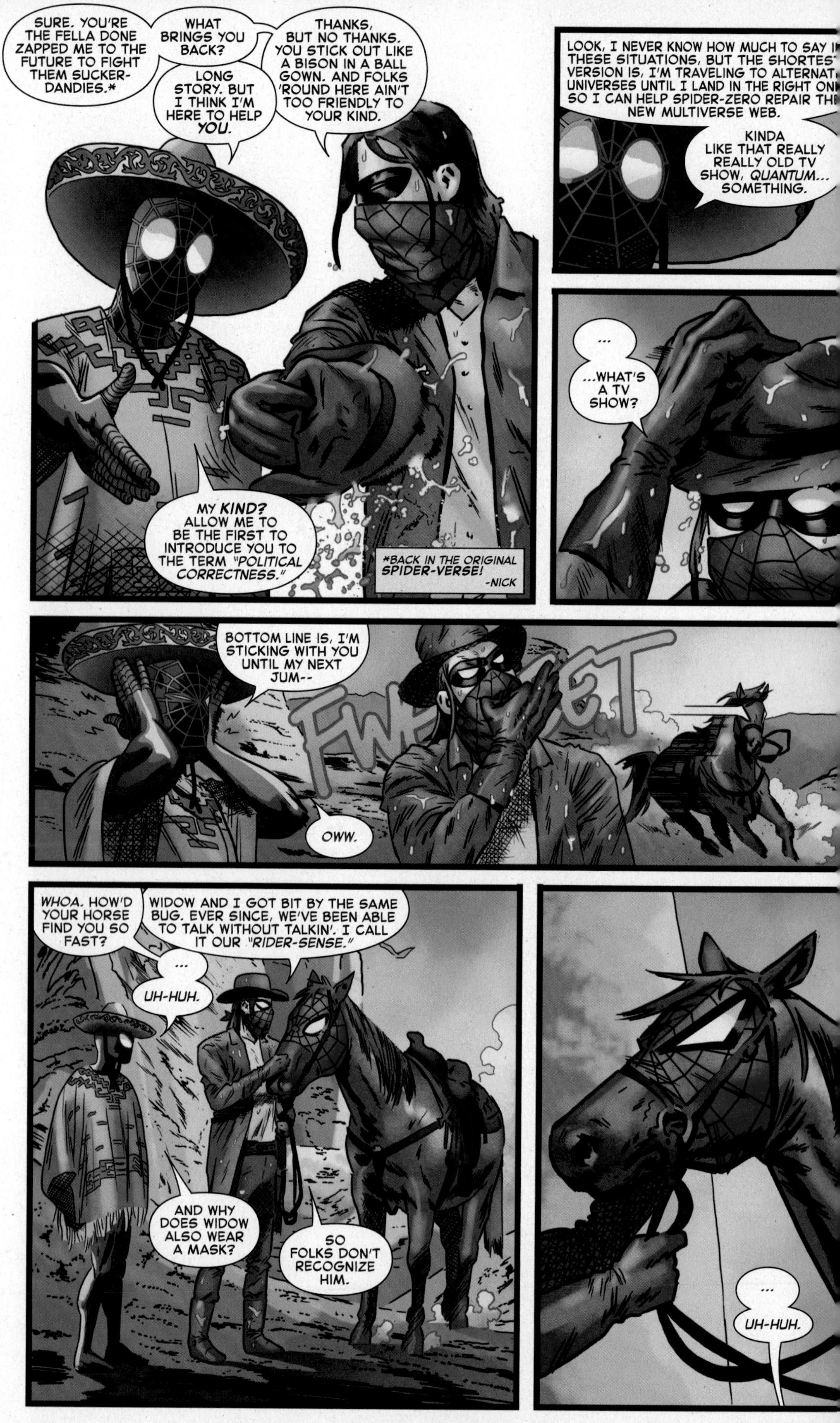
SURE. YOU'RE THE FELLA DONE ZAPPED ME TO THE FUTURE TO FIGHT THEM SUCKER-DANDIES.*
WHAT BRINGS YOU BACK?
LONG STORY. BUT I THINK I'M HERE TO HELP YOU.
THANKS, BUT NO THANKS. YOU STICK OUT LIKE A BISON IN A BALL GOWN. AND FOLKS 'ROUND HERE AIN'T TOO FRIENDLY TO YOUR KIND.
MY KIND? ALLOW ME TO BE THE FIRST TO INTRODUCE YOU TO THE TERM "POLITICAL CORRECTNESS."
*BACK IN THE ORIGINAL SPIDER-VERSE! -NICK
LOOK, I NEVER KNOW HOW MUCH TO SAY IN THESE SITUATIONS, BUT THE SHORTEST VERSION IS, I'M TRAVELING TO ALTERNATE UNIVERSES UNTIL I LAND IN THE RIGHT ONE SO I CAN HELP SPIDER-ZERO REPAIR THE NEW MULTIVERSE WEB.
KINDA LIKE THAT REALLY REALLY OLD TV SHOW, QUANTUM... SOMETHING.
...
...WHAT'S A TV SHOW?
BOTTOM LINE IS, I'M STICKING WITH YOU UNTIL MY NEXT JUM--
FWEEEET
OWW.
WHOA. HOW'D YOUR HORSE FIND YOU SO FAST?
WIDOW AND I GOT BIT BY THE SAME BUG. EVER SINCE, WE'VE BEEN ABLE TO TALK WITHOUT TALKIN'. I CALL IT OUR "RIDER-SENSE."
...
UH-HUH.
AND WHY DOES WIDOW ALSO WEAR A MASK?
SO FOLKS DON'T RECOGNIZE HIM.
...
UH-HUH.

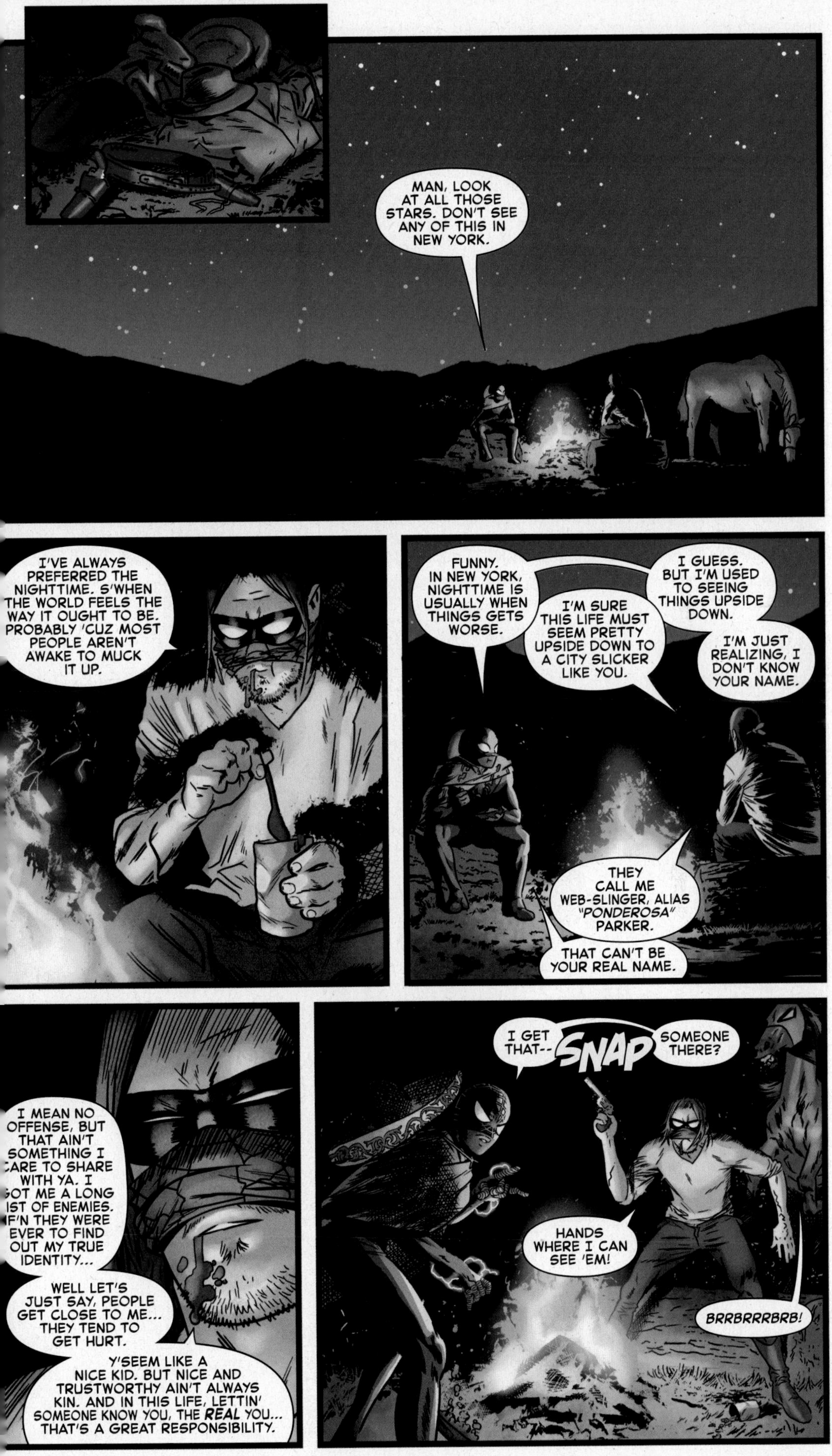
MAN, LOOK AT ALL THOSE STARS. DON'T SEE ANY OF THIS IN NEW YORK.
I'VE ALWAYS PREFERRED THE NIGHTTIME. S'WHEN THE WORLD FEELS THE WAY IT OUGHT TO BE. PROBABLY 'CUZ MOST PEOPLE AREN'T AWAKE TO MUCK IT UP.
FUNNY. IN NEW YORK, NIGHTTIME IS USUALLY WHEN THINGS GETS WORSE.
I'M SURE THIS LIFE MUST SEEM PRETTY UPSIDE DOWN TO A CITY SLICKER LIKE YOU.
I GUESS. BUT I'M USED TO SEEING THINGS UPSIDE DOWN.
I'M JUST REALIZING, I DON'T KNOW YOUR NAME.
THEY CALL ME WEB-SLINGER, ALIAS *"PONDEROSA"* PARKER.
THAT CAN'T BE YOUR REAL NAME.
I MEAN NO OFFENSE, BUT THAT AIN'T SOMETHING I CARE TO SHARE WITH YA. I GOT ME A LONG LIST OF ENEMIES. IF'N THEY WERE EVER TO FIND OUT MY TRUE IDENTITY...
WELL LET'S JUST SAY, PEOPLE GET CLOSE TO ME... THEY TEND TO GET HURT.
Y'SEEM LIKE A NICE KID. BUT NICE AND TRUSTWORTHY AIN'T ALWAYS KIN. AND IN THIS LIFE, LETTIN' SOMEONE KNOW YOU, THE *REAL* YOU... THAT'S A GREAT RESPONSIBILITY.
I GET THAT--
SNAP
SOMEONE THERE?
HANDS WHERE I CAN SEE 'EM!
BRRBRRRBRB!

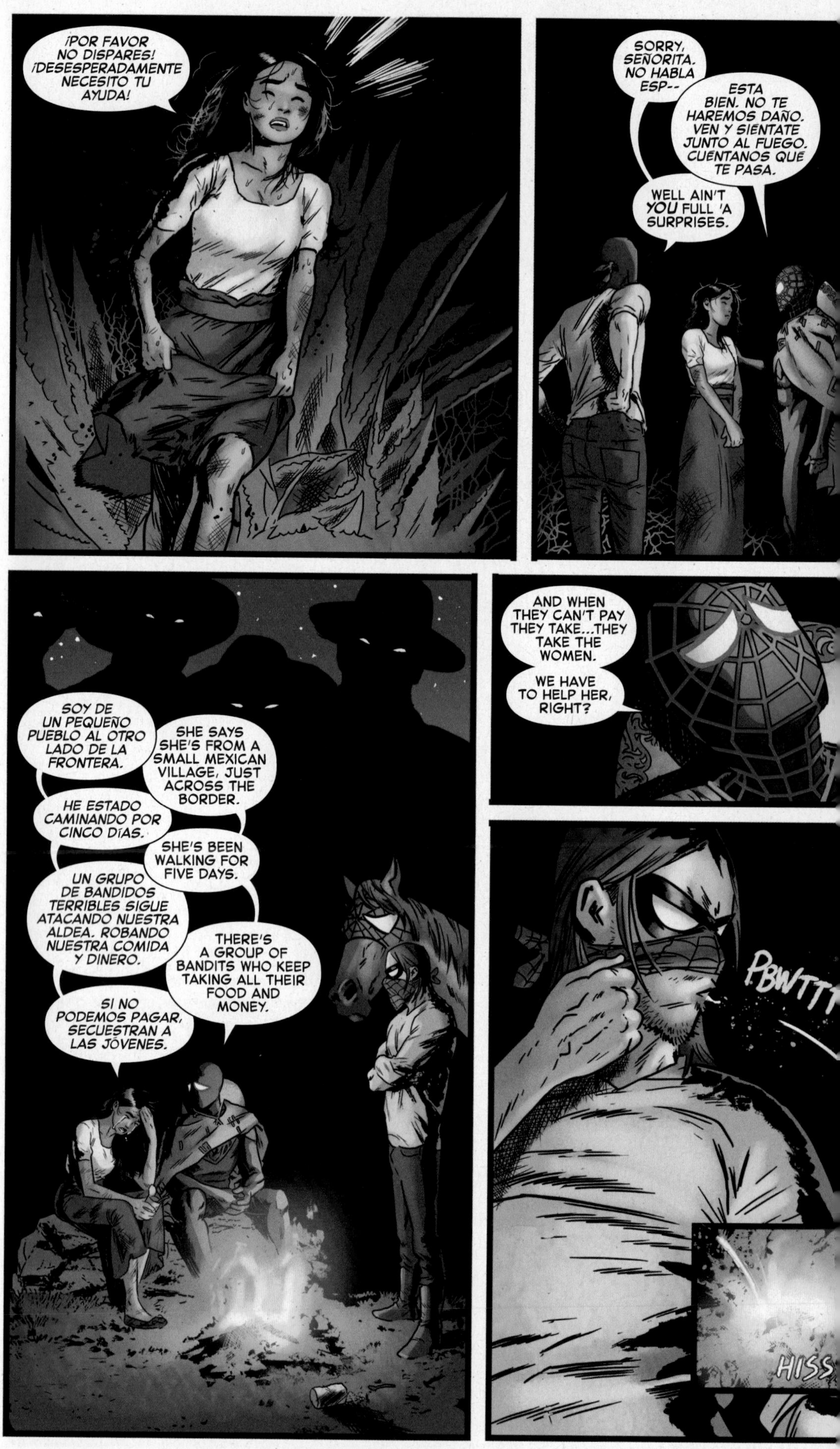
¡POR FAVOR NO DISPARES! ¡DESESPERADAMENTE NECESITO TU AYUDA!
SORRY, SEÑORITA. NO HABLA ESP--
ESTA BIEN. NO TE HAREMOS DAÑO. VEN Y SIENTATE JUNTO AL FUEGO. CUENTANOS QUÉ TE PASA.
WELL AIN'T *YOU* FULL 'A SURPRISES.
SOY DE UN PEQUEÑO PUEBLO AL OTRO LADO DE LA FRONTERA.
SHE SAYS SHE'S FROM A SMALL MEXICAN VILLAGE, JUST ACROSS THE BORDER.
HE ESTADO CAMINANDO POR CINCO DÍAS.
SHE'S BEEN WALKING FOR FIVE DAYS.
UN GRUPO DE BANDIDOS TERRIBLES SIGUE ATACANDO NUESTRA ALDEA. ROBANDO NUESTRA COMIDA Y DINERO.
THERE'S A GROUP OF BANDITS WHO KEEP TAKING ALL THEIR FOOD AND MONEY.
SI NO PODEMOS PAGAR, SECUESTRAN A LAS JÓVENES.
AND WHEN THEY CAN'T PAY THEY TAKE...THEY TAKE THE WOMEN.
WE HAVE TO HELP HER, RIGHT?
PBWTTT
HISS

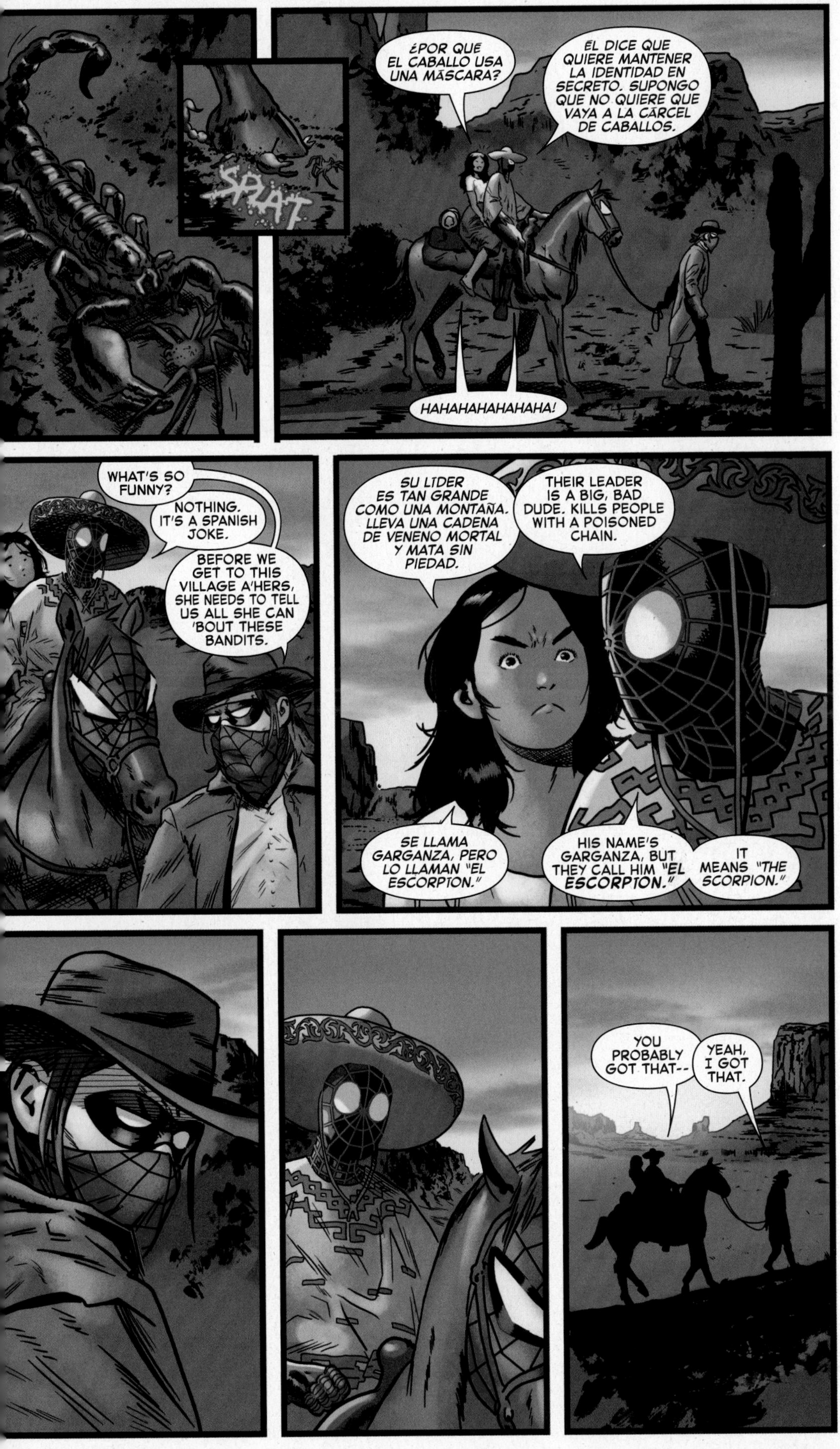
SPLAT
¿POR QUÉ EL CABALLO USA UNA MÁSCARA?
ÉL DICE QUE QUIERE MANTENER LA IDENTIDAD EN SECRETO. SUPONGO QUE NO QUIERE QUE VAYA A LA CÁRCEL DE CABALLOS.
HAHAHAHAHAHAHA!
WHAT'S SO FUNNY?
NOTHING. IT'S A SPANISH JOKE.
BEFORE WE GET TO THIS VILLAGE A'HERS, SHE NEEDS TO TELL US ALL SHE CAN 'BOUT THESE BANDITS.
SU LÍDER ES TAN GRANDE COMO UNA MONTAÑA. LLEVA UNA CADENA DE VENENO MORTAL Y MATA SIN PIEDAD.
THEIR LEADER IS A BIG, BAD DUDE. KILLS PEOPLE WITH A POISONED CHAIN.
SE LLAMA GARGANZA, PERO LO LLAMAN "EL ESCORPIÓN."
HIS NAME'S GARGANZA, BUT THEY CALL HIM "EL ESCORPIÓN."
IT MEANS "THE SCORPION."
YOU PROBABLY GOT THAT--
YEAH, I GOT THAT.

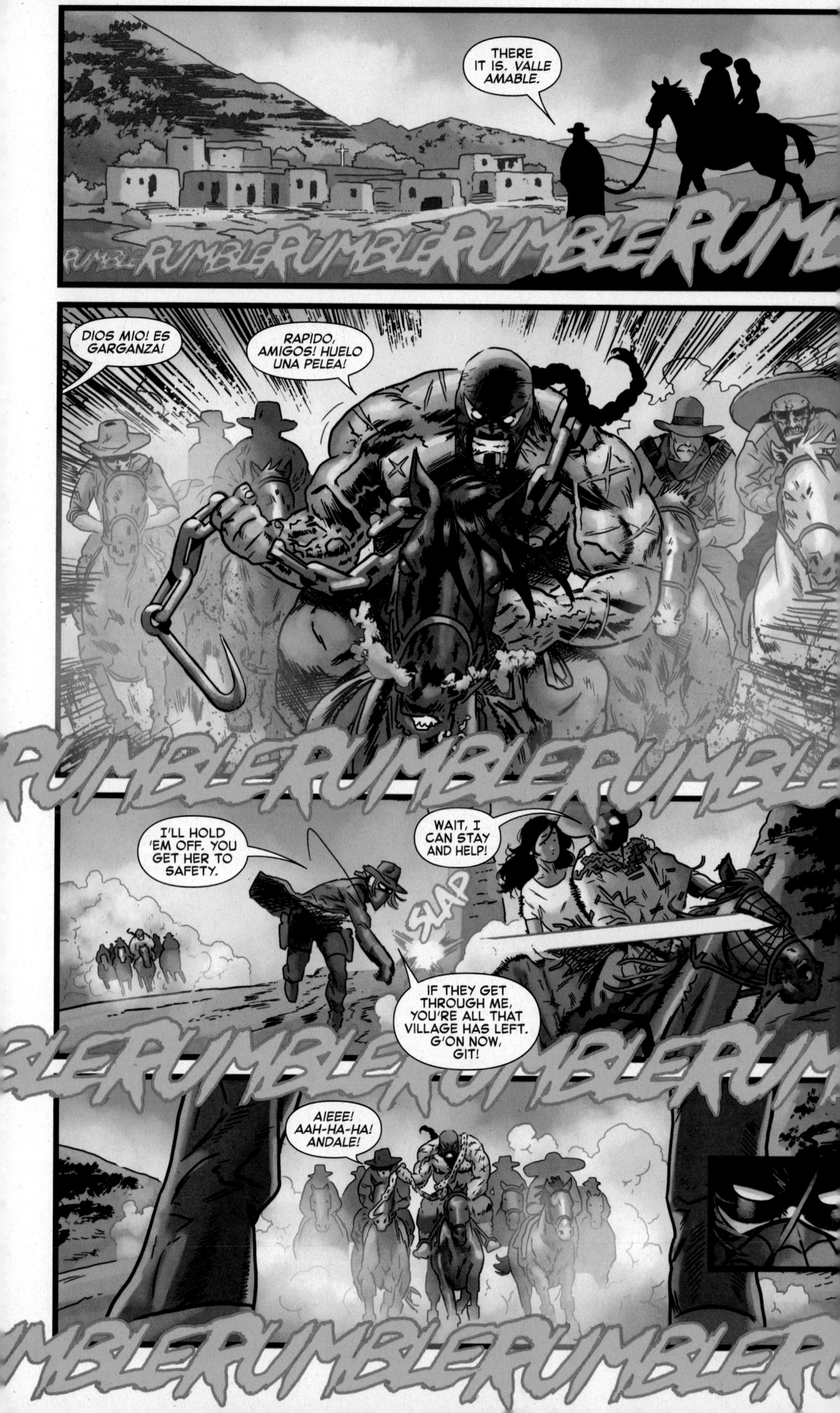
THERE IT IS. VALLE AMABLE.
RUMBLE RUMBLE RUMBLE RUMBLE
DIOS MIO! ES GARGANZA!
RAPIDO, AMIGOS! HUELO UNA PELEA!
RUMBLE RUMBLE RUMBLE
I'LL HOLD 'EM OFF. YOU GET HER TO SAFETY.
WAIT, I CAN STAY AND HELP!
SLAP
IF THEY GET THROUGH ME, YOU'RE ALL THAT VILLAGE HAS LEFT. G'ON NOW, GIT!
RUMBLE RUMBLE
AIEEE! AAH-HA-HA! ANDALE!
RUMBLE RUMBLE

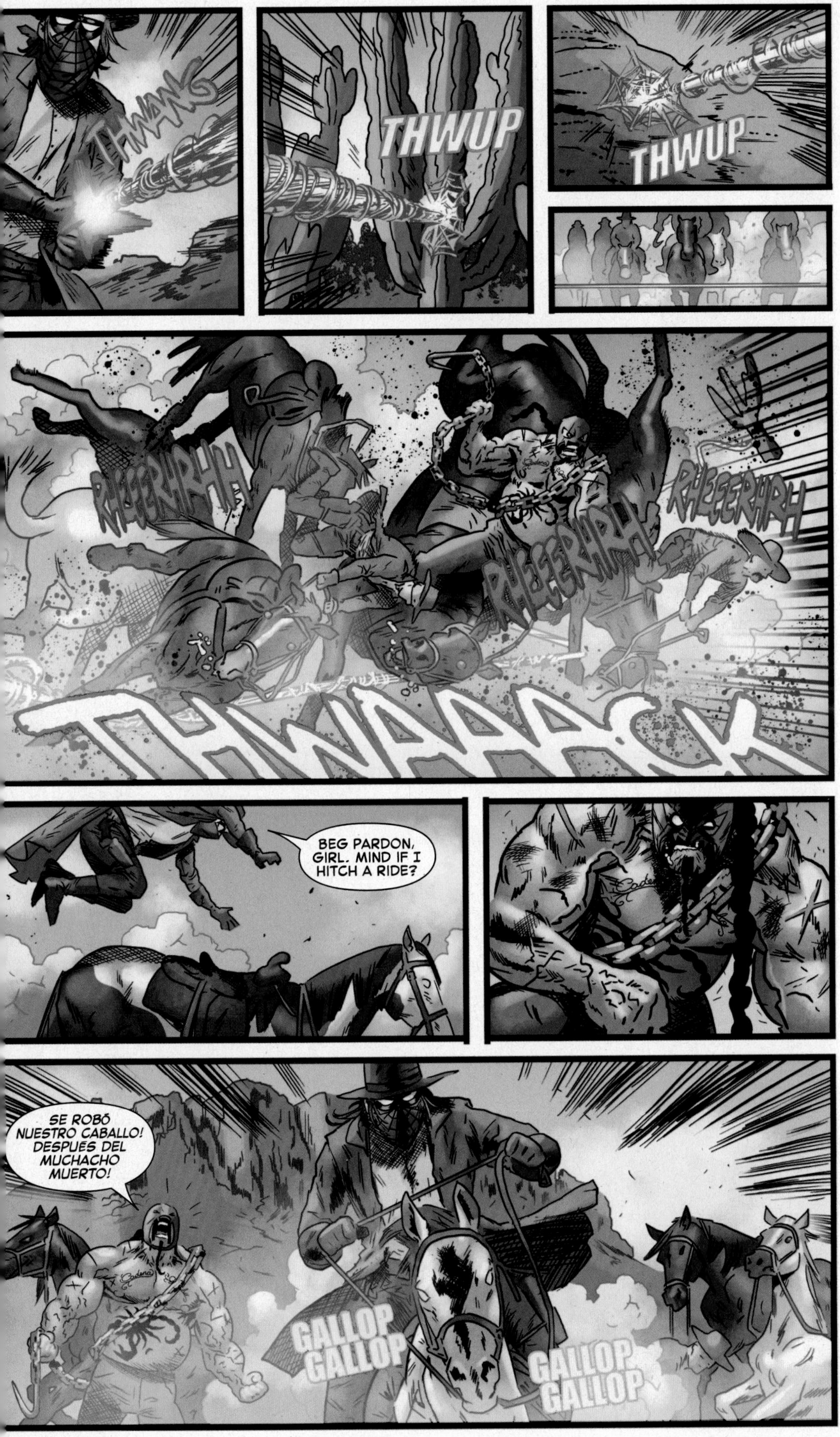
THWANG
THWUP
THWUP
RHEEERHRH
RHEEERHRH
RHEEERHRH
THWAACK
BEG PARDON, GIRL. MIND IF I HITCH A RIDE?
SE ROBÓ NUESTRO CABALLO! DESPUÉS DEL MUCHACHO MUERTO!
GALLOP GALLOP
GALLOP GALLOP

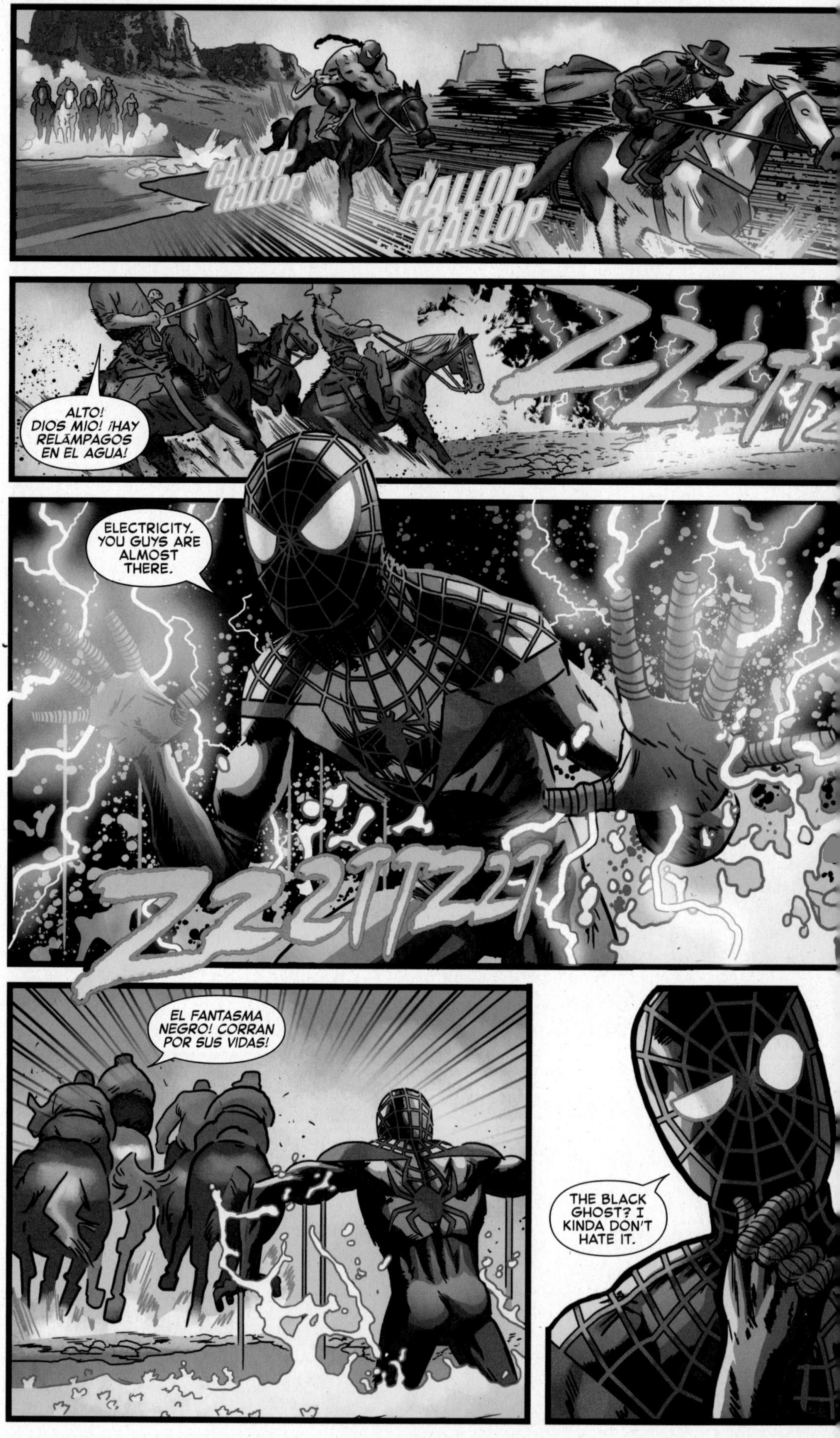
GALLOP GALLOP
GALLOP GALLOP
ALTO! DIOS MIO! ¡HAY RELÁMPAGOS EN EL AGUA!
ZZZITZ
ELECTRICITY. YOU GUYS ARE ALMOST THERE.
ZZZITZZT
EL FANTASMA NEGRO! CORRAN POR SUS VIDAS!
THE BLACK GHOST? I KINDA DON'T HATE IT.

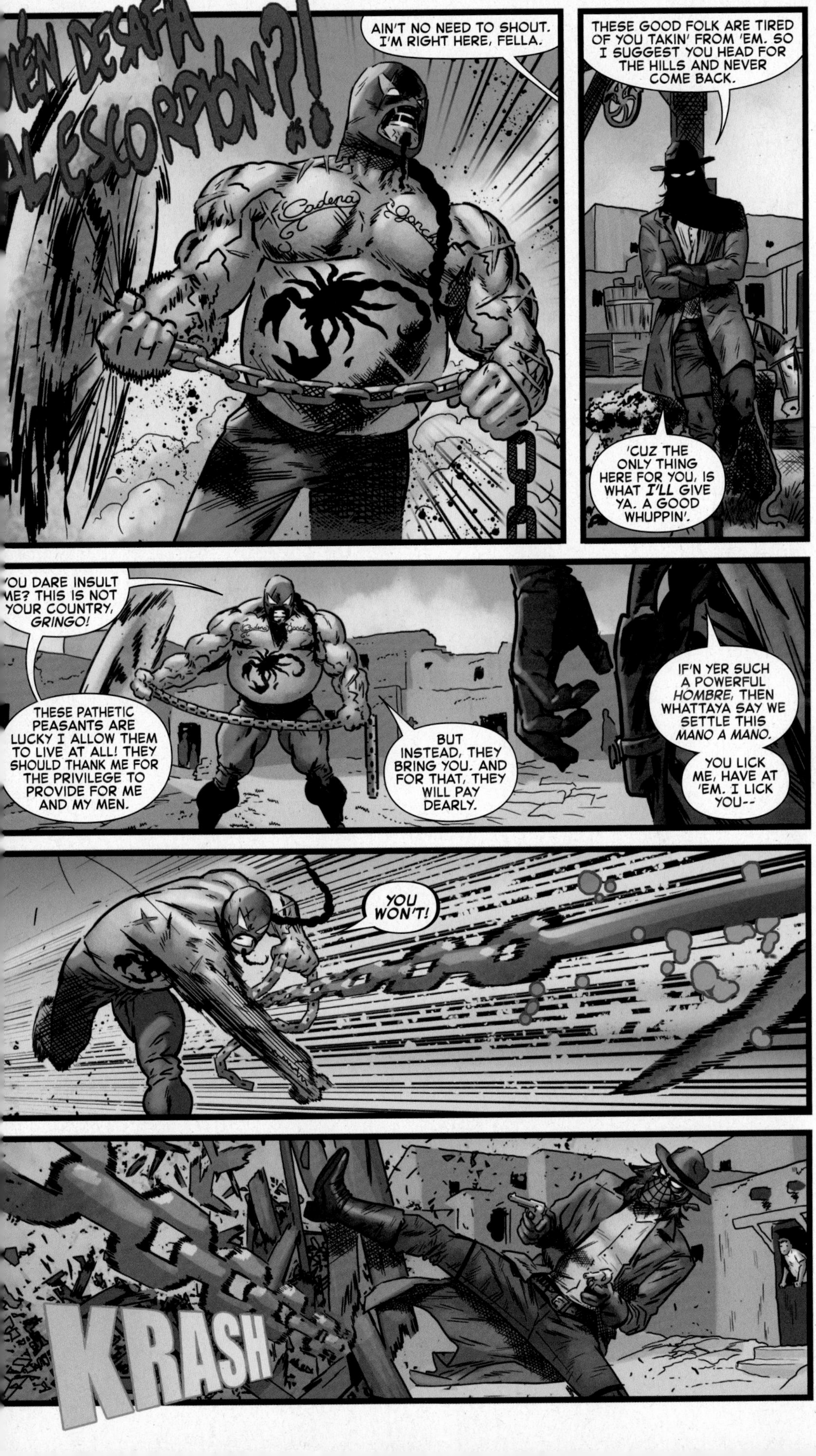

¿QUIÉN DESAFÍA AL ESCORPIÓN?!
AIN'T NO NEED TO SHOUT. I'M RIGHT HERE, FELLA.
THESE GOOD FOLK ARE TIRED OF YOU TAKIN' FROM 'EM. SO I SUGGEST YOU HEAD FOR THE HILLS AND NEVER COME BACK.
'CUZ THE ONLY THING HERE FOR YOU, IS WHAT *I'LL* GIVE YA. A GOOD WHUPPIN'.
YOU DARE INSULT ME? THIS IS NOT YOUR COUNTRY, *GRINGO!*
THESE PATHETIC PEASANTS ARE LUCKY I ALLOW THEM TO LIVE AT ALL! THEY SHOULD THANK ME FOR THE PRIVILEGE TO PROVIDE FOR ME AND MY MEN.
BUT INSTEAD, THEY BRING YOU. AND FOR THAT, THEY WILL PAY DEARLY.
IF'N YER SUCH A POWERFUL *HOMBRE,* THEN WHATTAYA SAY WE SETTLE THIS *MANO A MANO.*
YOU LICK ME, HAVE AT 'EM. I LICK YOU--
YOU WON'T!
KRASH

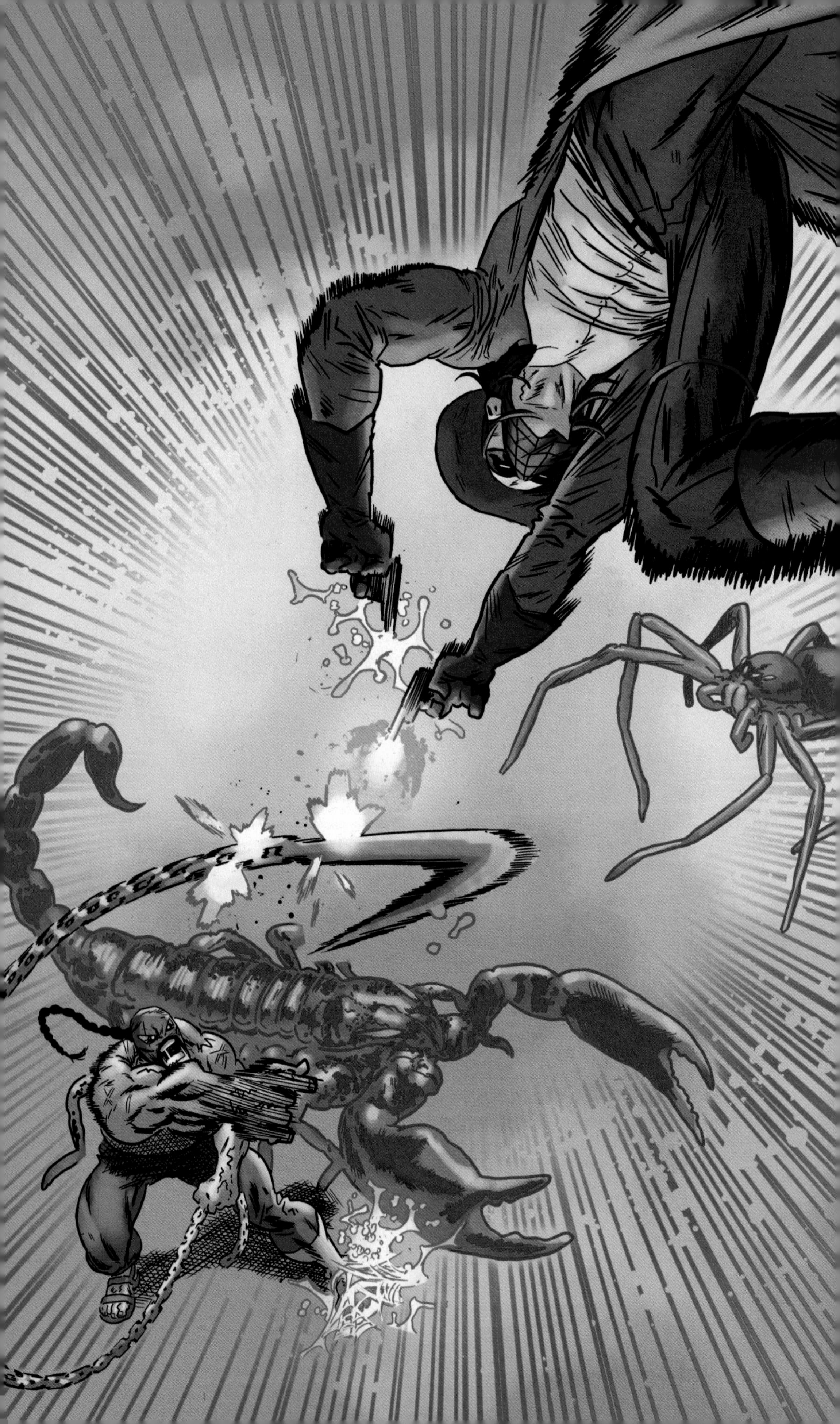

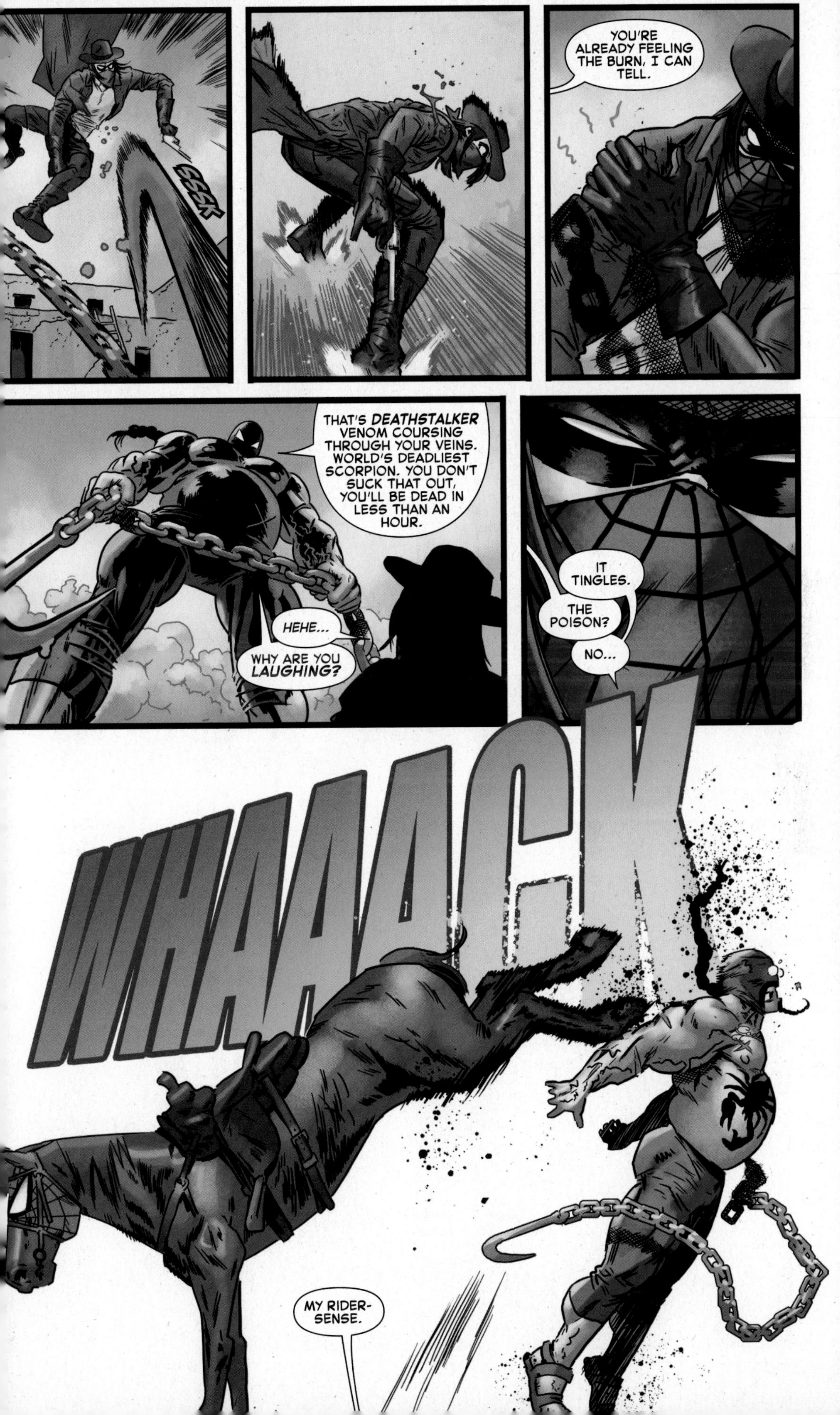
SSSK
YOU'RE ALREADY FEELING THE BURN, I CAN TELL.
THAT'S DEATHSTALKER VENOM COURSING THROUGH YOUR VEINS. WORLD'S DEADLIEST SCORPION. YOU DON'T SUCK THAT OUT, YOU'LL BE DEAD IN LESS THAN AN HOUR.
HEHE...
WHY ARE YOU LAUGHING?
IT TINGLES.
THE POISON?
NO...
WHAAACK
MY RIDER-SENSE.

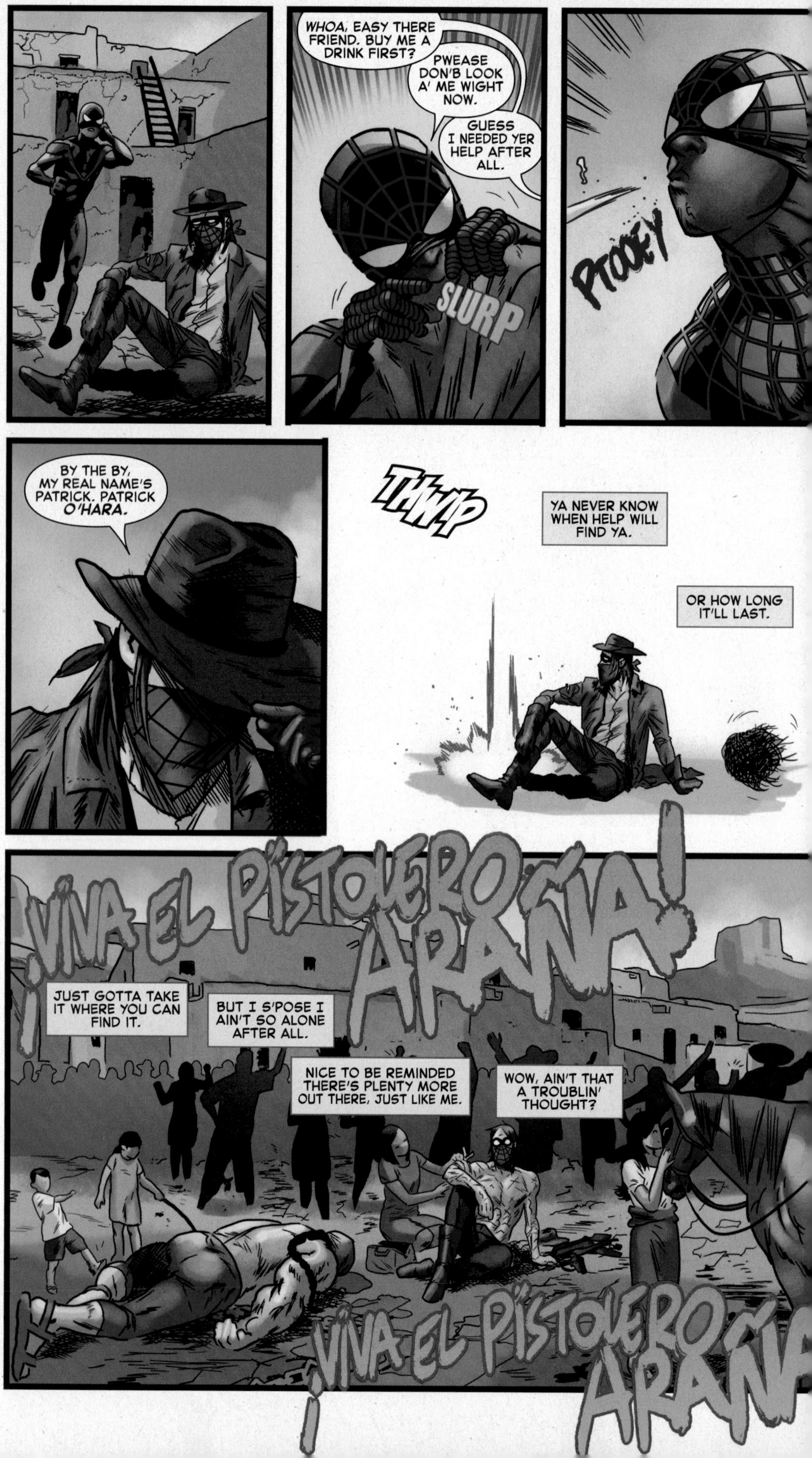
WHOA, EASY THERE FRIEND. BUY ME A DRINK FIRST?
PWEASE DON'B LOOK A' ME WIGHT NOW.
GUESS I NEEDED YER HELP AFTER ALL.
SLURP
PTOOEY
BY THE BY, MY REAL NAME'S PATRICK. PATRICK O'HARA.
THWIP
YA NEVER KNOW WHEN HELP WILL FIND YA.
OR HOW LONG IT'LL LAST.
¡VIVA EL PISTOLERO ARAÑA!
JUST GOTTA TAKE IT WHERE YOU CAN FIND IT.
BUT I S'POSE I AIN'T SO ALONE AFTER ALL.
NICE TO BE REMINDED THERE'S PLENTY MORE OUT THERE, JUST LIKE ME.
WOW, AIN'T THAT A TROUBLIN' THOUGHT?
¡VIVA EL PISTOLERO ARAÑA

SPIDERSONA:

REN

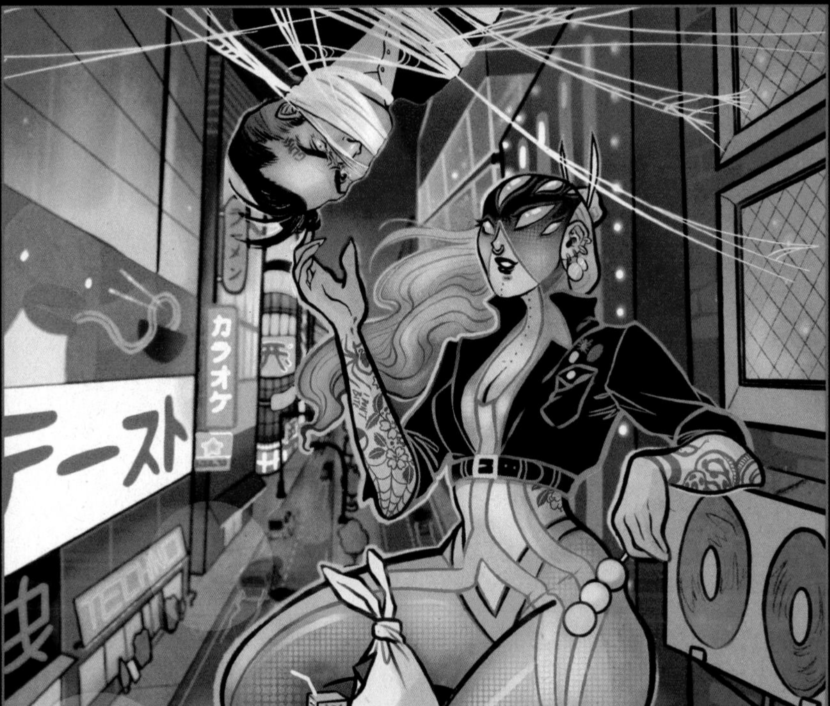

カラオケ
TECHNO

Art & Text by AUDRA AUCLAIR

Canada

A Canadian living in Japan, Ren has the special ability to manipulate emotions, born from a desire to control her own sadness. I wanted to create a character who could help those in emotionally difficult positions and also use emotions like sadness and anger to disrupt her enemies.

SPIDERSONA:
SPINNER

Art & Text by C.R. SCANNELL
United States

Cassandra Kelly was blessed with the powers of a spider by the goddess Athena, also giving her clairvoyance and the ability to weave light itself. This hasn't particularly helped pay the rent on her New York City apartment or get her career as an abstract textile artist off the ground, but her powers can come in handy when it comes to catching criminals.

SPIDERSONA:
HALLOW

Art & Text by ABRAHAM LOPEZ
United States

*My love of all things Halloween inspired the design of this wall-crawler!
Hallow lives in modern Boston, Massachusetts—close to Salem, of course.
In addition to the usual spider-powers, he has knowledge of the occult.*

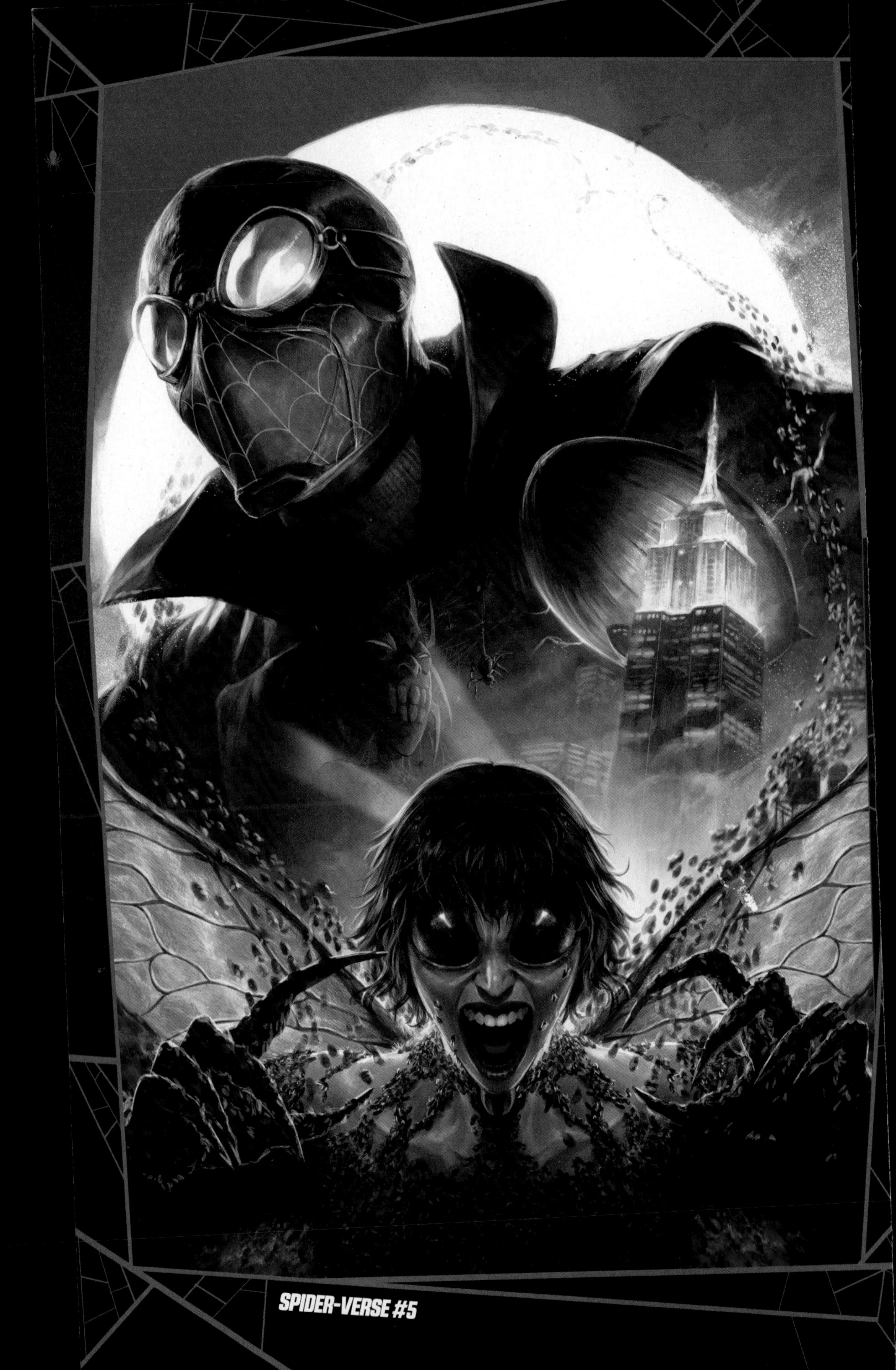

SPIDER-VERSE #5

NAME'S *PETER PARKER*. I'M A PRIVATE EYE.

[HA]VEN'T HAD THE [LICE]NSE LONG, BUT [I'V]E BEEN DOING [RE]LATED WORK [F]OR A WHILE.

"AND I'VE SEEN STUFF THAT'D MAKE VETERANS OF THE GREAT WAR LOSE THEIR BREAKFAST, LUNCH *AND* DINNER.

"MY LIFE GOT EVEN STRANGER WHEN I WAS BITTEN BY A MAGIC SPIDER THAT CAME OUT OF SOME ANCIENT IDOL.

"SURE, GIVE ME THAT LOOK, SEE IF I CARE. IT'S *TRUE.*

"I DUNNO IF THIS WAS REAL OR SOME KINDA FEVER DREAM, BUT I *SAW* THE SPIDER-GOD. IT PRETTY MUCH SAID I WORKED FOR IT NOW.

"WE BOTH HAD A THING FOR JUSTICE. SO I GOT IT THE ONLY WAY YOU CAN IN THIS TOWN...BY *CRACKING SKULLS.*

"THEN I MET OTHER SPIDER-FOLKS, ON OTHER WORLDS. AND ON ONE OF 'EM, I *DIED.*

"FIGURED THAT WAS IT. END OF THE LINE.

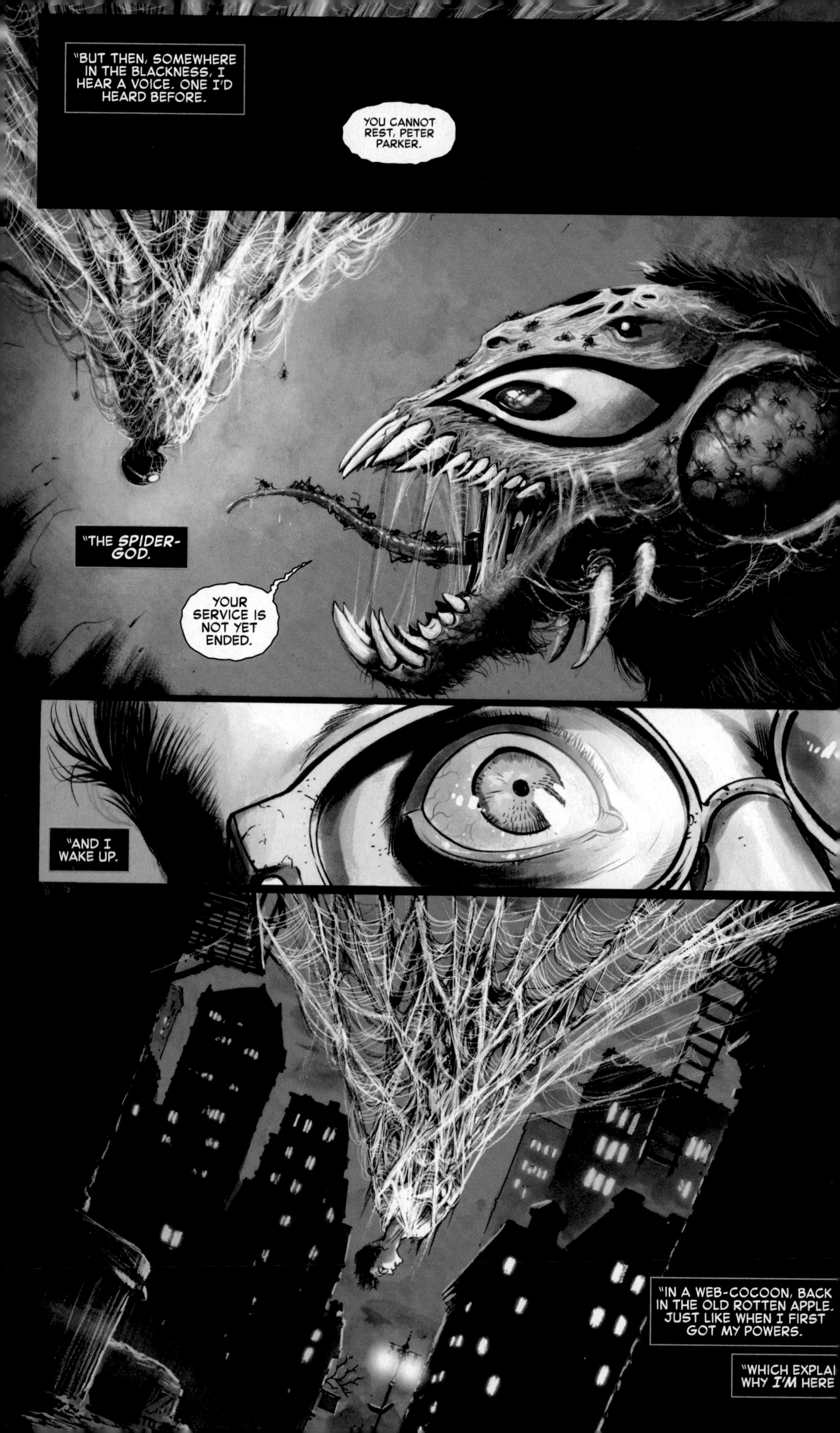
"BUT THEN, SOMEWHERE IN THE BLACKNESS, I HEAR A VOICE. ONE I'D HEARD BEFORE.
YOU CANNOT REST, PETER PARKER.
"THE SPIDER-GOD.
YOUR SERVICE IS NOT YET ENDED.
"AND I WAKE UP.
"IN A WEB-COCOON, BACK IN THE OLD ROTTEN APPLE. JUST LIKE WHEN I FIRST GOT MY POWERS.
"WHICH EXPLAI
WHY I'M HERE

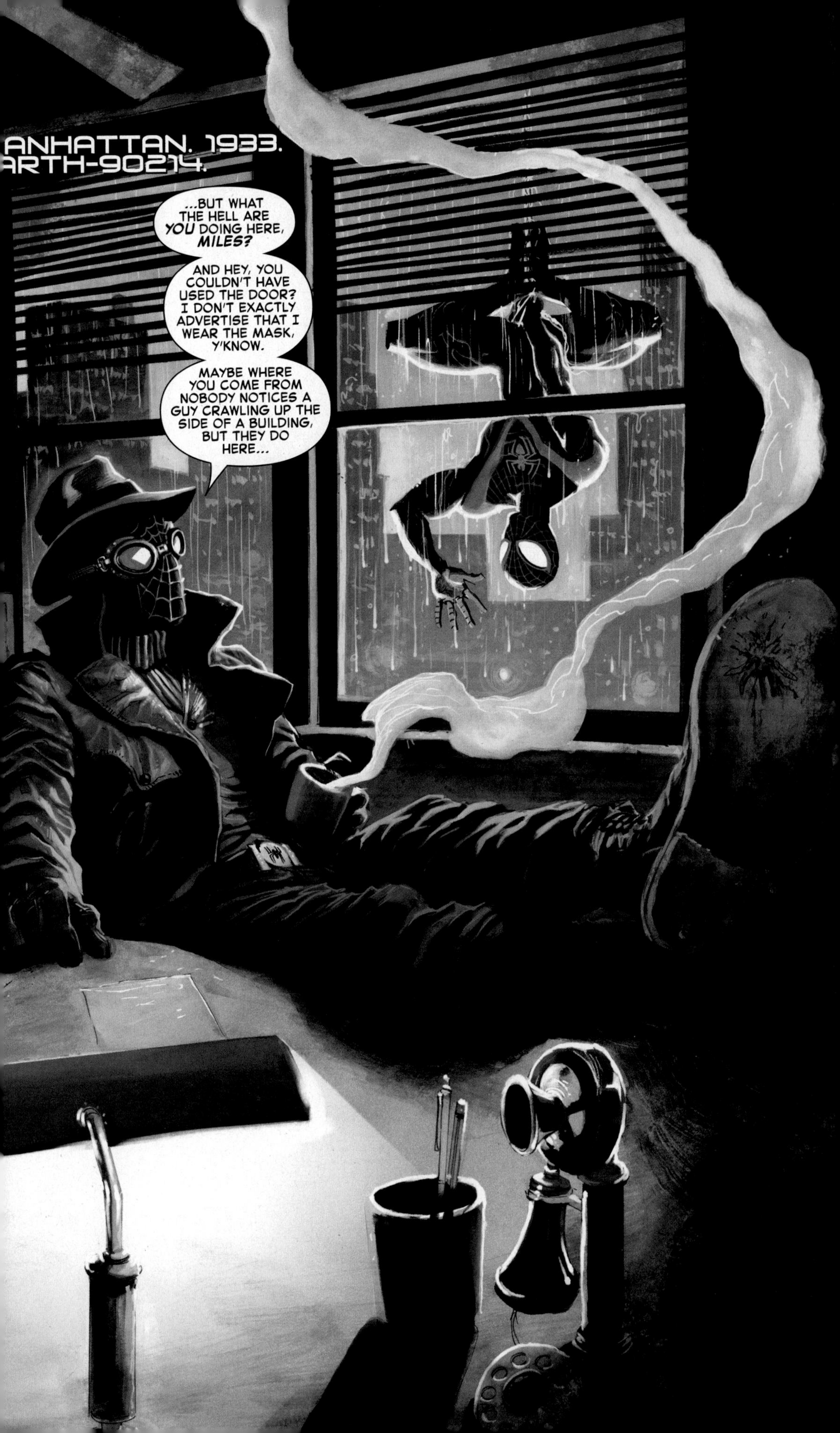

ANHATTAN. 1933.
ARTH-90214.
...BUT WHAT THE HELL ARE YOU DOING HERE, MILES?
AND HEY, YOU COULDN'T HAVE USED THE DOOR? I DON'T EXACTLY ADVERTISE THAT I WEAR THE MASK, Y'KNOW.
MAYBE WHERE YOU COME FROM NOBODY NOTICES A GUY CRAWLING UP THE SIDE OF A BUILDING, BUT THEY DO HERE...

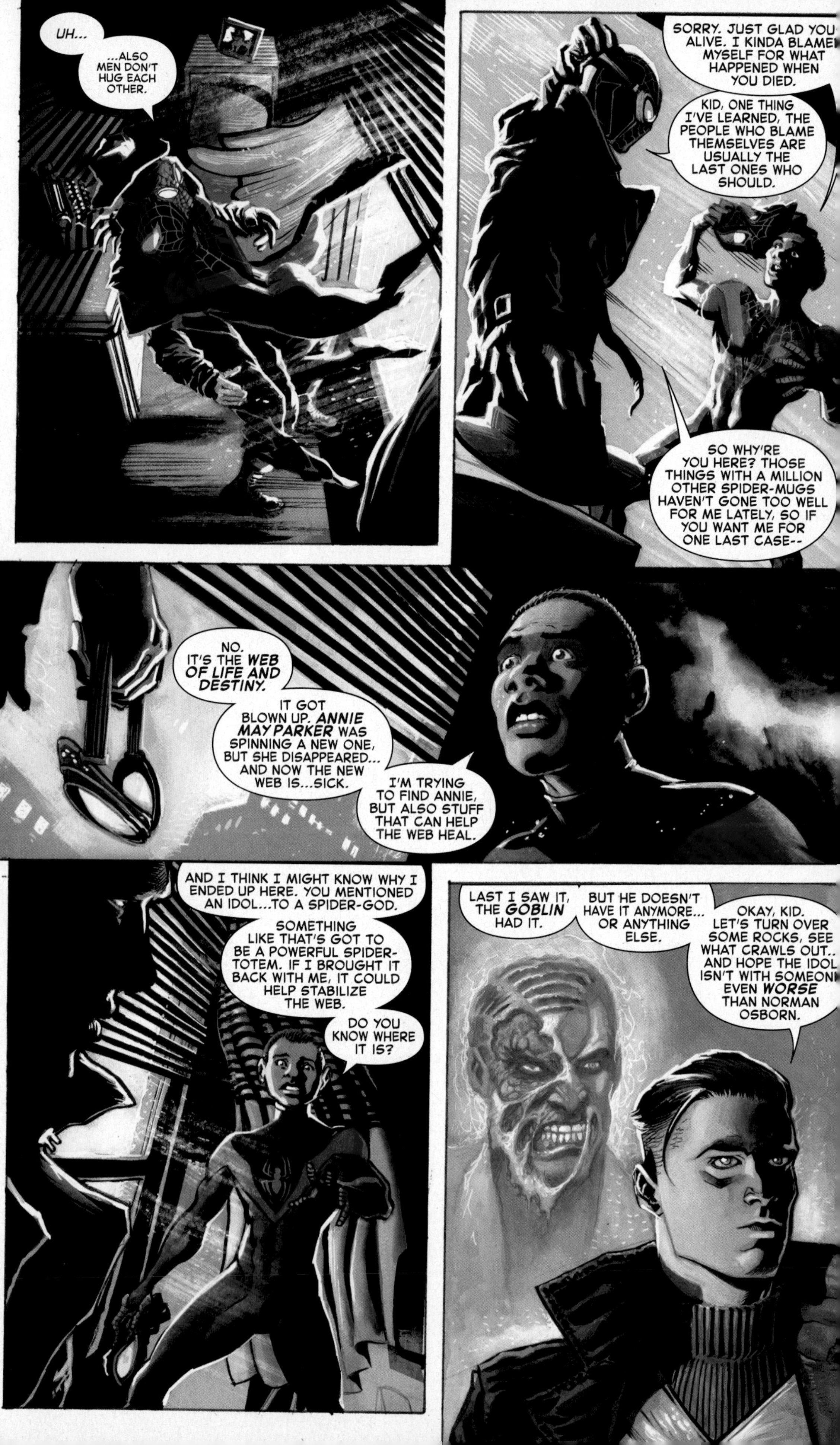

UH...
...ALSO MEN DON'T HUG EACH OTHER.
SORRY. JUST GLAD YOU ALIVE. I KINDA BLAME MYSELF FOR WHAT HAPPENED WHEN YOU DIED.
KID, ONE THING I'VE LEARNED, THE PEOPLE WHO BLAME THEMSELVES ARE USUALLY THE LAST ONES WHO SHOULD.
SO WHY'RE YOU HERE? THOSE THINGS WITH A MILLION OTHER SPIDER-MUGS HAVEN'T GONE TOO WELL FOR ME LATELY, SO IF YOU WANT ME FOR ONE LAST CASE--
NO. IT'S THE WEB OF LIFE AND DESTINY.
IT GOT BLOWN UP. ANNIE MAY PARKER WAS SPINNING A NEW ONE, BUT SHE DISAPPEARED... AND NOW THE NEW WEB IS...SICK.
I'M TRYING TO FIND ANNIE, BUT ALSO STUFF THAT CAN HELP THE WEB HEAL.
AND I THINK I MIGHT KNOW WHY I ENDED UP HERE. YOU MENTIONED AN IDOL...TO A SPIDER-GOD.
SOMETHING LIKE THAT'S GOT TO BE A POWERFUL SPIDER-TOTEM. IF I BROUGHT IT BACK WITH ME, IT COULD HELP STABILIZE THE WEB.
DO YOU KNOW WHERE IT IS?
LAST I SAW IT, THE GOBLIN HAD IT.
BUT HE DOESN'T HAVE IT ANYMORE... OR ANYTHING ELSE.
OKAY, KID. LET'S TURN OVER SOME ROCKS, SEE WHAT CRAWLS OUT.. AND HOPE THE IDOL ISN'T WITH SOMEONE EVEN WORSE THAN NORMAN OSBORN.

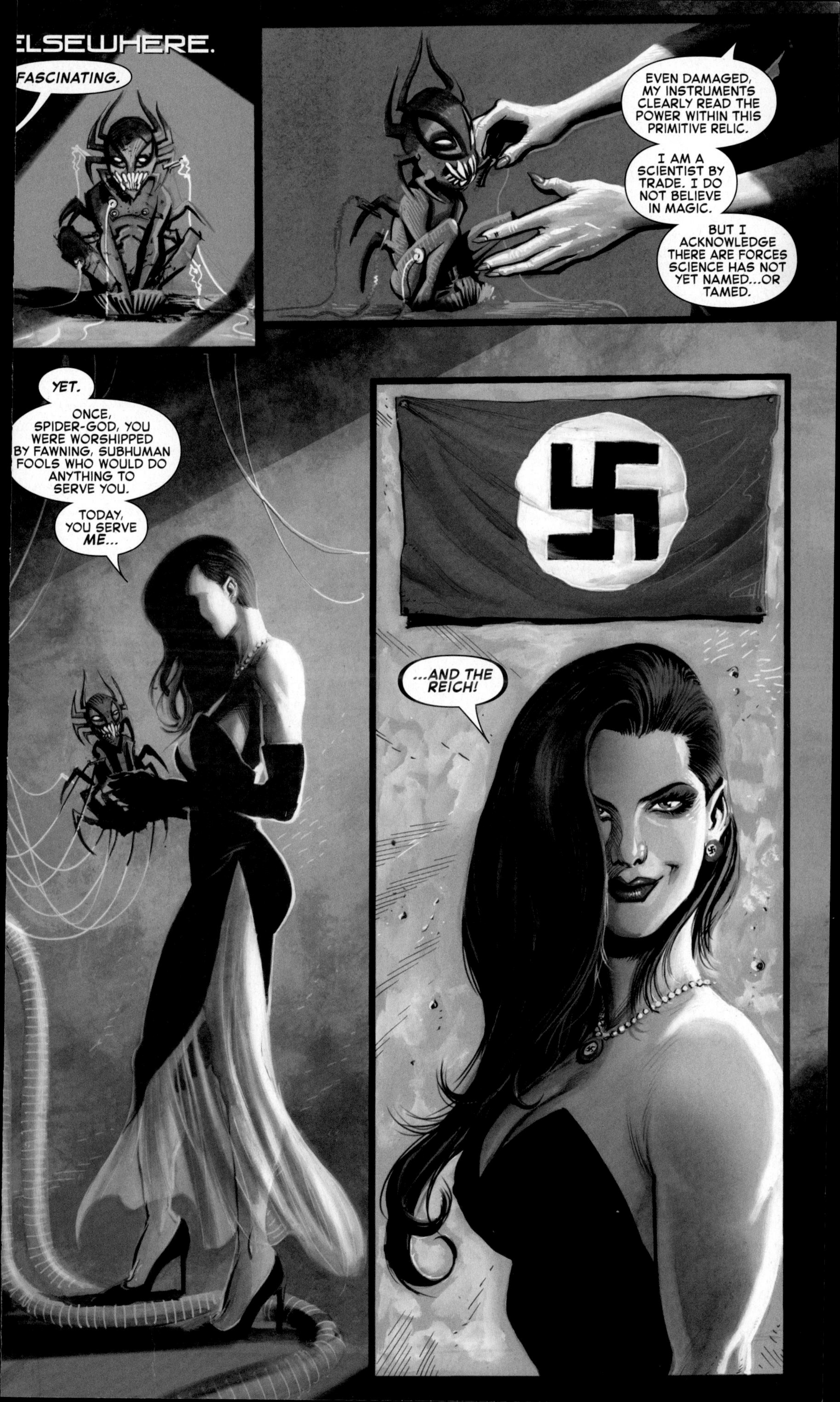
ELSEWHERE.
FASCINATING.
EVEN DAMAGED, MY INSTRUMENTS CLEARLY READ THE POWER WITHIN THIS PRIMITIVE RELIC.
I AM A SCIENTIST BY TRADE. I DO NOT BELIEVE IN MAGIC.
BUT I ACKNOWLEDGE THERE ARE FORCES SCIENCE HAS NOT YET NAMED...OR TAMED.
YET.
ONCE, SPIDER-GOD, YOU WERE WORSHIPPED BY FAWNING, SUBHUMAN FOOLS WHO WOULD DO ANYTHING TO SERVE YOU.
TODAY, YOU SERVE *ME*...
...AND THE REICH!

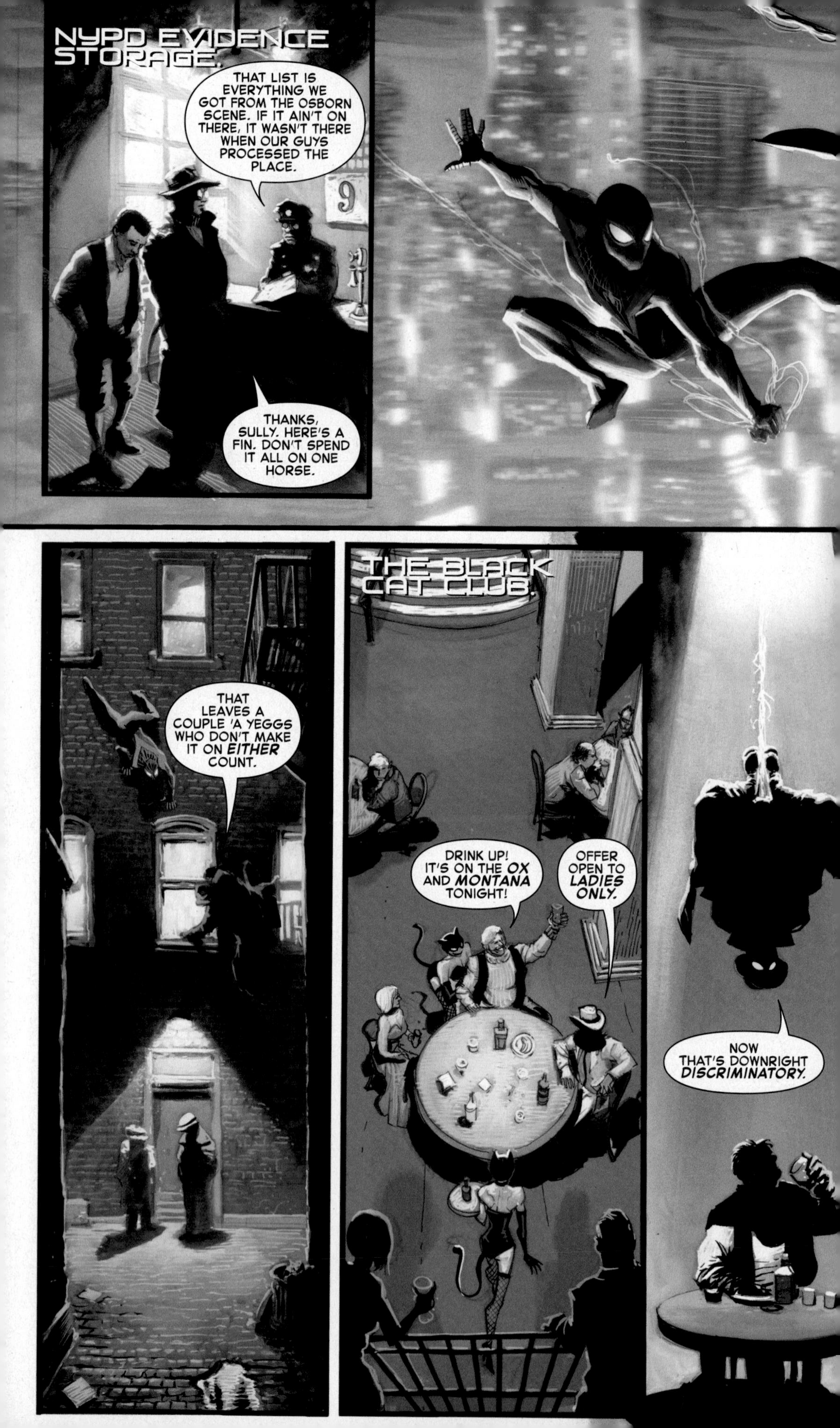
NYPD EVIDENCE STORAGE.
THAT LIST IS EVERYTHING WE GOT FROM THE OSBORN SCENE. IF IT AIN'T ON THERE, IT WASN'T THERE WHEN OUR GUYS PROCESSED THE PLACE.
9
THANKS, SULLY. HERE'S A FIN. DON'T SPEND IT ALL ON ONE HORSE.
THAT LEAVES A COUPLE 'A YEGGS WHO DON'T MAKE IT ON EITHER COUNT.
THE BLACK CAT CLUB.
DRINK UP! IT'S ON THE OX AND MONTANA TONIGHT!
OFFER OPEN TO LADIES ONLY.
NOW THAT'S DOWNRIGHT DISCRIMINATORY.

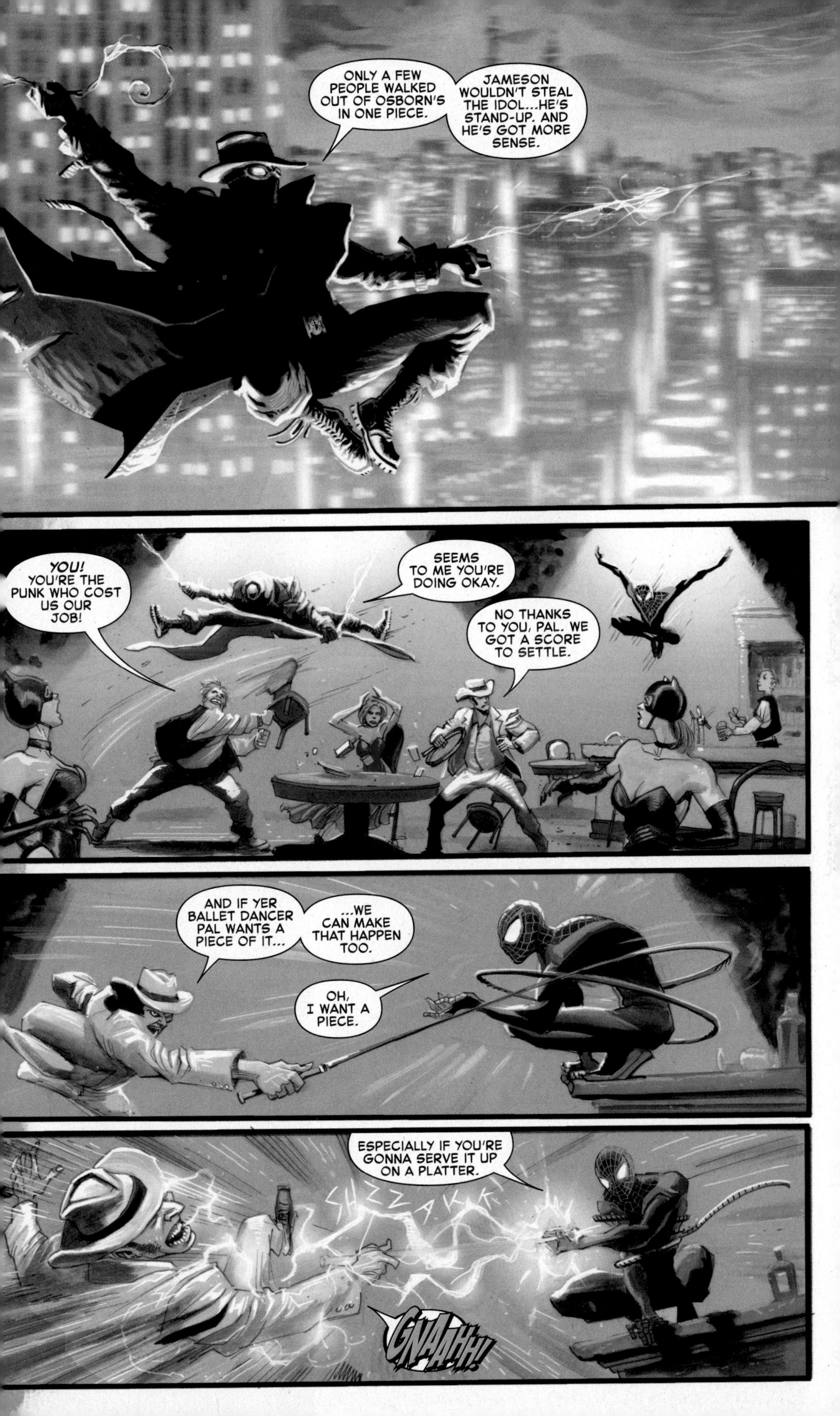

ONLY A FEW PEOPLE WALKED OUT OF OSBORN'S IN ONE PIECE.
JAMESON WOULDN'T STEAL THE IDOL...HE'S STAND-UP. AND HE'S GOT MORE SENSE.
YOU! YOU'RE THE PUNK WHO COST US OUR JOB!
SEEMS TO ME YOU'RE DOING OKAY.
NO THANKS TO YOU, PAL. WE GOT A SCORE TO SETTLE.
AND IF YER BALLET DANCER PAL WANTS A PIECE OF IT...
...WE CAN MAKE THAT HAPPEN TOO.
OH, I WANT A PIECE.
ESPECIALLY IF YOU'RE GONNA SERVE IT UP ON A PLATTER.
SHZZAKK
GNAAHH!

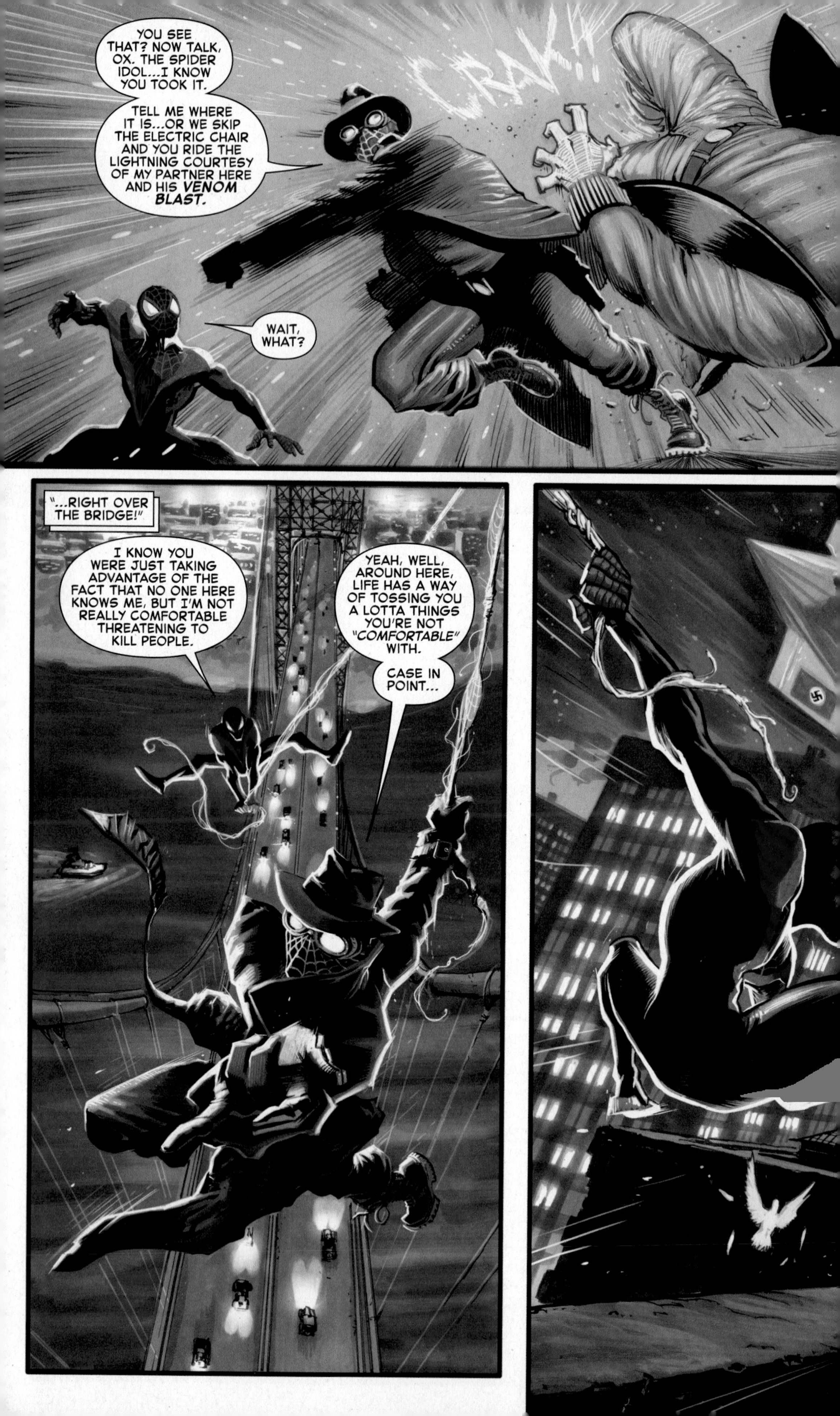
YOU SEE THAT? NOW TALK, OX. THE SPIDER IDOL...I KNOW YOU TOOK IT.
TELL ME WHERE IT IS...OR WE SKIP THE ELECTRIC CHAIR AND YOU RIDE THE LIGHTNING COURTESY OF MY PARTNER HERE AND HIS *VENOM BLAST.*
CRAK!!
WAIT, WHAT?
"...RIGHT OVER THE BRIDGE!"
I KNOW YOU WERE JUST TAKING ADVANTAGE OF THE FACT THAT NO ONE HERE KNOWS ME, BUT I'M NOT REALLY COMFORTABLE THREATENING TO KILL PEOPLE.
YEAH, WELL, AROUND HERE, LIFE HAS A WAY OF TOSSING YOU A LOTTA THINGS YOU'RE NOT *"COMFORTABLE"* WITH.
CASE IN POINT...

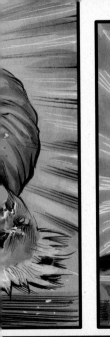

N-NO...I'LL TELL YA! THAT DAMN THING WAS NO PICNIC TA SELL...

...UNTIL WE MET A KRAUT NAMED *STURM.* WHAT I HEAR, IT'S FOR ADOLF HIMSELF.

IF YOU'RE TELLING ME IT'S IN GERMANY, THIS ISN'T GONNA END POLITELY.

NO! SHE HADDA WAIT 'TIL THE NEXT CARGO SHIP. YOU GOT TIME! SHE HAS A PLACE IN TOWN...

...I'M NOT PARTIAL TO *NAZI BLIMPS* FLYING OVER MANHATTAN, BUT HERE WE ARE.

DAMN. WHEN OX SAID *"CARGO SHIP"* I THOUGHT...NOT THAT.

THEY'RE GONNA GET THERE BEFORE US...

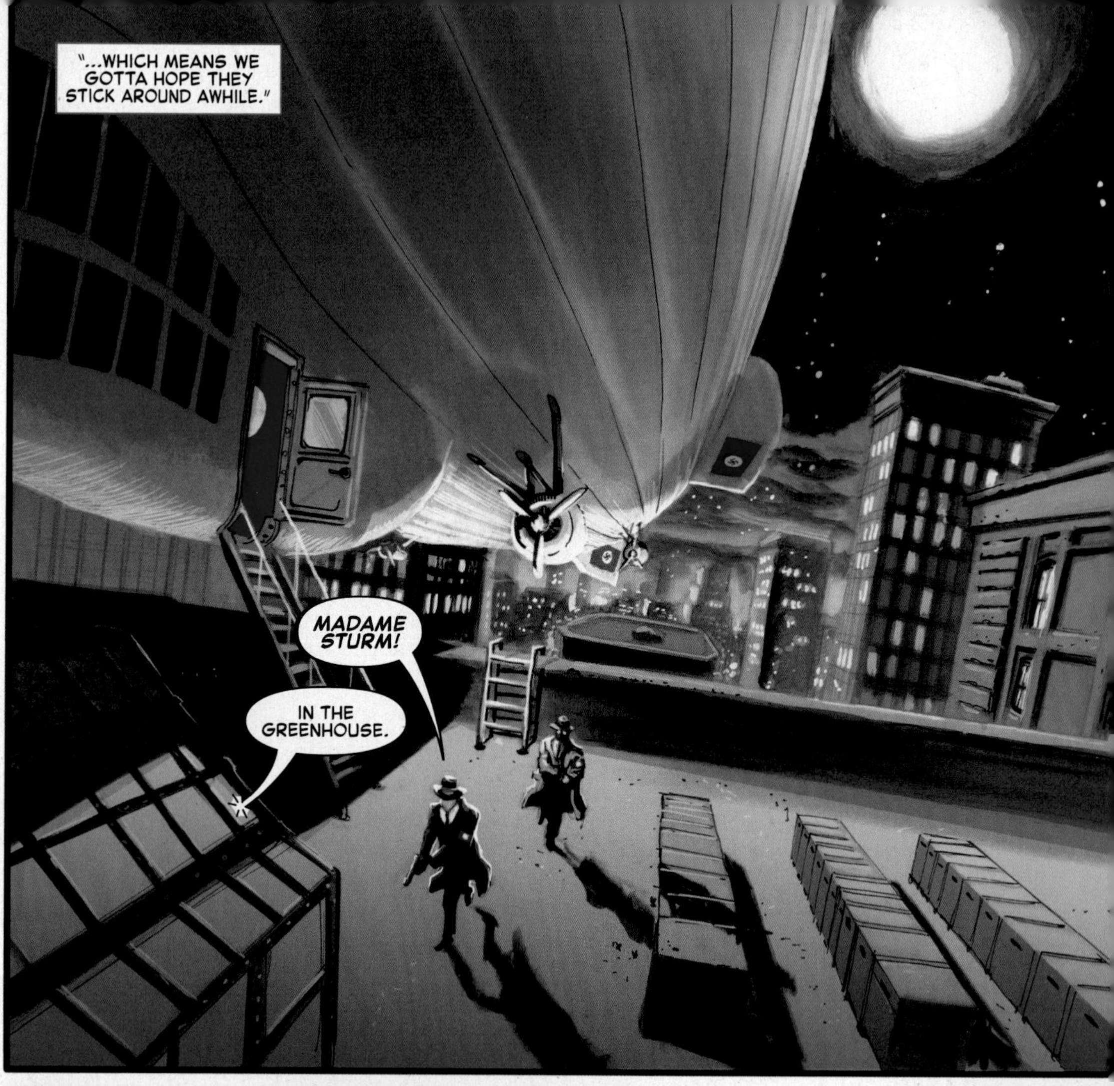
"...WHICH MEANS WE GOTTA HOPE THEY STICK AROUND AWHILE."
MADAME STURM!
IN THE GREENHOUSE.

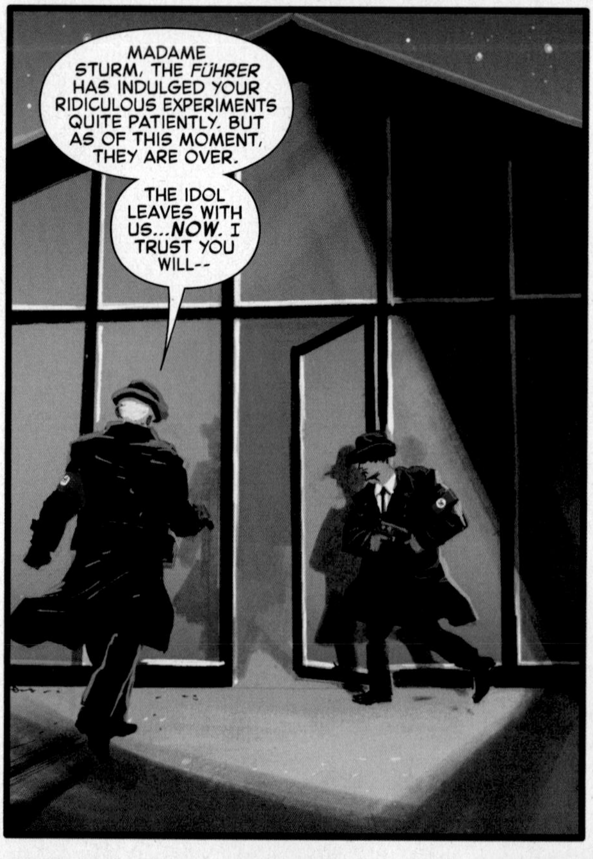
MADAME STURM, THE FÜHRER HAS INDULGED YOUR RIDICULOUS EXPERIMENTS QUITE PATIENTLY. BUT AS OF THIS MOMENT, THEY ARE OVER.
THE IDOL LEAVES WITH US...NOW. I TRUST YOU WILL--

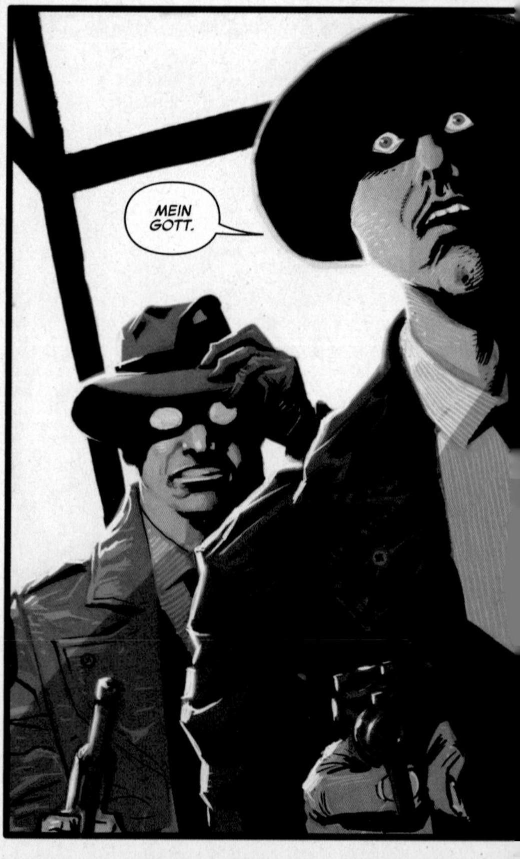
MEIN GOTT.

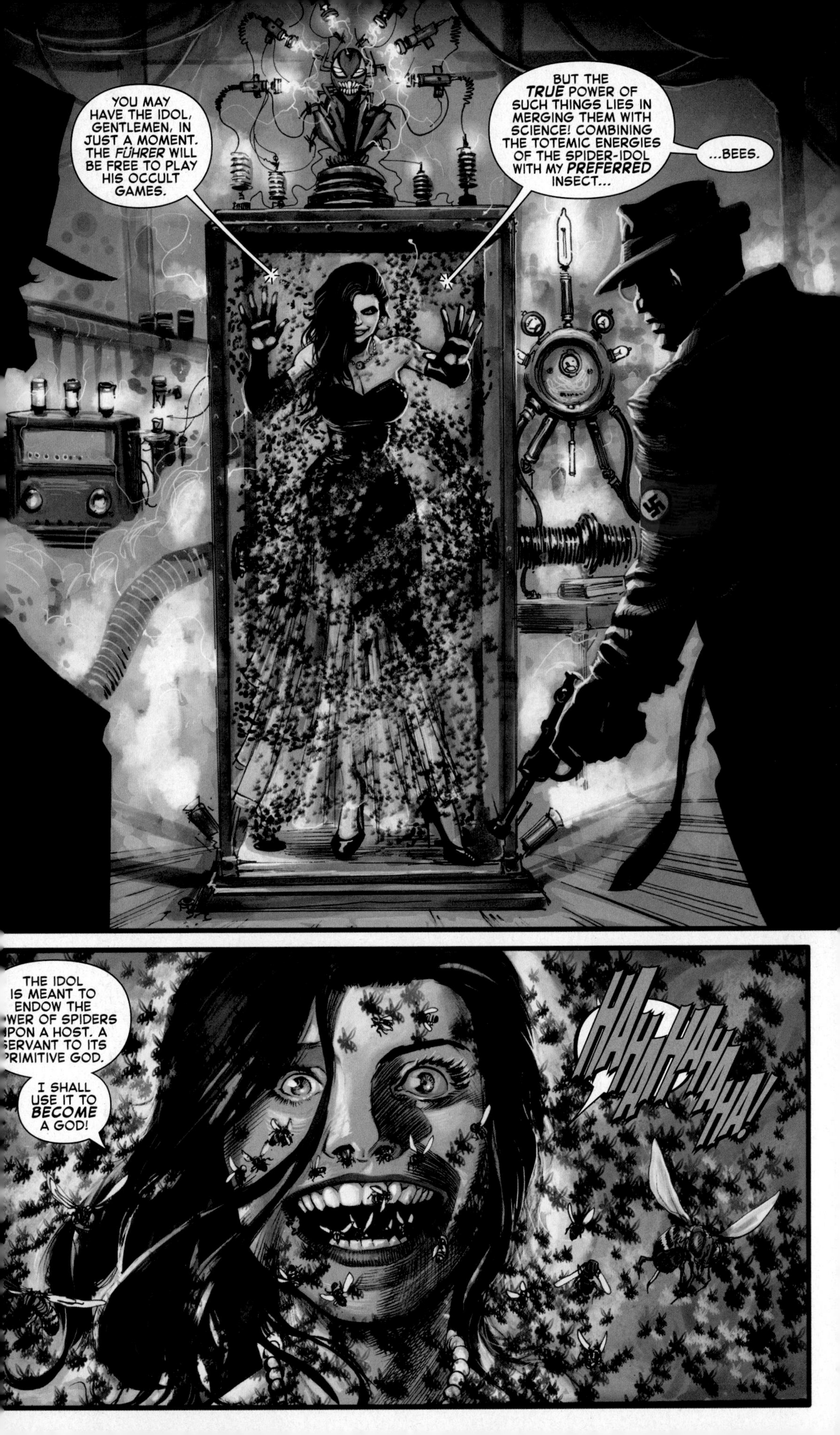
YOU MAY HAVE THE IDOL, GENTLEMEN, IN JUST A MOMENT. THE FÜHRER WILL BE FREE TO PLAY HIS OCCULT GAMES.
BUT THE TRUE POWER OF SUCH THINGS LIES IN MERGING THEM WITH SCIENCE! COMBINING THE TOTEMIC ENERGIES OF THE SPIDER-IDOL WITH MY PREFERRED INSECT...
...BEES.
THE IDOL IS MEANT TO ENDOW THE WER OF SPIDERS PON A HOST. A ERVANT TO ITS RIMITIVE GOD.
I SHALL USE IT TO BECOME A GOD!
HAHAHAHAHA!

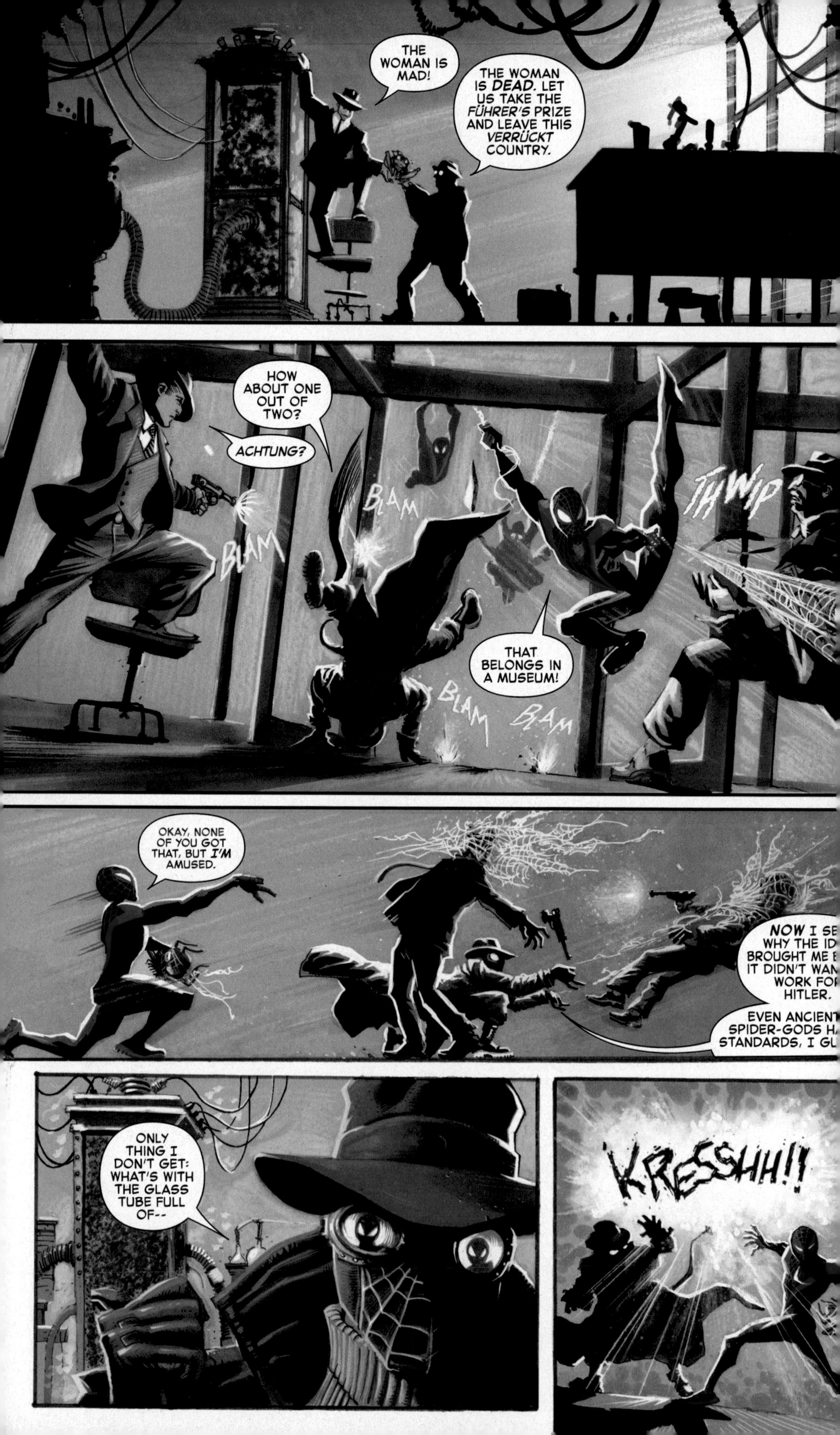
THE WOMAN IS MAD!
THE WOMAN IS DEAD. LET US TAKE THE FÜHRER'S PRIZE AND LEAVE THIS VERRÜCKT COUNTRY.
HOW ABOUT ONE OUT OF TWO?
ACHTUNG?
BLAM
BLAM
THWIP
THAT BELONGS IN A MUSEUM!
BLAM
BLAM
OKAY, NONE OF YOU GOT THAT, BUT I'M AMUSED.
NOW I SE WHY THE ID BROUGHT ME I IT DIDN'T WAN WORK FOI HITLER.
EVEN ANCIENT SPIDER-GODS HA STANDARDS, I GU
ONLY THING I DON'T GET: WHAT'S WITH THE GLASS TUBE FULL OF--
KRESSHH!!

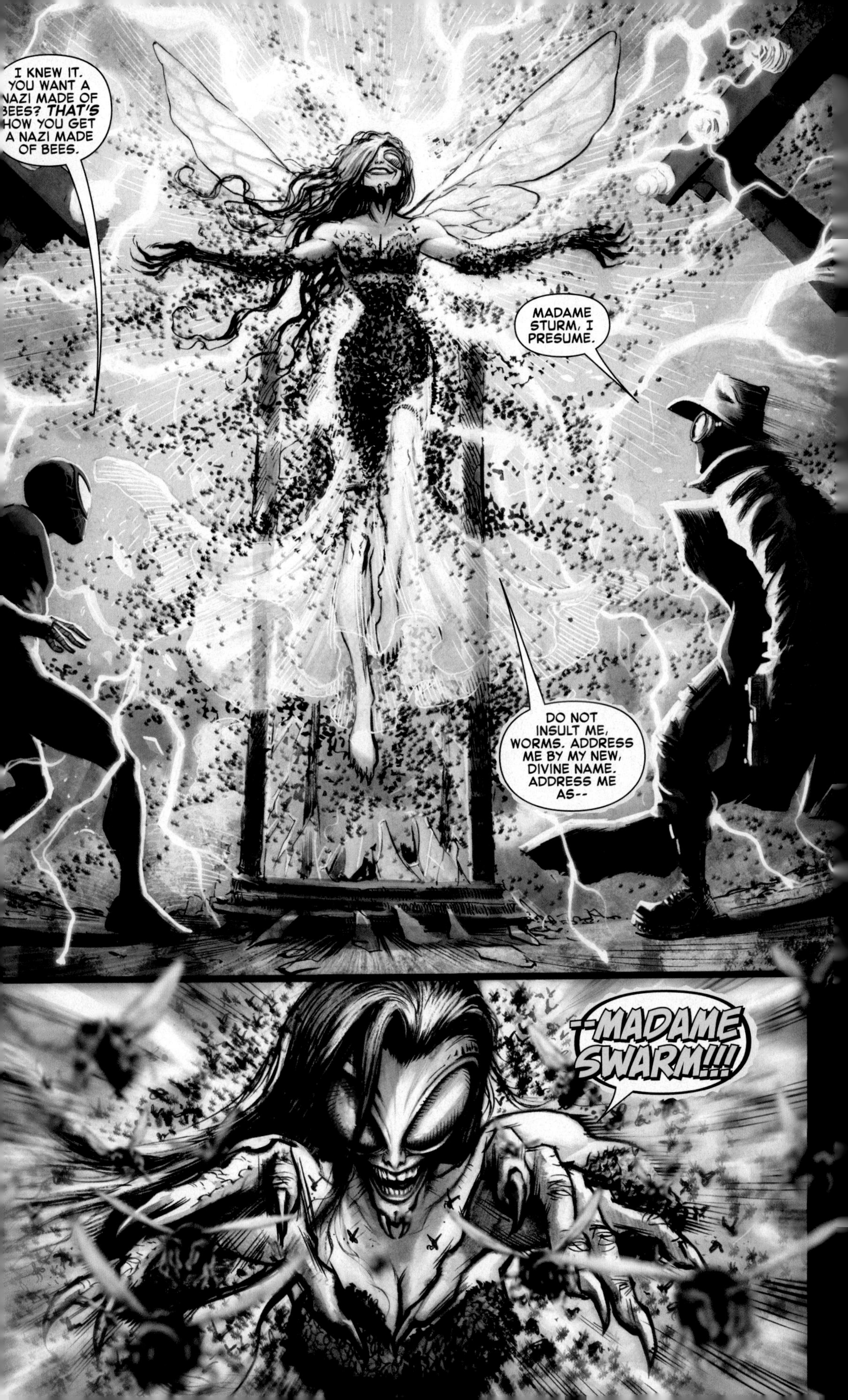
I KNEW IT. YOU WANT A NAZI MADE OF BEES? THAT'S HOW YOU GET A NAZI MADE OF BEES.
MADAME STURM, I PRESUME.
DO NOT INSULT ME, WORMS. ADDRESS ME BY MY NEW, DIVINE NAME. ADDRESS ME AS--
--MADAME SWARM!!!

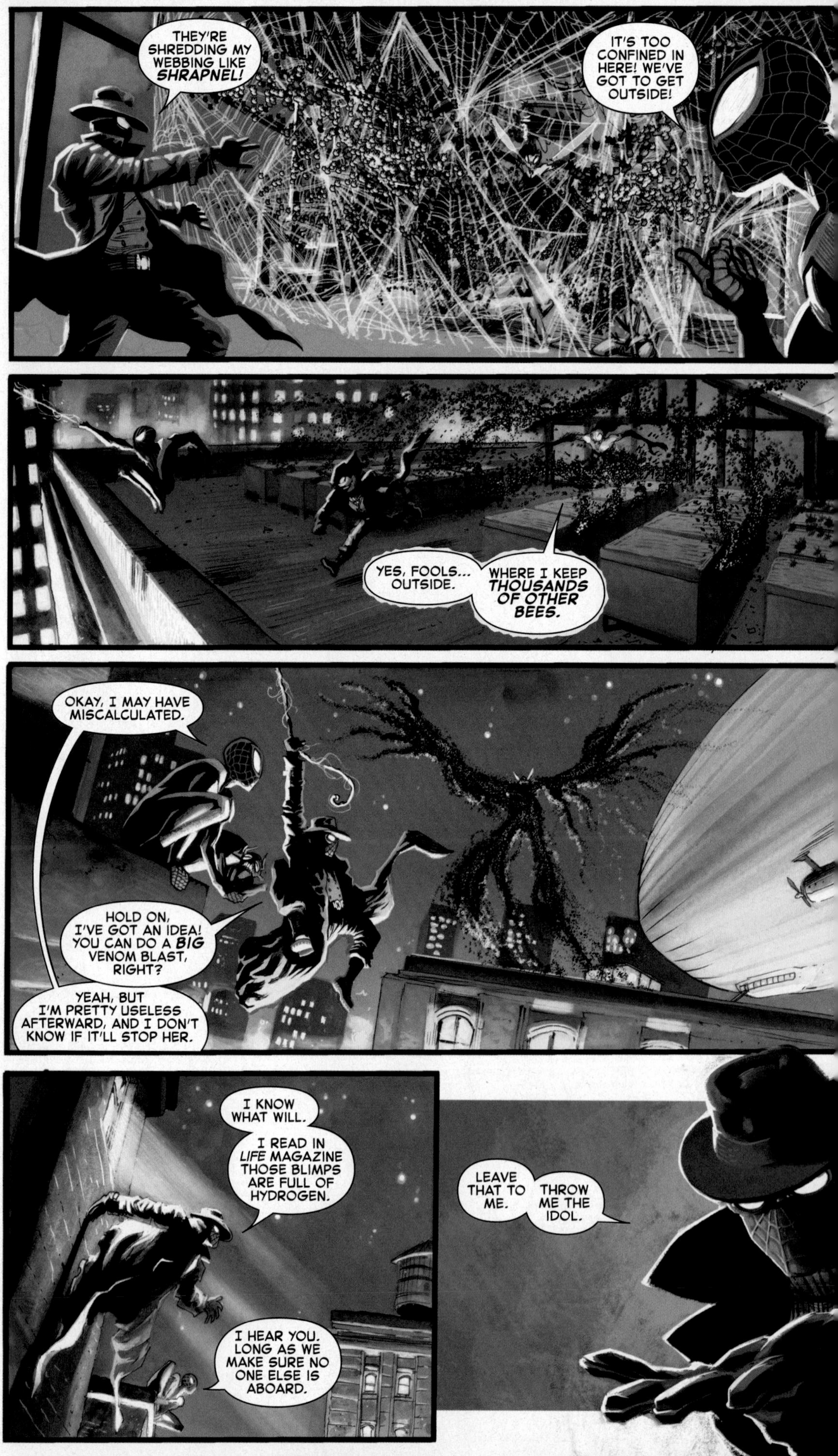
THEY'RE SHREDDING MY WEBBING LIKE SHRAPNEL!
IT'S TOO CONFINED IN HERE! WE'VE GOT TO GET OUTSIDE!
YES, FOOLS... OUTSIDE.
WHERE I KEEP THOUSANDS OF OTHER BEES.
OKAY, I MAY HAVE MISCALCULATED.
HOLD ON, I'VE GOT AN IDEA! YOU CAN DO A BIG VENOM BLAST, RIGHT?
YEAH, BUT I'M PRETTY USELESS AFTERWARD, AND I DON'T KNOW IF IT'LL STOP HER.
I KNOW WHAT WILL.
I READ IN LIFE MAGAZINE THOSE BLIMPS ARE FULL OF HYDROGEN.
I HEAR YOU. LONG AS WE MAKE SURE NO ONE ELSE IS ABOARD.
LEAVE THAT TO ME.
THROW ME THE IDOL.

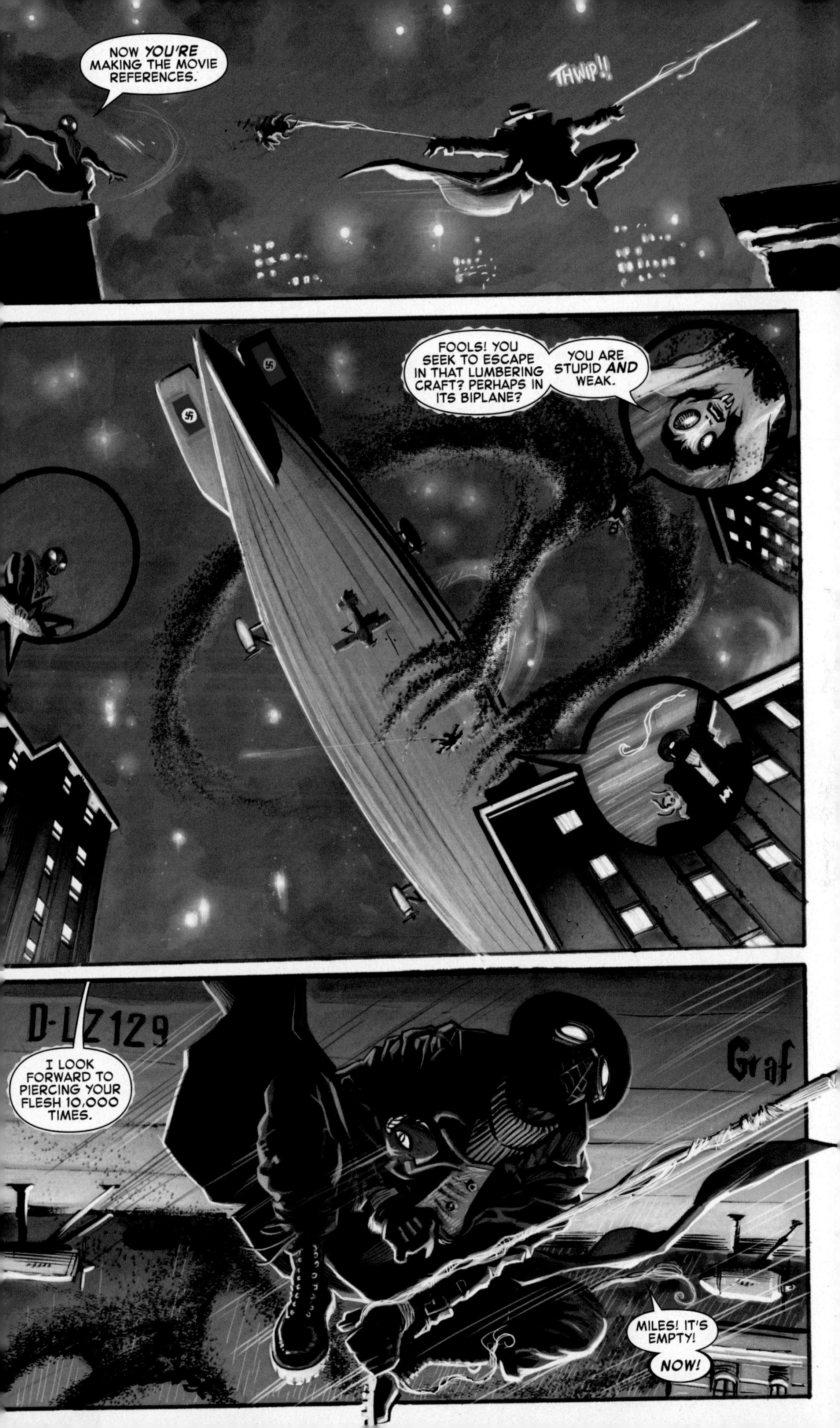
NOW YOU'RE MAKING THE MOVIE REFERENCES.
THWIP!!
FOOLS! YOU SEEK TO ESCAPE IN THAT LUMBERING CRAFT? PERHAPS IN ITS BIPLANE?
YOU ARE STUPID AND WEAK.
D-LZ129
Graf
I LOOK FORWARD TO PIERCING YOUR FLESH 10,000 TIMES.
MILES! IT'S EMPTY!
NOW!

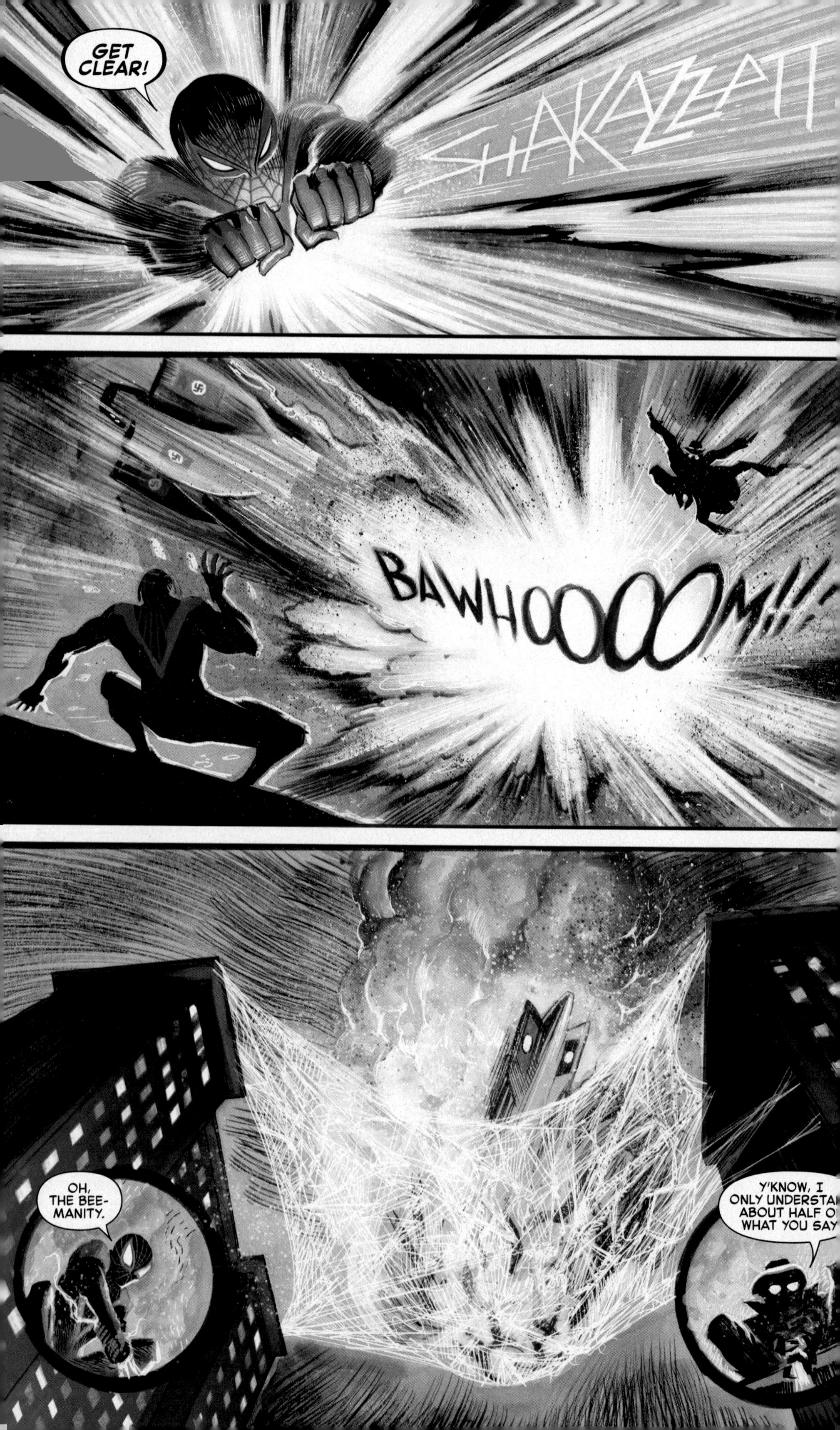
GET CLEAR!
SHAKAZZATT
BAWHOOOOOM!!!
OH, THE BEE-MANITY.
Y'KNOW, I ONLY UNDERSTA ABOUT HALF O WHAT YOU SAY

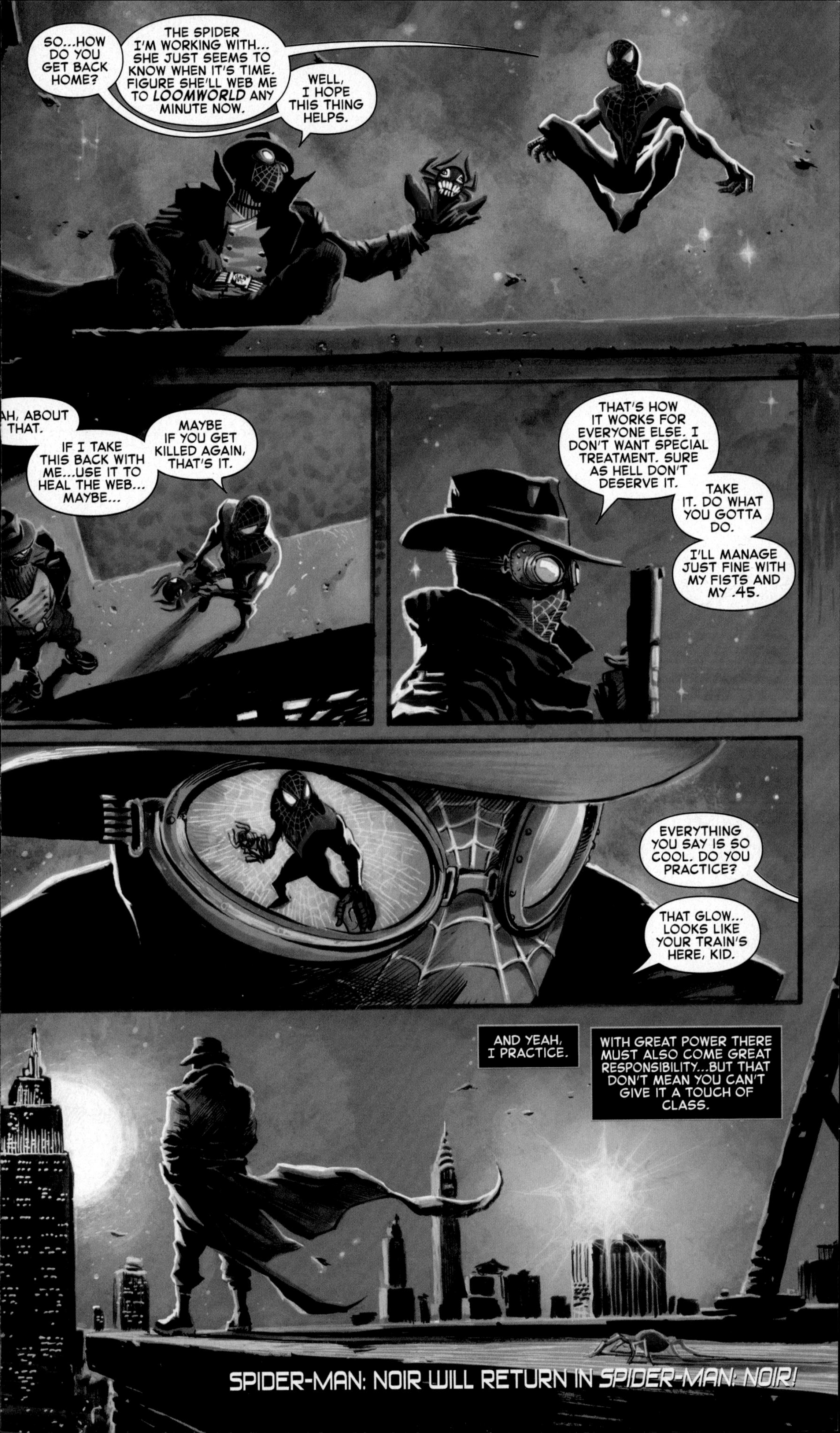

SO...HOW DO YOU GET BACK HOME?
THE SPIDER I'M WORKING WITH... SHE JUST SEEMS TO KNOW WHEN IT'S TIME. FIGURE SHE'LL WEB ME TO LOOMWORLD ANY MINUTE NOW.
WELL, I HOPE THIS THING HELPS.
AH, ABOUT THAT.
IF I TAKE THIS BACK WITH ME...USE IT TO HEAL THE WEB... MAYBE...
MAYBE IF YOU GET KILLED AGAIN, THAT'S IT.
THAT'S HOW IT WORKS FOR EVERYONE ELSE. I DON'T WANT SPECIAL TREATMENT. SURE AS HELL DON'T DESERVE IT.
TAKE IT. DO WHAT YOU GOTTA DO.
I'LL MANAGE JUST FINE WITH MY FISTS AND MY .45.
EVERYTHING YOU SAY IS SO COOL. DO YOU PRACTICE?
THAT GLOW... LOOKS LIKE YOUR TRAIN'S HERE, KID.
AND YEAH, I PRACTICE.
WITH GREAT POWER THERE MUST ALSO COME GREAT RESPONSIBILITY...BUT THAT DON'T MEAN YOU CAN'T GIVE IT A TOUCH OF CLASS.
SPIDER-MAN: NOIR WILL RETURN IN SPIDER-MAN: NOIR!

SPIDERSONA:

SPIDER-RAMEN

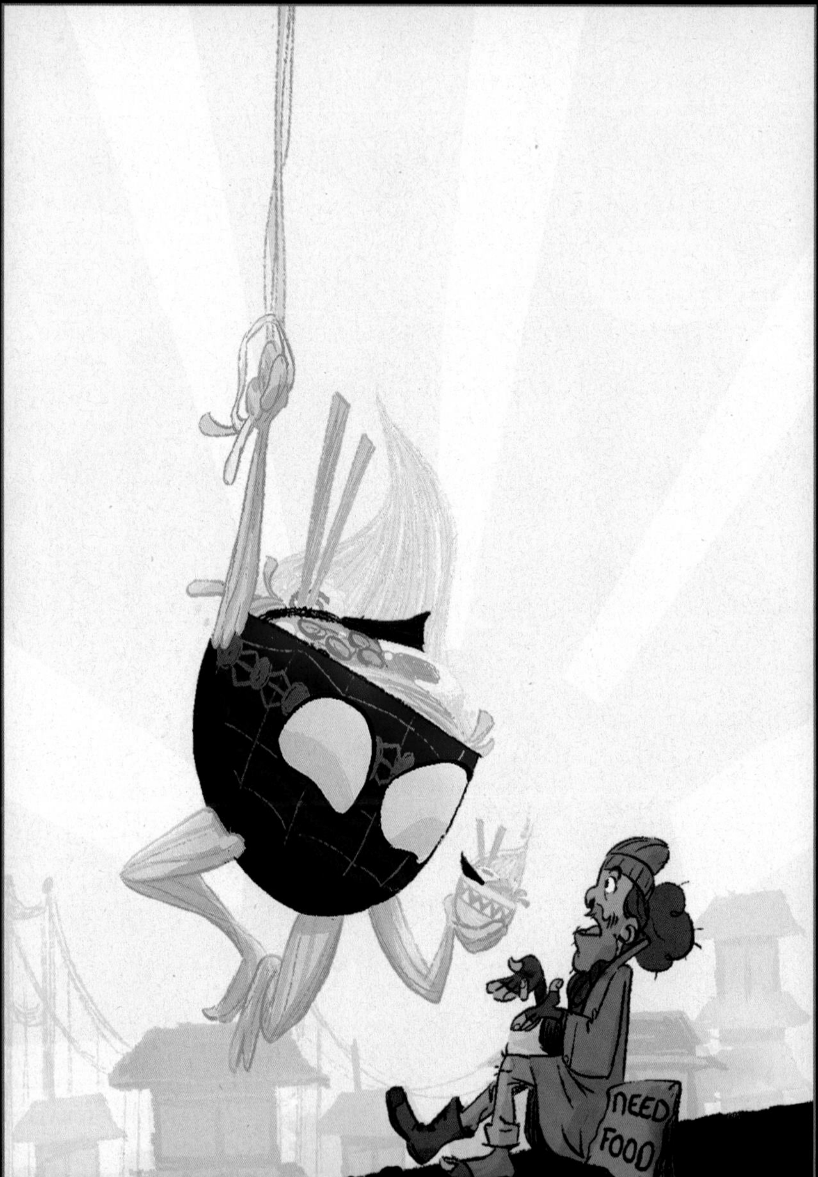
NEED
FOOD

Art & Text by STEVE POOLE

Ireland

Spider-Ramen lives in a future alternate timeline. He can generate multiple bowls of ramen, which he uses both as webbing and to help feed the city's hungry.

SPIDERSONA:

SPIDER-SPY

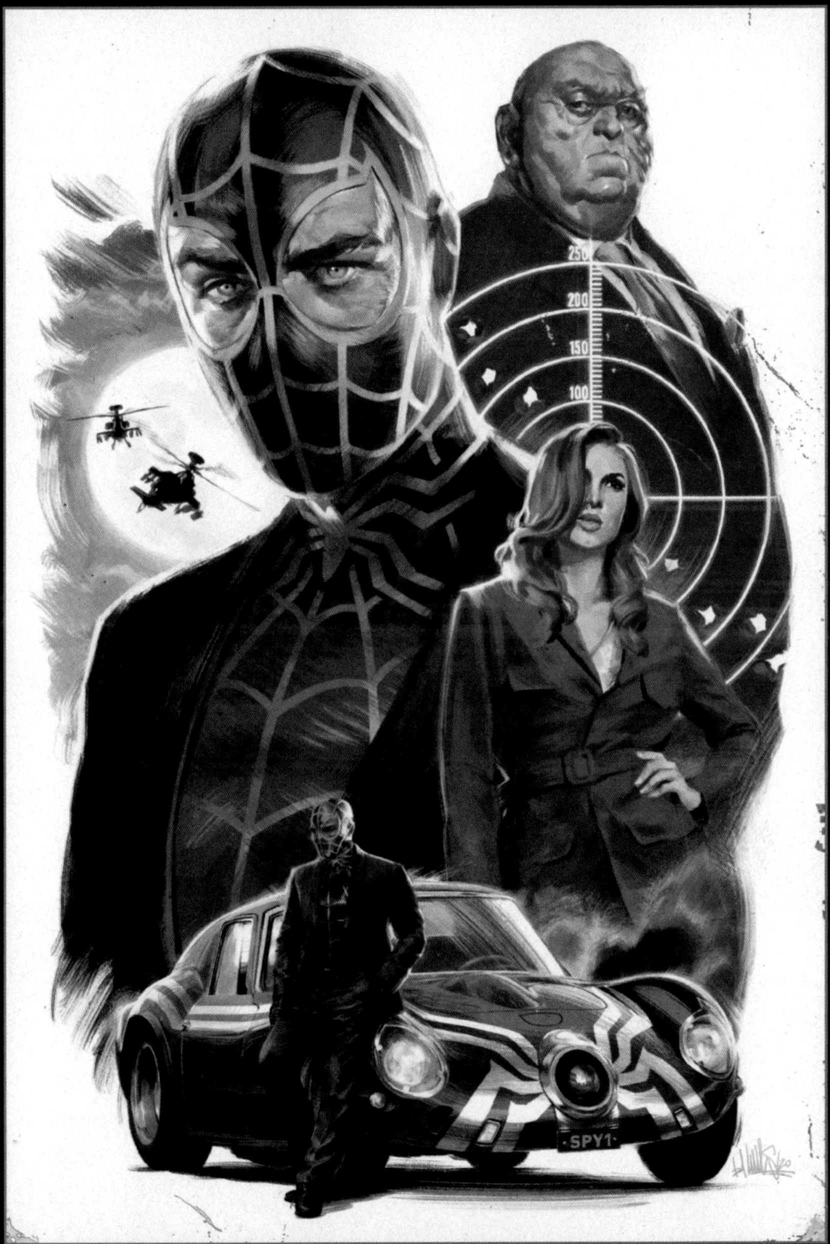

·SPY1·

Art & Text by DAVID "KOPFSTOFF" MÜLLER

Germany

Pierce Parker was just an average private detective until he was bitten by a lab spider during one of his investigations and gained super-powers. He now does his usual detective work by day but also uses his secret powers and gadgets as Spider-Spy at night. His partner, Marilyn, helps him to keep the streets of Noir New York safe!

SPIDERSONA:
SPIDER-WOOL

Art & Text by OH SHEEPS
United States

Dorothy "Dottie" Belle comes from a long line of shepherds and is now making a name for herself in New York City. Her powers include exceptional hearing and being able to communicate with animals. Her stubborn will and passion for life are what carry her through to winning. Her family was always musical, hence the banjo she carries with her most of the time.

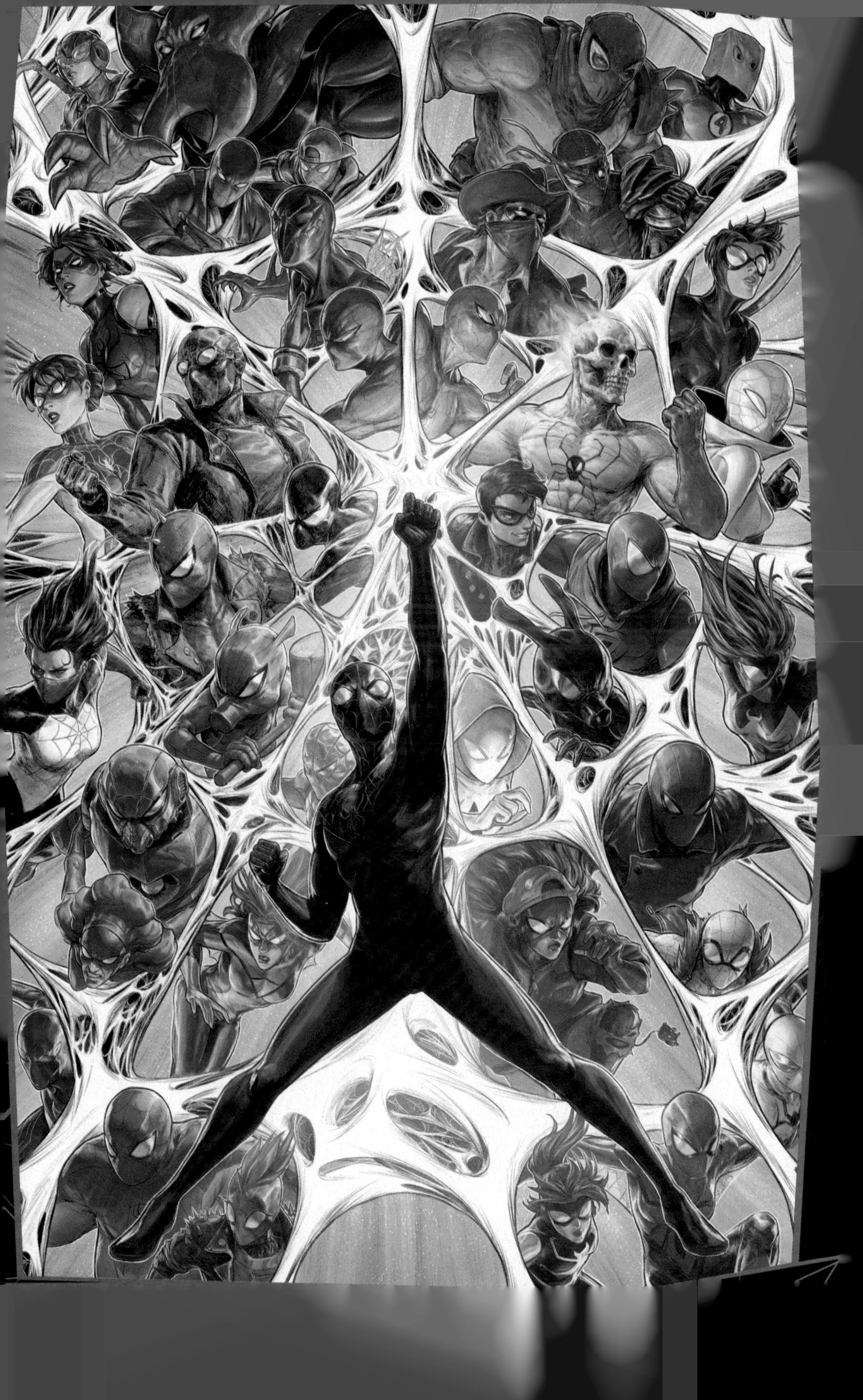

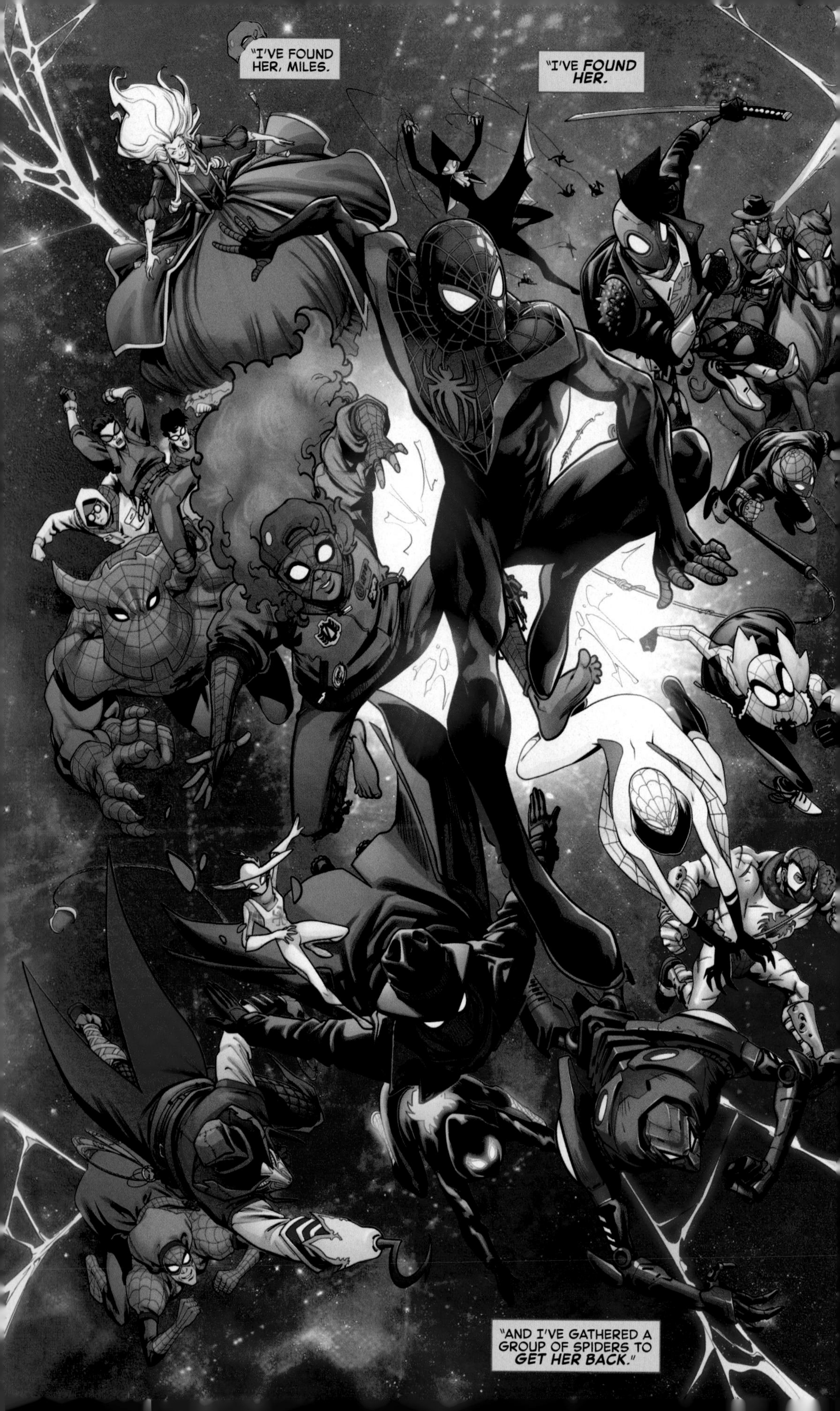
"I'VE FOUND HER, MILES.
"I'VE FOUND HER.
"AND I'VE GATHERED A GROUP OF SPIDERS TO GET HER BACK."

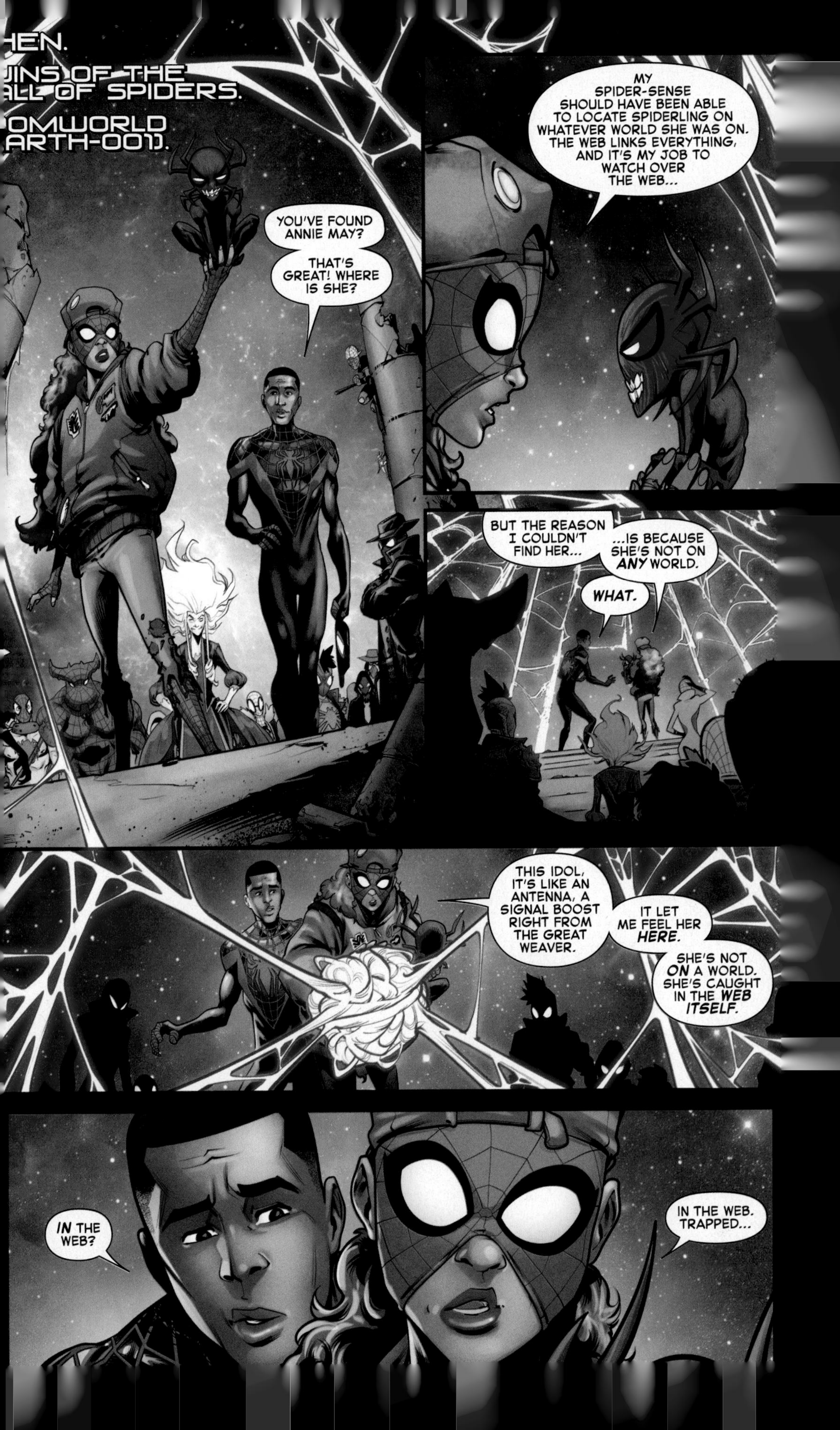

HEN.
UINS OF THE
ALL OF SPIDERS.
OMWORLD
ARTH-001).
YOU'VE FOUND ANNIE MAY?
THAT'S GREAT! WHERE IS SHE?
MY SPIDER-SENSE SHOULD HAVE BEEN ABLE TO LOCATE SPIDERLING ON WHATEVER WORLD SHE WAS ON. THE WEB LINKS EVERYTHING, AND IT'S MY JOB TO WATCH OVER THE WEB...
BUT THE REASON I COULDN'T FIND HER...
...IS BECAUSE SHE'S NOT ON ANY WORLD.
WHAT.
THIS IDOL, IT'S LIKE AN ANTENNA, A SIGNAL BOOST RIGHT FROM THE GREAT WEAVER.
IT LET ME FEEL HER HERE.
SHE'S NOT ON A WORLD. SHE'S CAUGHT IN THE WEB ITSELF.
IN THE WEB?
IN THE WEB. TRAPPED...

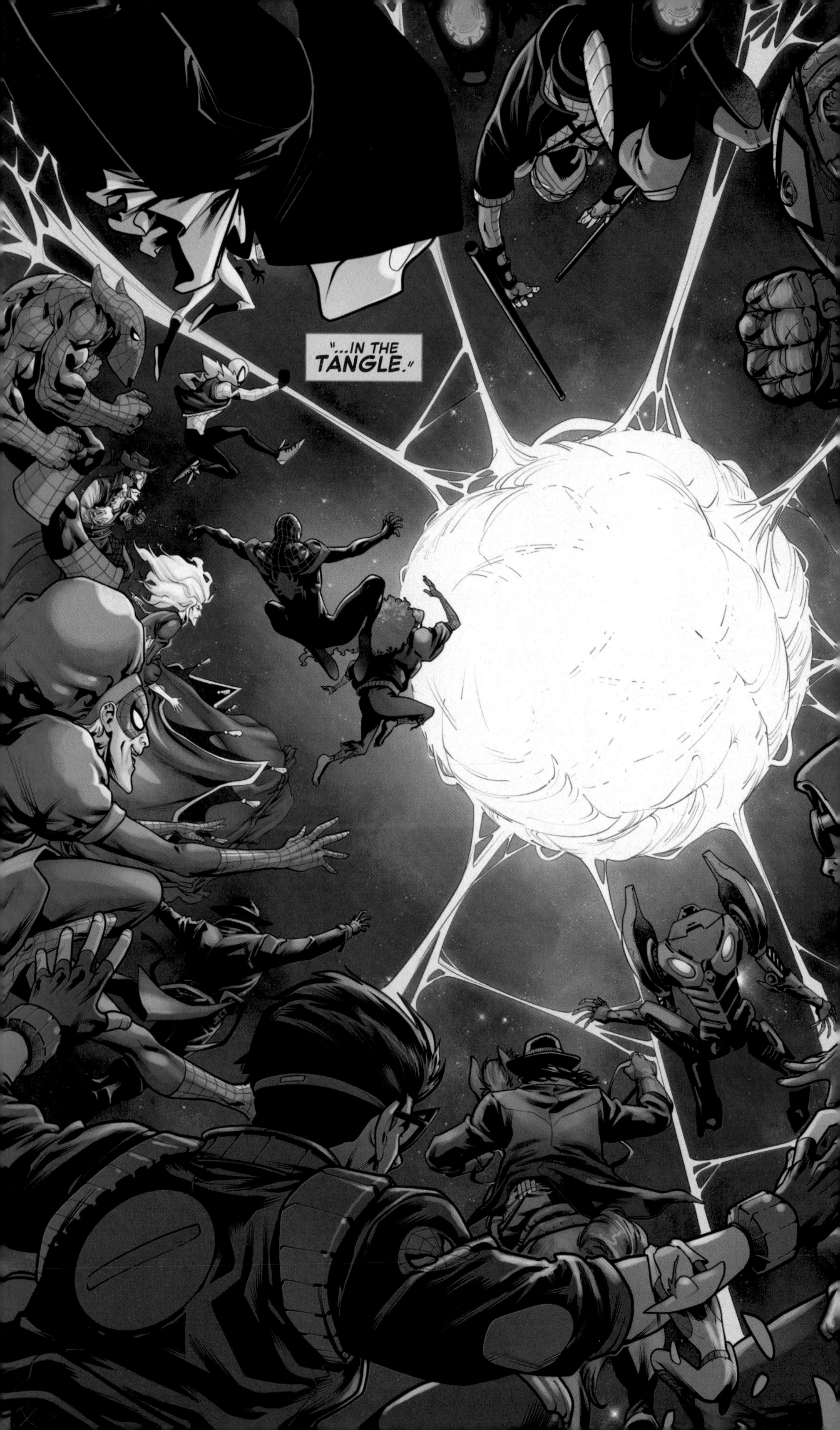
"...IN THE TANGLE."

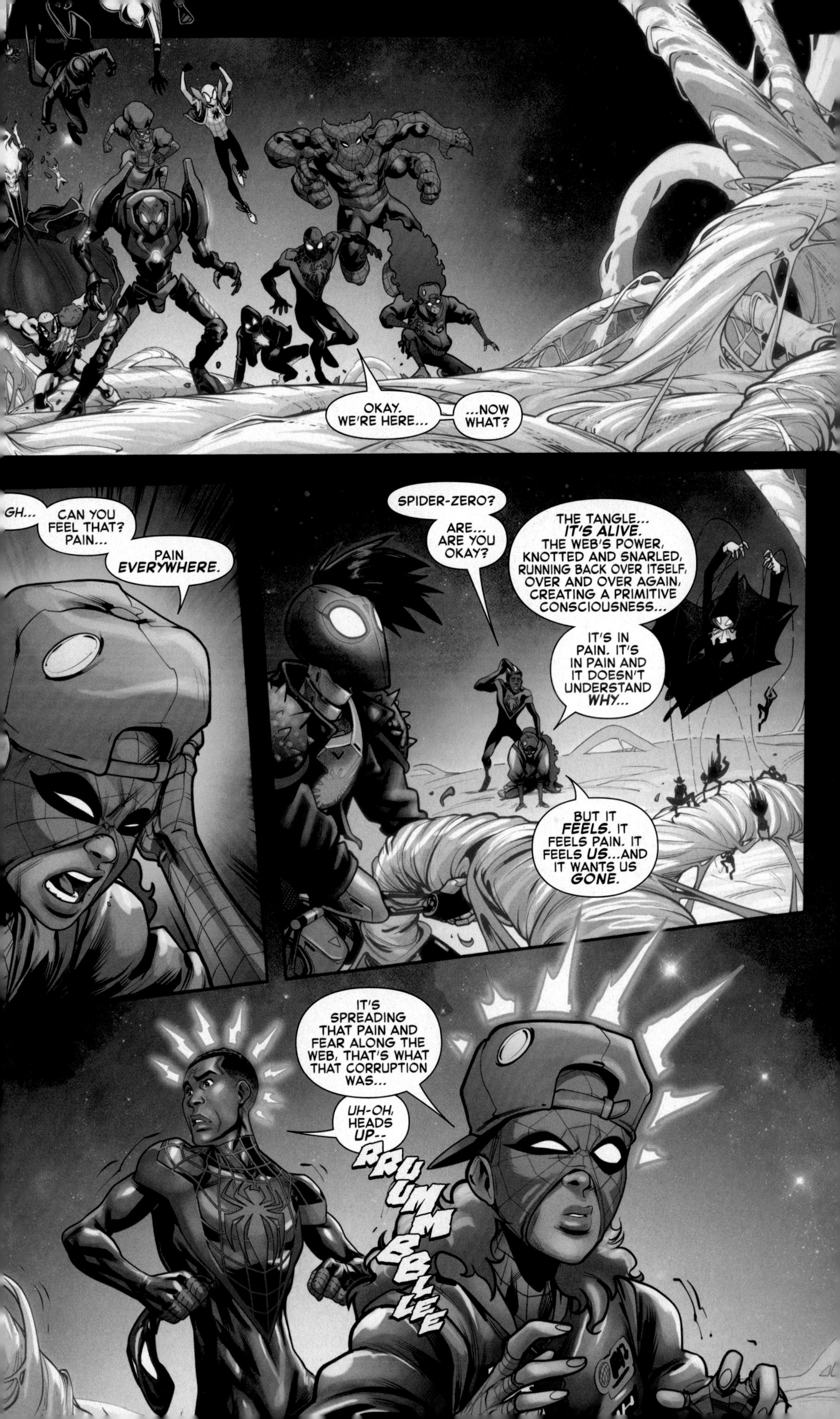
OKAY. WE'RE HERE...
...NOW WHAT?
GH...
CAN YOU FEEL THAT? PAIN...
PAIN EVERYWHERE.
SPIDER-ZERO?
ARE... ARE YOU OKAY?
THE TANGLE... IT'S ALIVE. THE WEB'S POWER, KNOTTED AND SNARLED, RUNNING BACK OVER ITSELF, OVER AND OVER AGAIN, CREATING A PRIMITIVE CONSCIOUSNESS...
IT'S IN PAIN. IT'S IN PAIN AND IT DOESN'T UNDERSTAND WHY...
BUT IT FEELS. IT FEELS PAIN. IT FEELS US...AND IT WANTS US GONE.
IT'S SPREADING THAT PAIN AND FEAR ALONG THE WEB, THAT'S WHAT THAT CORRUPTION WAS...
UH-OH, HEADS UP--
RRUMMBBLEE

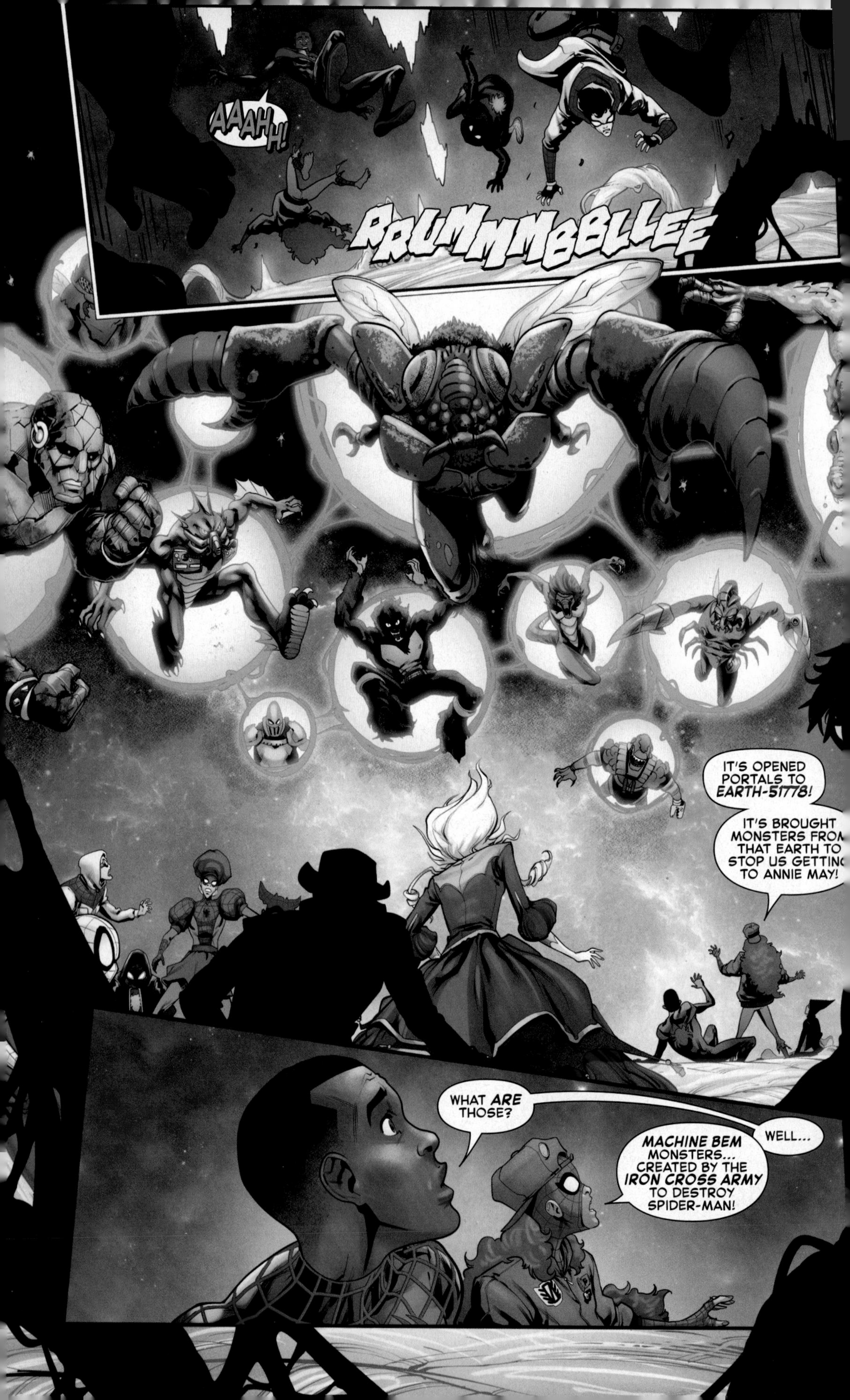
AAAHH!
RRUMMMBBLLEE
IT'S OPENED PORTALS TO EARTH-51778!
IT'S BROUGHT MONSTERS FROM THAT EARTH TO STOP US GETTING TO ANNIE MAY!
WHAT ARE THOSE?
WELL...
MACHINE BEM MONSTERS... CREATED BY THE IRON CROSS ARMY TO DESTROY SPIDER-MAN!

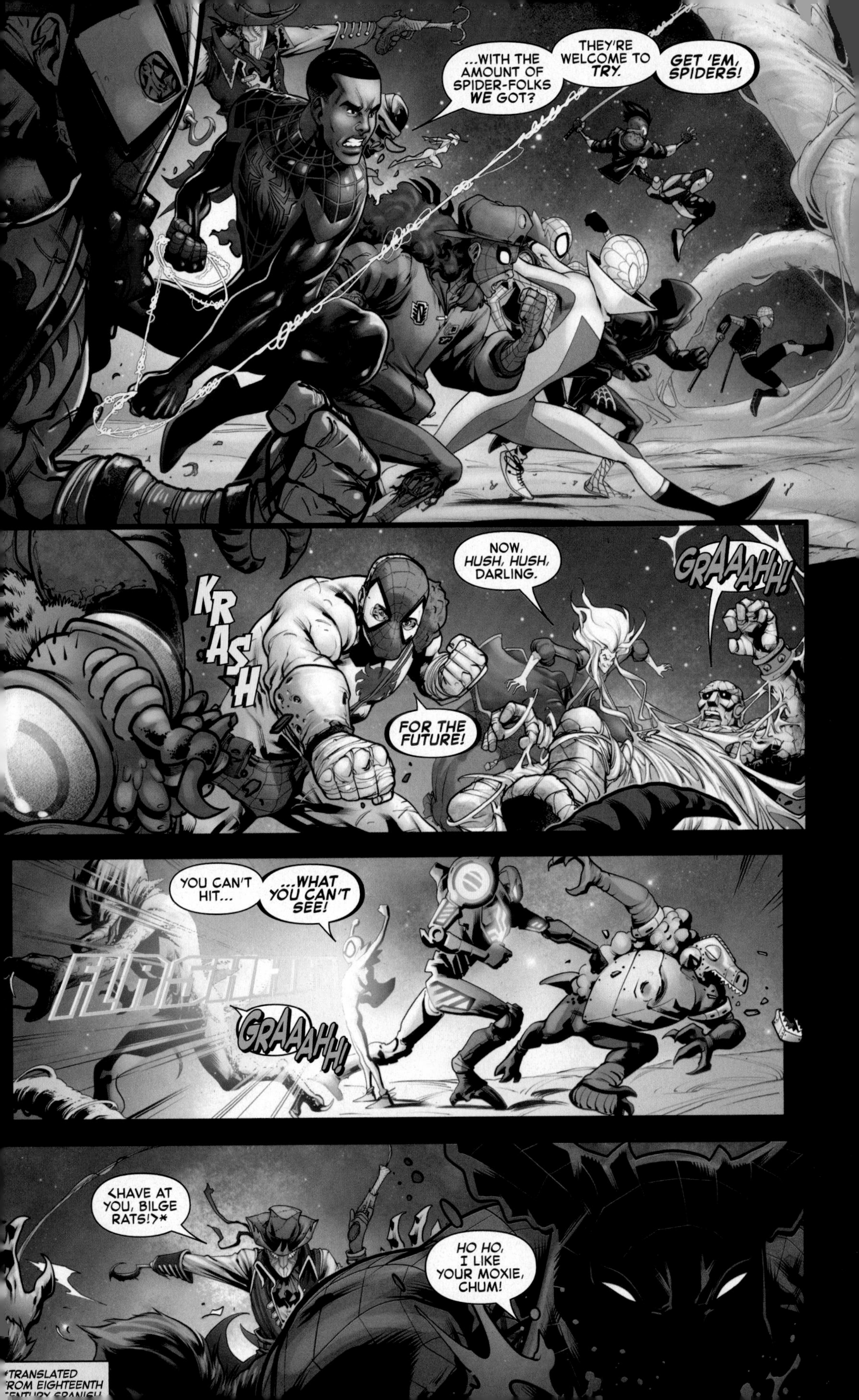

...WITH THE AMOUNT OF SPIDER-FOLKS WE GOT?
THEY'RE WELCOME TO TRY.
GET 'EM, SPIDERS!
KRASH
NOW, HUSH, HUSH, DARLING.
GRAAAHH!
FOR THE FUTURE!
YOU CAN'T HIT...
...WHAT YOU CAN'T SEE!
GRAAAHH!
<HAVE AT YOU, BILGE RATS!>*
HO HO, I LIKE YOUR MOXIE, CHUM!
*TRANSLATED
FROM EIGHTEENTH

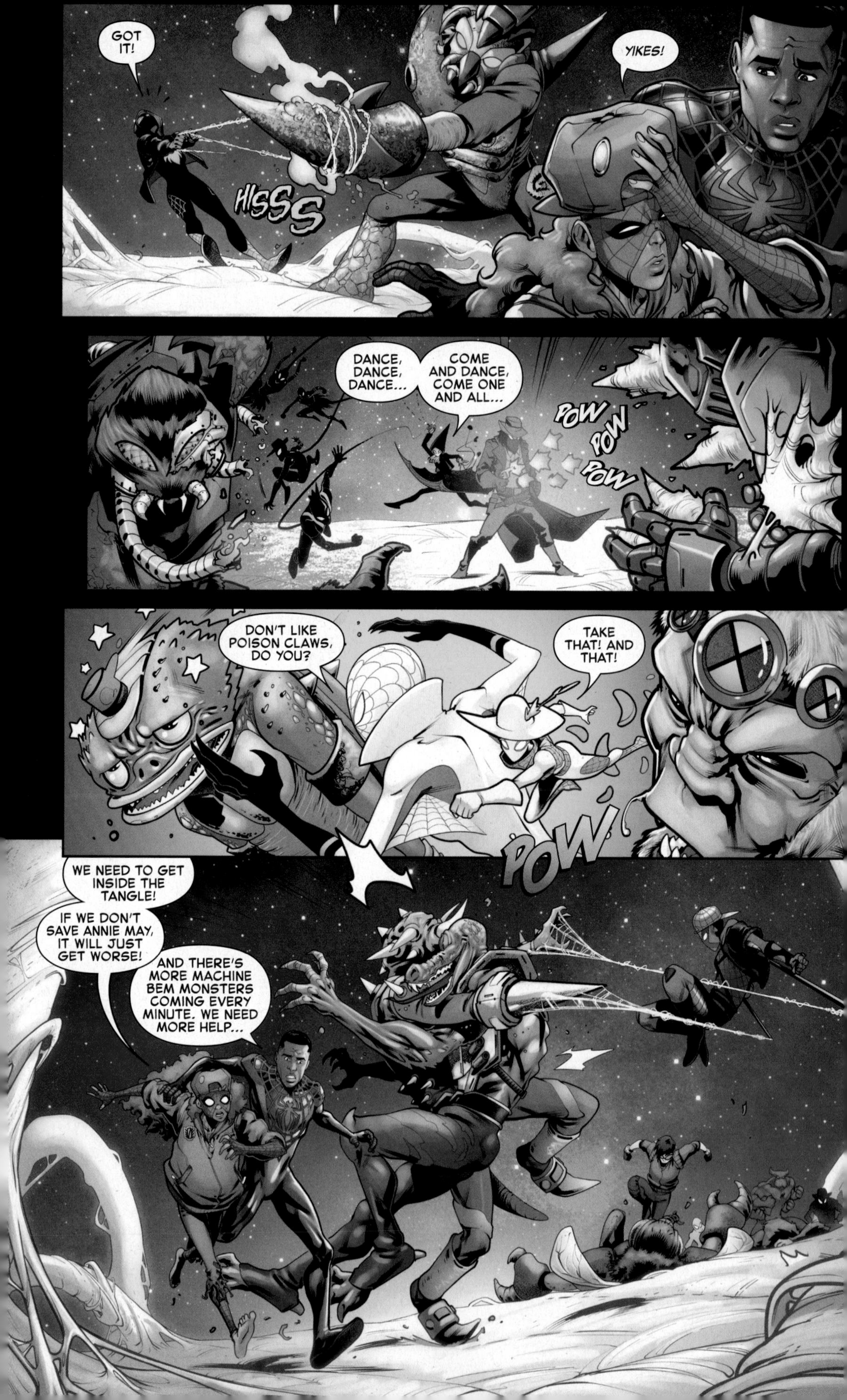
GOT IT!
YIKES!
HISSS
DANCE, DANCE, DANCE...
COME AND DANCE, COME ONE AND ALL...
POW
POW
POW
DON'T LIKE POISON CLAWS, DO YOU?
TAKE THAT! AND THAT!
POW
WE NEED TO GET INSIDE THE TANGLE!
IF WE DON'T SAVE ANNIE MAY, IT WILL JUST GET WORSE!
AND THERE'S MORE MACHINE BEM MONSTERS COMING EVERY MINUTE. WE NEED MORE HELP...

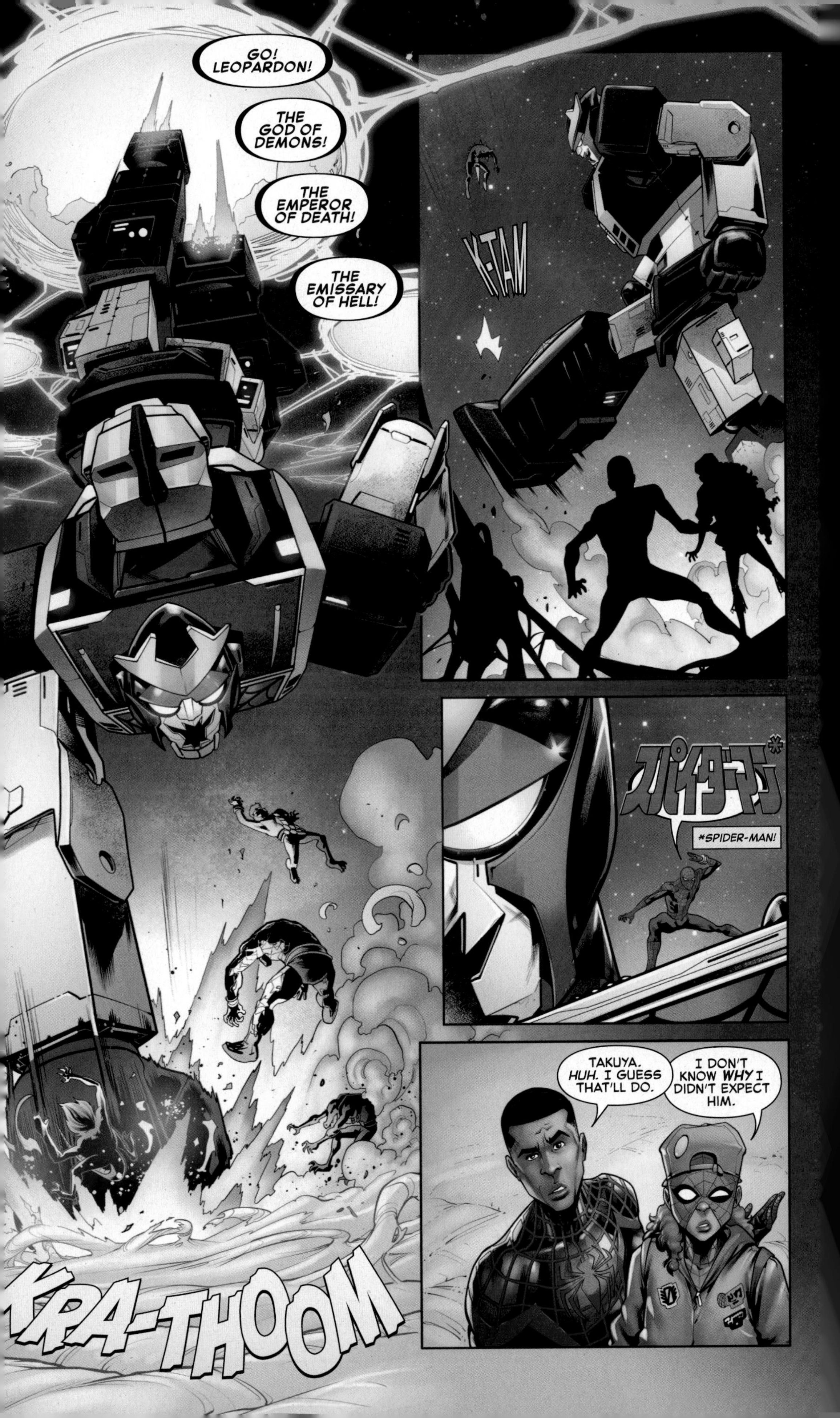
GO! LEOPARDON!
THE GOD OF DEMONS!
THE EMPEROR OF DEATH!
THE EMISSARY OF HELL!
K-TAM
KRA-THOOM
スパイダーマン*
*SPIDER-MAN!
TAKUYA. HUH. I GUESS THAT'LL DO.
I DON'T KNOW WHY I DIDN'T EXPECT HIM.

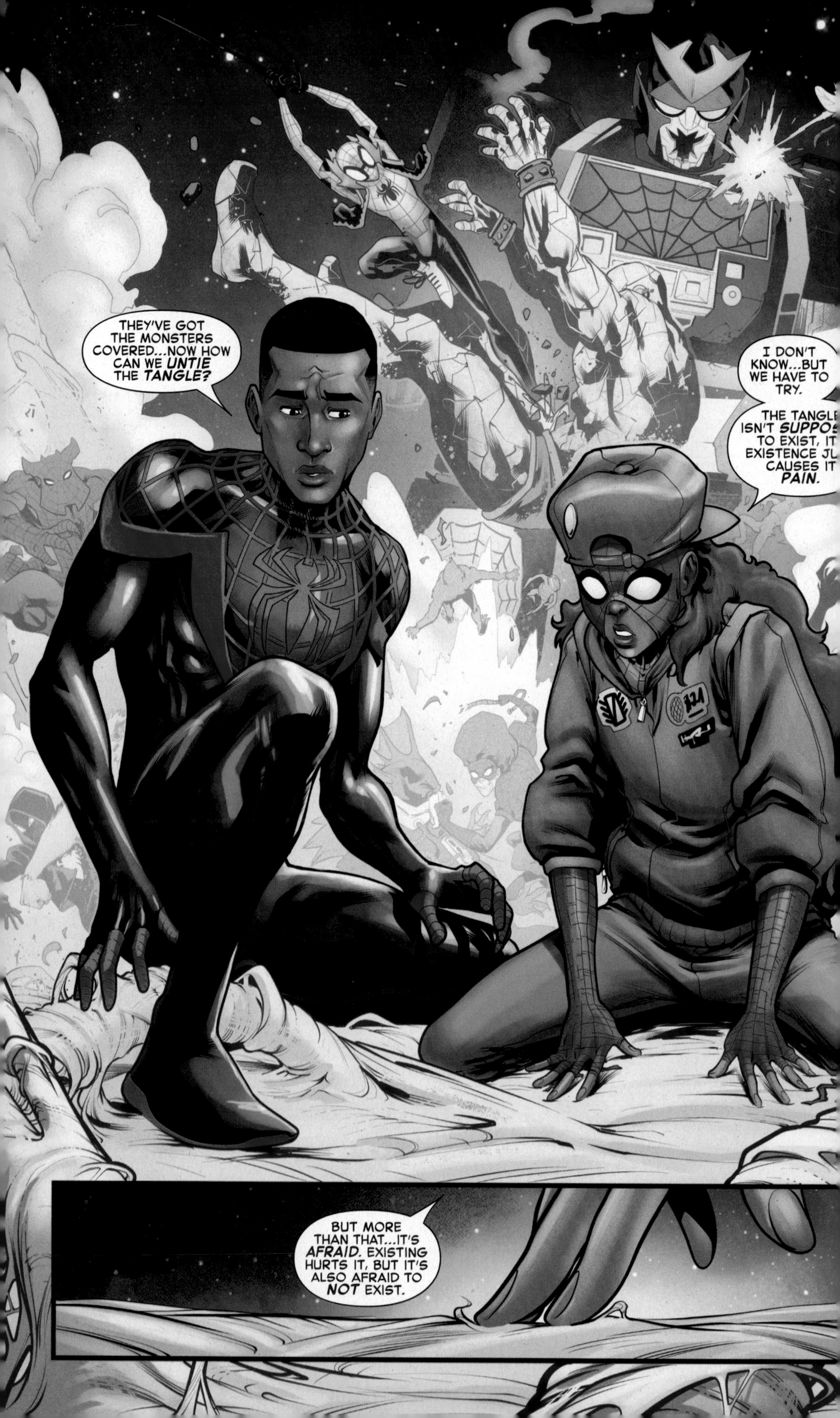
THEY'VE GOT THE MONSTERS COVERED...NOW HOW CAN WE UNTIE THE TANGLE?
I DON'T KNOW...BUT WE HAVE TO TRY.
THE TANGLE ISN'T SUPPO TO EXIST, IT EXISTENCE JU CAUSES IT PAIN.
BUT MORE THAN THAT...IT'S AFRAID. EXISTING HURTS IT, BUT IT'S ALSO AFRAID TO NOT EXIST.

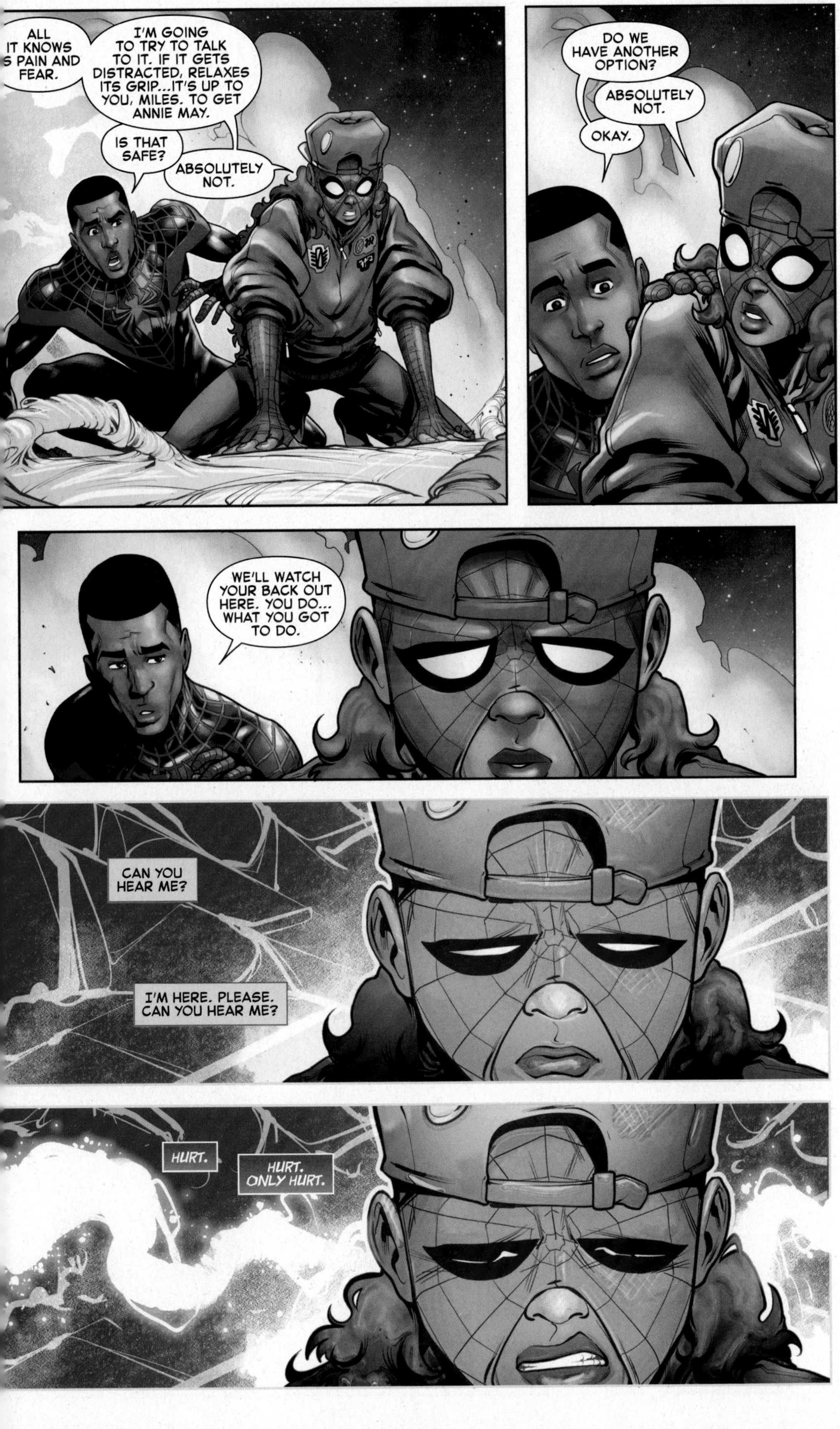

ALL IT KNOWS S PAIN AND FEAR.
I'M GOING TO TRY TO TALK TO IT. IF IT GETS DISTRACTED, RELAXES ITS GRIP...IT'S UP TO YOU, MILES. TO GET ANNIE MAY.
IS THAT SAFE?
ABSOLUTELY NOT.
DO WE HAVE ANOTHER OPTION?
ABSOLUTELY NOT.
OKAY.
WE'LL WATCH YOUR BACK OUT HERE. YOU DO... WHAT YOU GOT TO DO.
CAN YOU HEAR ME?
I'M HERE. PLEASE. CAN YOU HEAR ME?
HURT.
HURT. ONLY HURT.

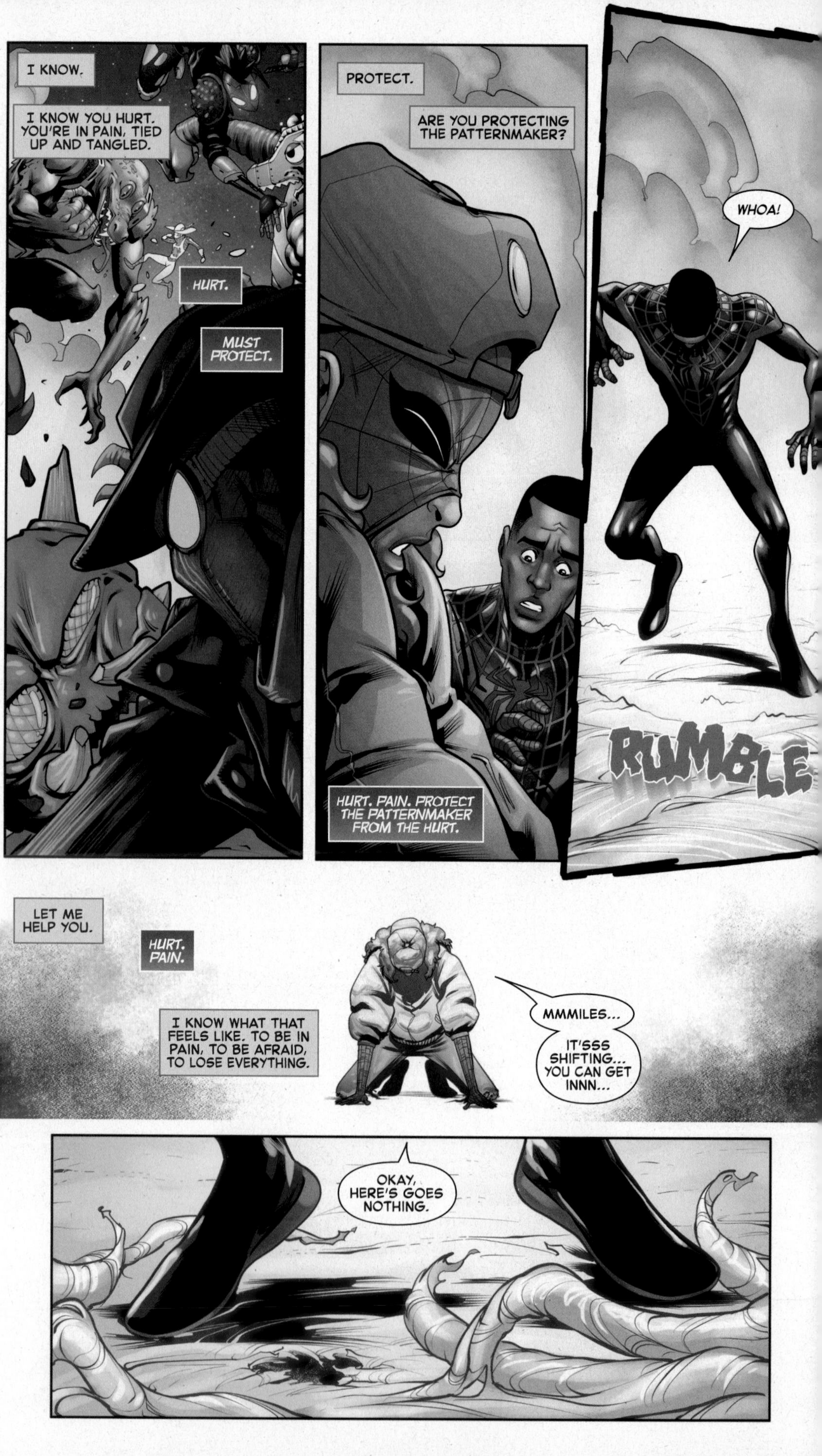
I KNOW.
I KNOW YOU HURT. YOU'RE IN PAIN, TIED UP AND TANGLED.
HURT.
MUST PROTECT.
PROTECT.
ARE YOU PROTECTING THE PATTERNMAKER?
HURT. PAIN. PROTECT THE PATTERNMAKER FROM THE HURT.
WHOA!
RUMBLE
LET ME HELP YOU.
HURT. PAIN.
I KNOW WHAT THAT FEELS LIKE. TO BE IN PAIN, TO BE AFRAID, TO LOSE EVERYTHING.
MMMILES...
IT'SSS SHIFTING... YOU CAN GET INNN...
OKAY, HERE'S GOES NOTHING.

WHAT IS...

THIS IS ME.

THIS IS WHEN I LOST EVERYTHING.

HEFF!

GRFF!

WHEN MY WORLD ENDED.

HURT?

HEFF!

HEFF!

MORE THAN ANYTHING.

...CAN'T GO MUCH FARTHER...

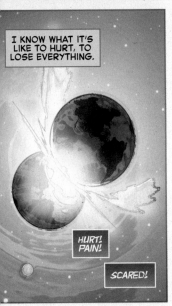

I KNOW WHAT IT'S LIKE TO HURT, TO LOSE EVERYTHING.

HURT! PAIN!

SCARED!

THAT'S HOW I FELT.

THAT'S HOW I FEEL.

EVERY DAY SINCE I WAS CHOSEN FOR THIS ROLE AND SAVED.

EVERY DAY SINCE I LEFT THEM BEHIND TO DIE.

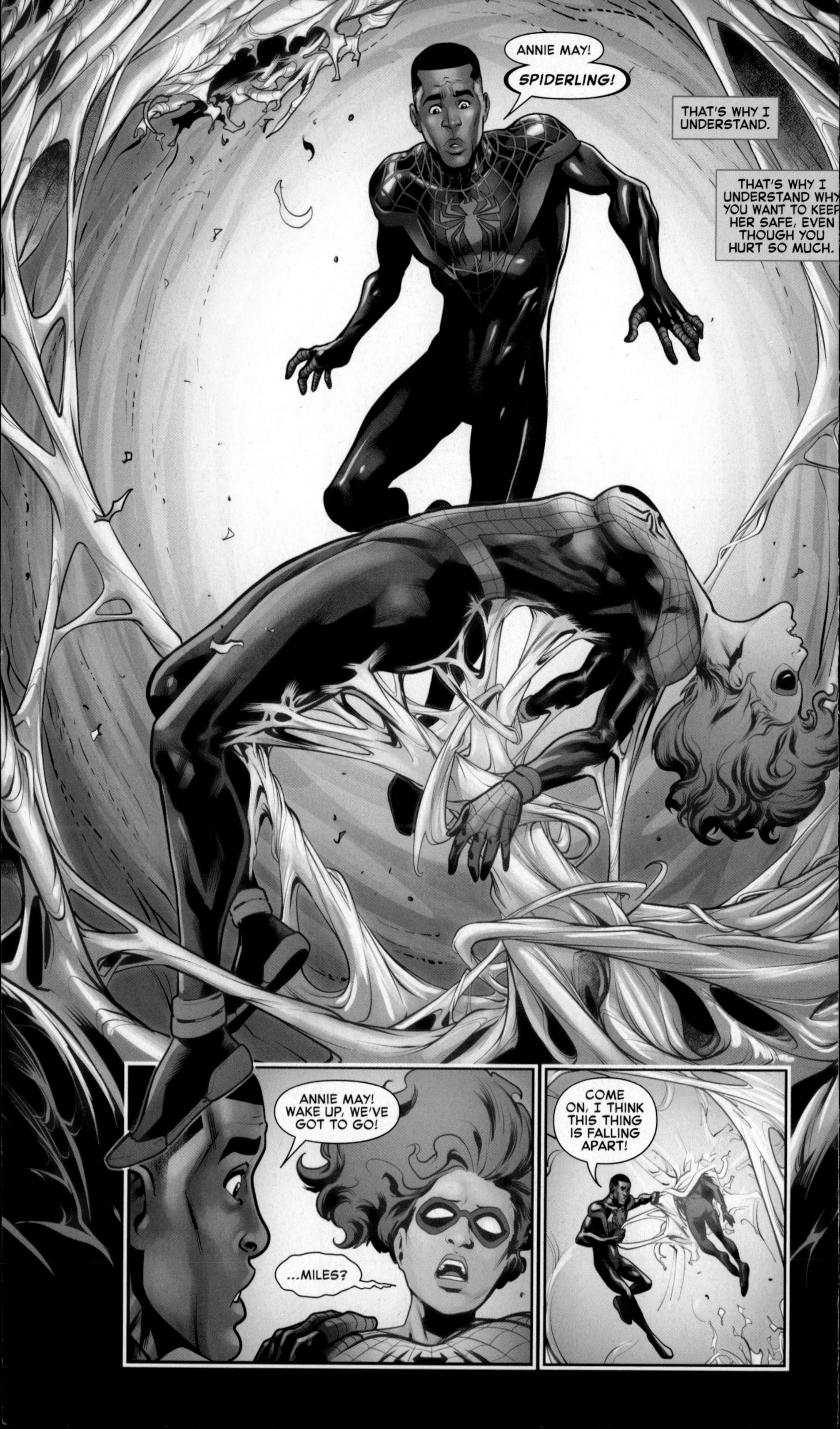
ANNIE MAY!
SPIDERLING!
THAT'S WHY I UNDERSTAND.
THAT'S WHY I UNDERSTAND WHY YOU WANT TO KEEP HER SAFE, EVEN THOUGH YOU HURT SO MUCH.
ANNIE MAY! WAKE UP, WE'VE GOT TO GO!
...MILES?
COME ON, I THINK THIS THING IS FALLING APART!

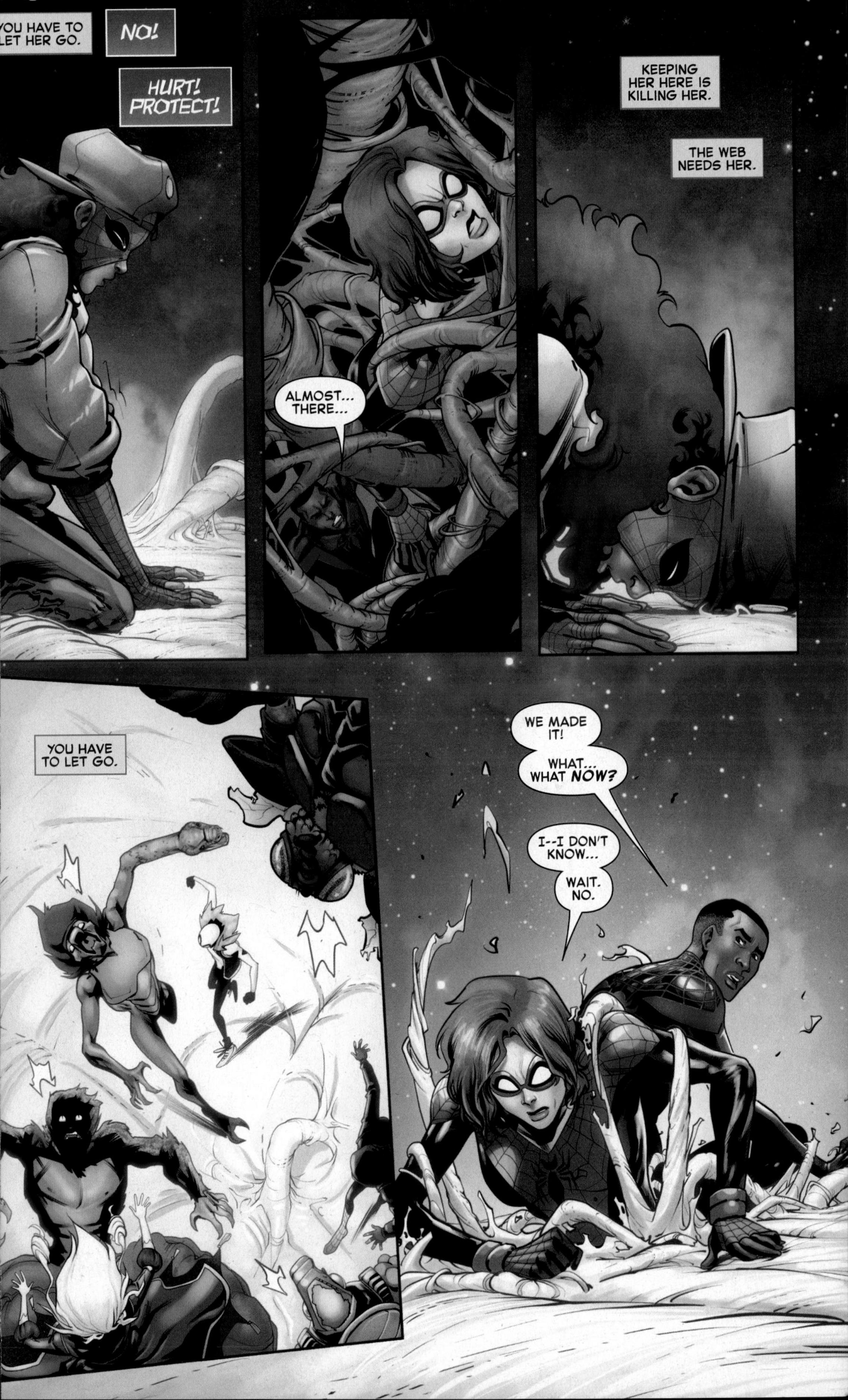
YOU HAVE TO LET HER GO.
NO!
HURT! PROTECT!
ALMOST... THERE...
KEEPING HER HERE IS KILLING HER.
THE WEB NEEDS HER.
YOU HAVE TO LET GO.
WE MADE IT!
WHAT... WHAT NOW?
I--I DON'T KNOW...
WAIT. NO.

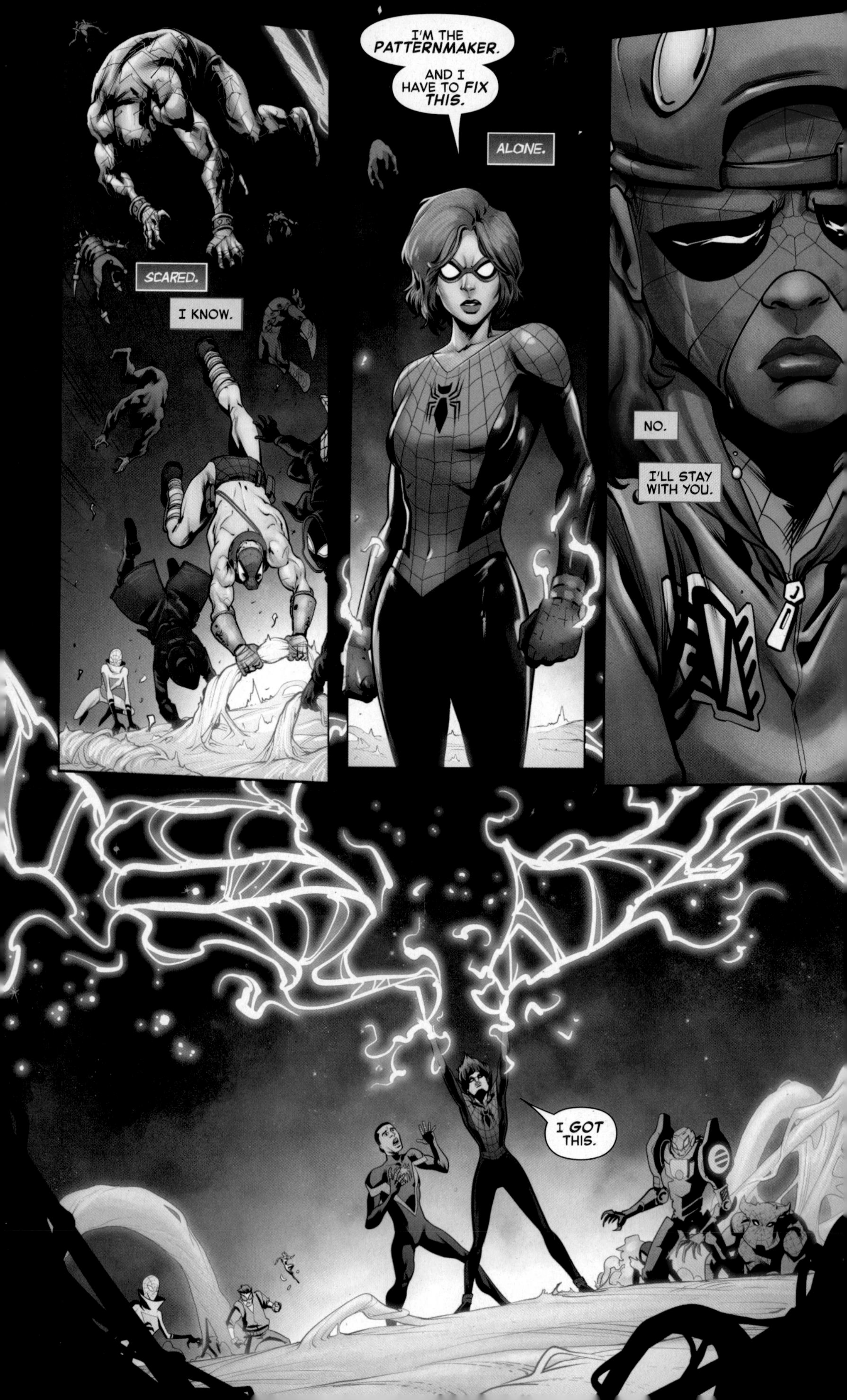

SCARED.
I KNOW.
I'M THE PATTERNMAKER.
AND I HAVE TO FIX THIS.
ALONE.
NO.
I'LL STAY WITH YOU.
I GOT THIS.

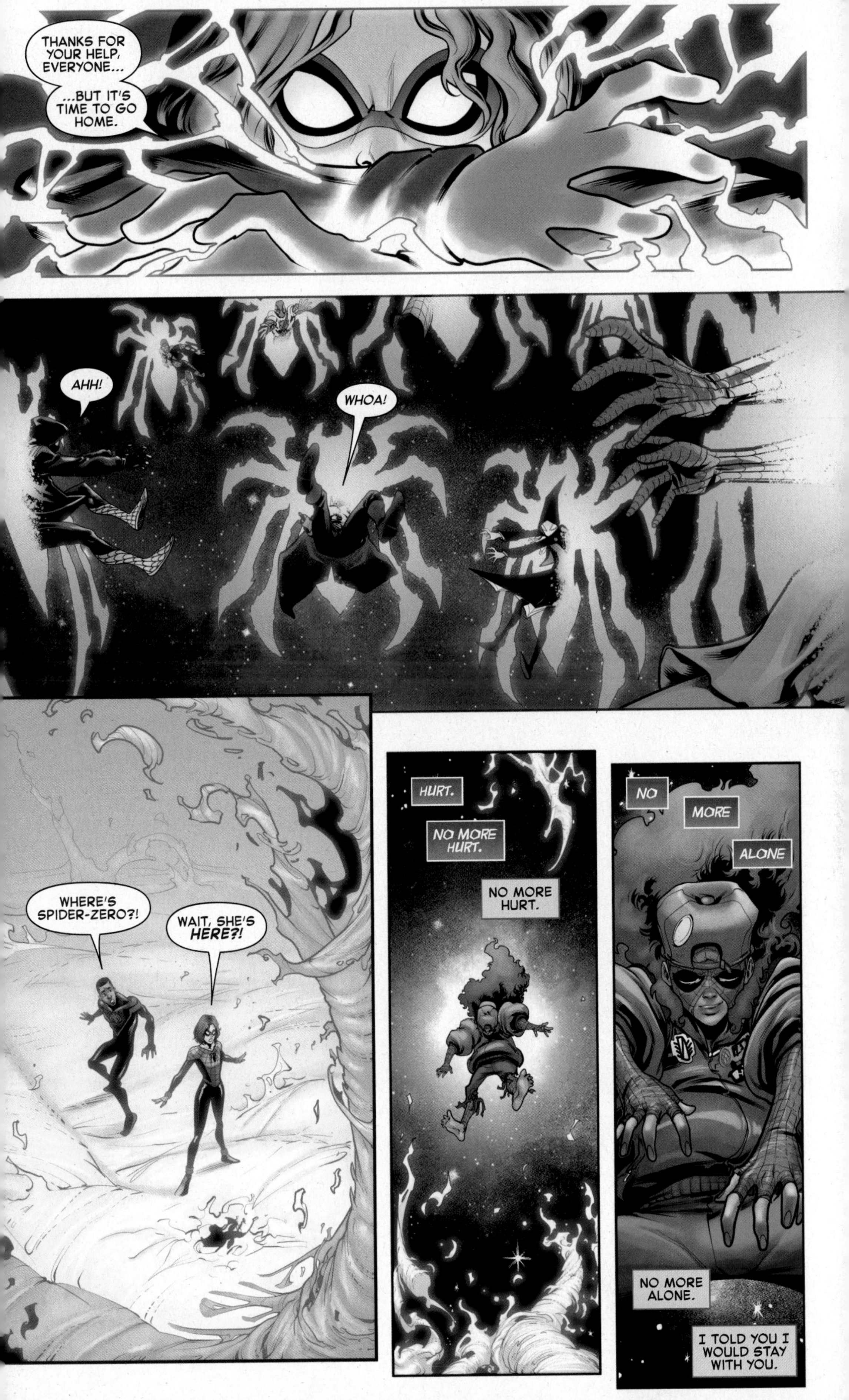

THANKS FOR YOUR HELP, EVERYONE...
...BUT IT'S TIME TO GO HOME.
AHH!
WHOA!
WHERE'S SPIDER-ZERO?!
WAIT, SHE'S *HERE?!*
HURT.
NO MORE HURT.
NO MORE HURT.
NO
MORE
ALONE
NO MORE ALONE.
I TOLD YOU I WOULD STAY WITH YOU.

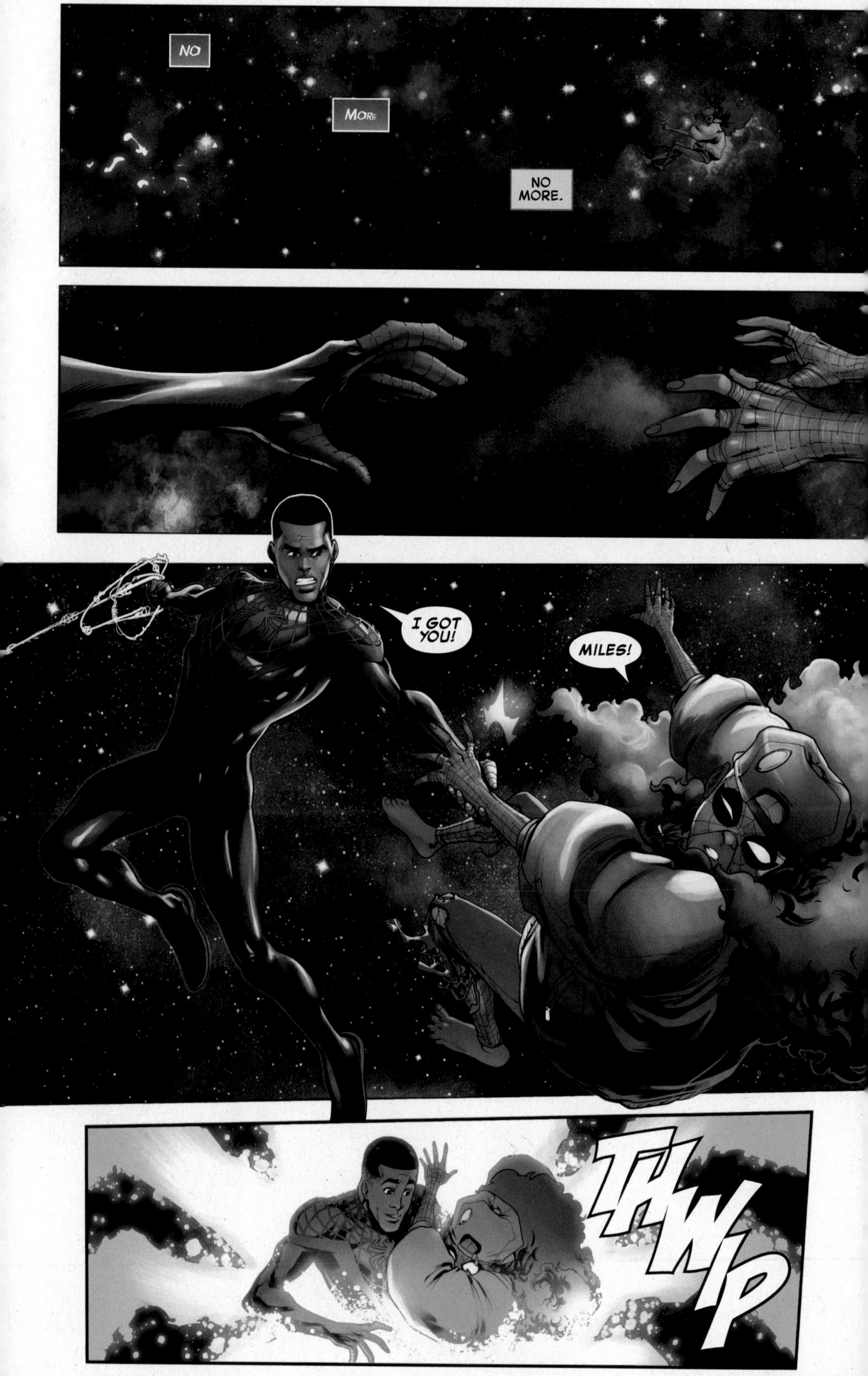
NO
MORE
NO MORE.
I GOT YOU!
MILES!
THWIP

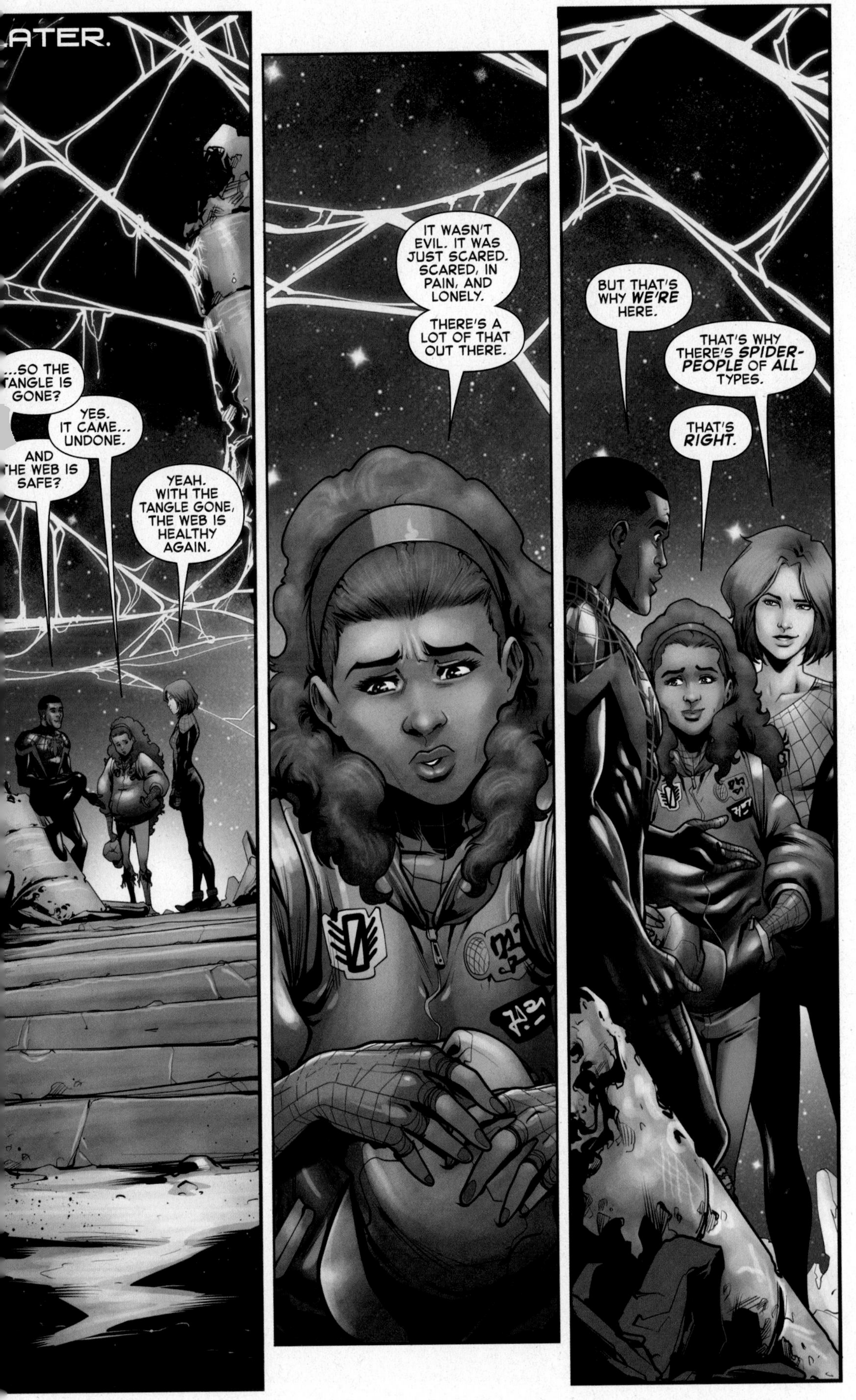
ATER.
...SO THE TANGLE IS GONE?
YES. IT CAME... UNDONE.
AND THE WEB IS SAFE?
YEAH. WITH THE TANGLE GONE, THE WEB IS HEALTHY AGAIN.
IT WASN'T EVIL. IT WAS JUST SCARED. SCARED, IN PAIN, AND LONELY.
THERE'S A LOT OF THAT OUT THERE.
BUT THAT'S WHY WE'RE HERE.
THAT'S WHY THERE'S SPIDER-PEOPLE OF ALL TYPES.
THAT'S RIGHT.

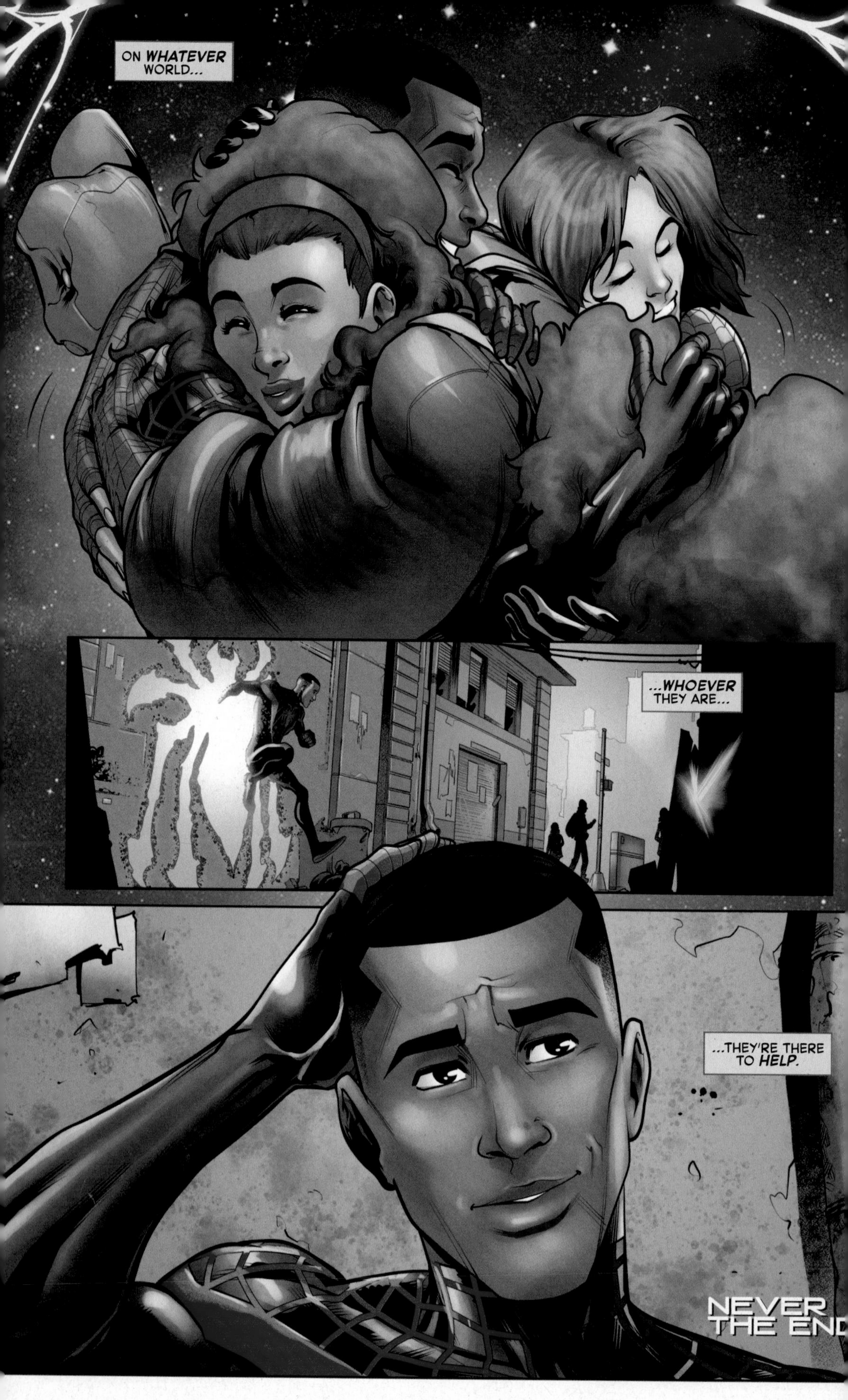
ON WHATEVER WORLD...
...WHOEVER THEY ARE...
...THEY'RE THERE TO HELP.
NEVER THE END

SPIDERSONA:
SPIDER-MANLY

Art & Text by KEVIN BOLK
United States

Spider-Manly walks with the desert wind and slays the foes of righteousness with his mighty Arachne-Ax! The design started with the concept for his weapon and then the character was formed around that.

SPIDERSONA:
WEB-WITCH

Art & Text by CAIT ZELLERS
United States

The Web-Witch is a sorceress who has learned to walk the fragile webs of possibility that link the worlds of the Spider-Verse. The cards she carries bear the symbols of the other Spider-Heroes she's encountered, so she can call on them when she finds a world that needs their help.

SPIDERSONA:
RECLUSE

Art & Text by CHRIS WILSON
United States

Recluse lives in an alternate future version of New York City that has been placed under martial law by S.H.I.E.LD. His design, including his legs and claws, was inspired by brown recluse and trapdoor spiders.

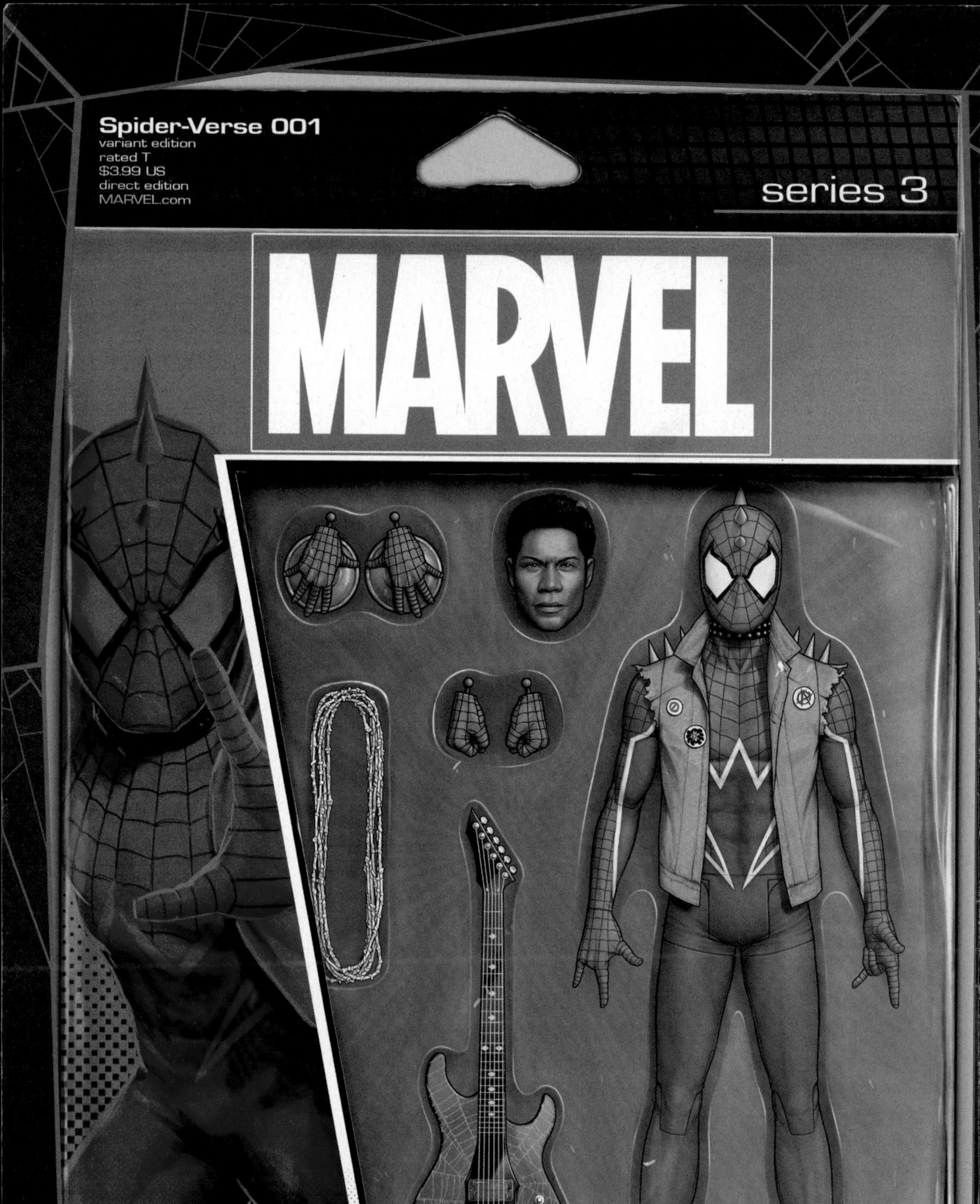
Spider-Verse 001
variant edition
rated T
$3.99 US
direct edition
MARVEL.com
series 3
MARVEL
SPIDER-VERSE
SPIDER-MAN
spider-punk

SPIDER-VERSE #1 ACTION FIGURE VARIANT BY
JOHN TYLER CHRISTOPHER

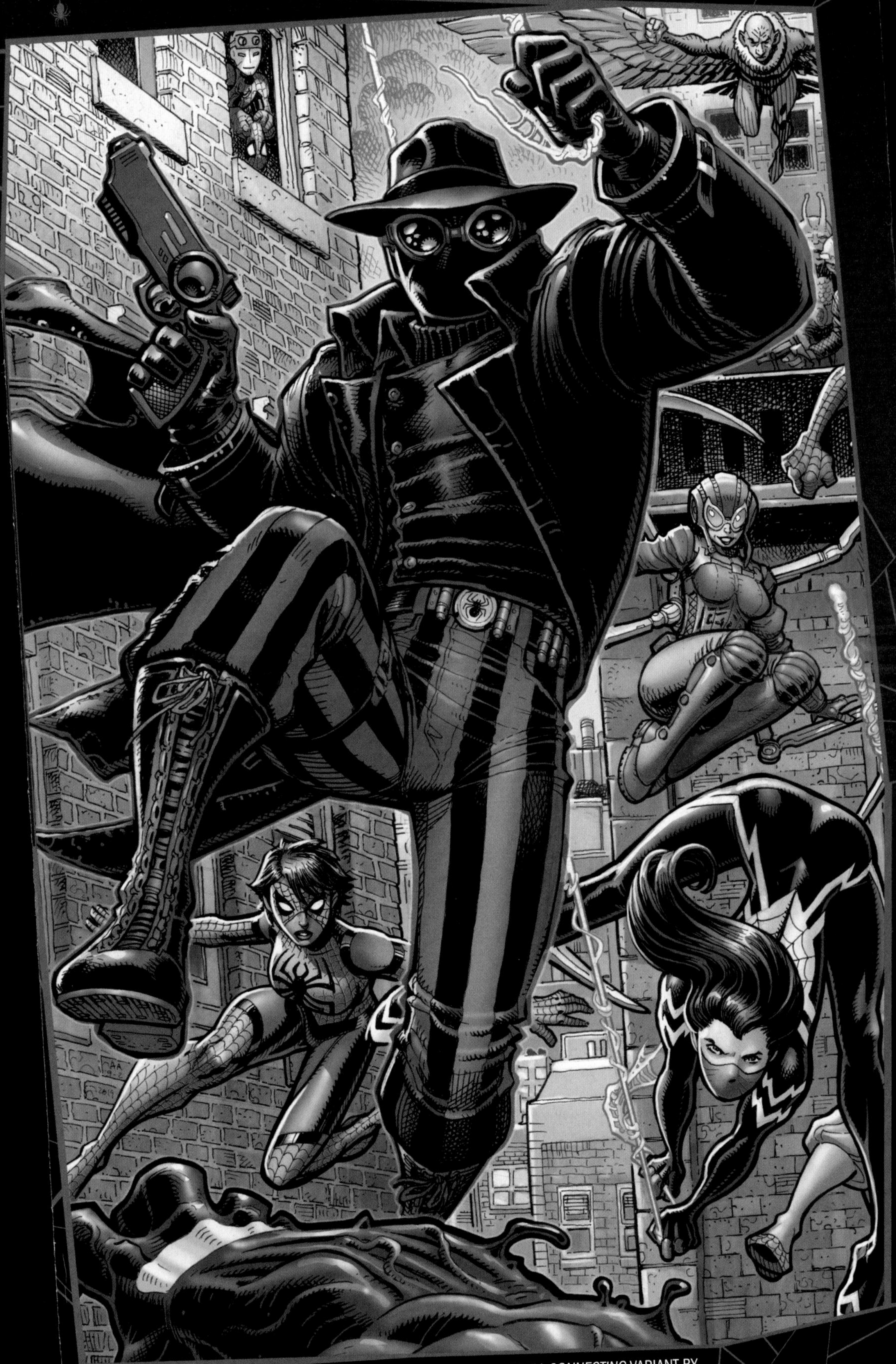

SPIDER-VERSE #1 CONNECTING VARIANT BY
ARTHUR ADAMS & EDGAR DELGADO

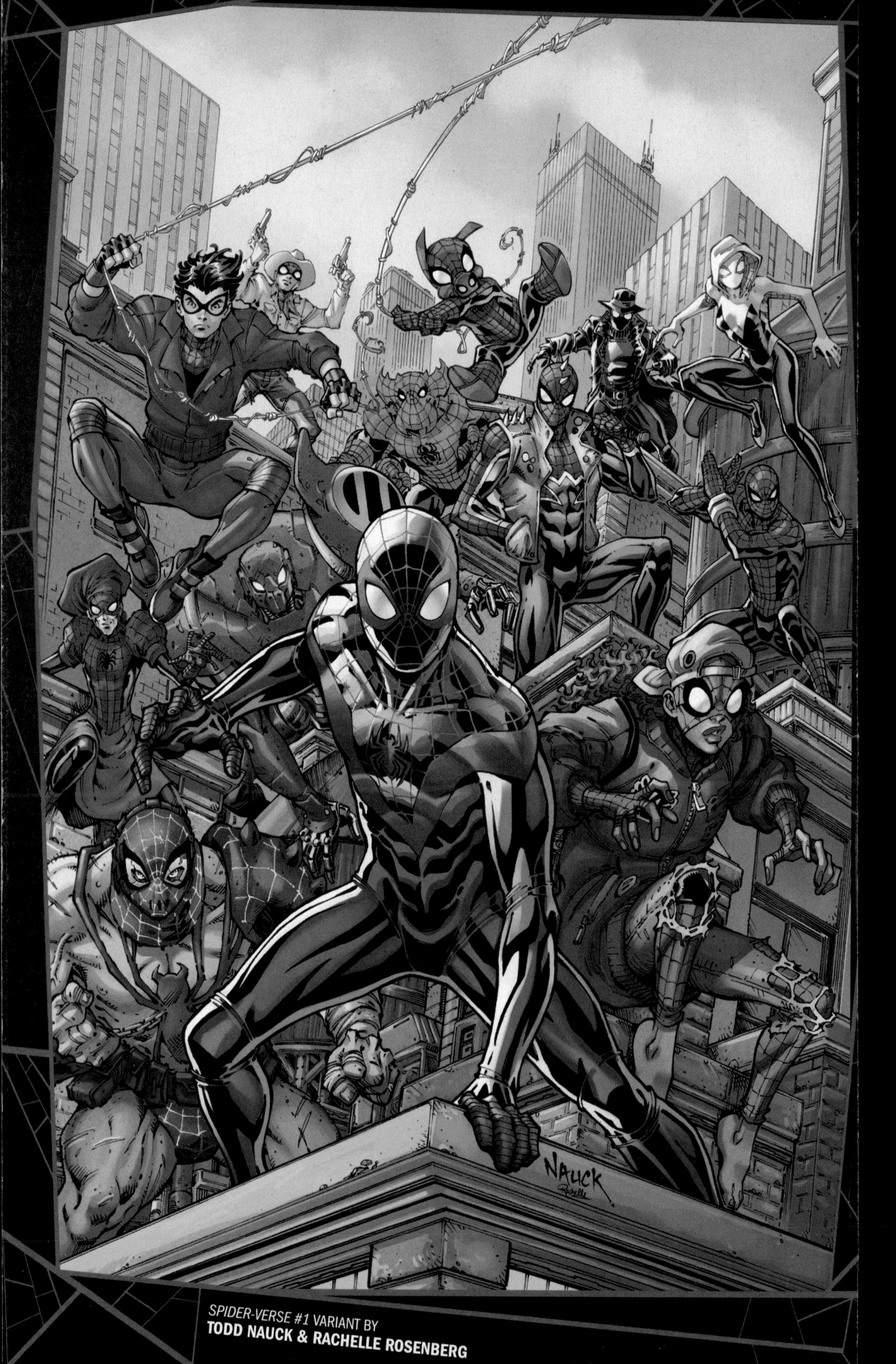
NAUCK

SPIDER-VERSE #1 VARIANT BY
TODD NAUCK & RACHELLE ROSENBERG